The Essential
Abraham Lincoln

★

The Essential Abraham Lincoln

★

EDITED, WITH AN INTRODUCTION, BY

John Gabriel Hunt

GRAMERCY BOOKS
New York

This 1999 edition is published by Gramercy Books,™
an imprint of Random House Value Publishing, Inc.,
201 East 50th Street, New York, New York 10022.

Gramercy Books™ and design are trademarks of
Random House Value Publishing, Inc.

Random House
New York • Toronto • London • Sydney • Auckland
http://www.randomhouse.com/

Printed and bound in the United States of America

Library of Congress Cataloging-in-Publication Data
Lincoln, Abraham, 1809–1865.
The essential Abraham Lincoln.
p. cm.
ISBN 0-517-09345-6
1. United States—Politics and government—1845–1861.
2. United States—Politics and government—Civil War, 1861–1865.
I. Title.
E457.92 1993b   93-3373
973.6—dc20   CIP

9 8 7 6 5 4 3 2

CONTENTS

INTRODUCTION

ABRAHAM LINCOLN was an ambitious, skillful politician as well as a man of conscience whose soul cried out against American slavery. While his early letters and speeches reflect the more regional concerns of his home state of Illinois, by the 1850s his opposition to slavery had become the focal point of his career.

Born in Kentucky in 1809, Lincoln at the age of twenty-one moved with his family to Illinois. He worked as a store clerk and as a postmaster; he studied law and fought in the Black Hawk War. From 1834 to 1841 he served as a state legislator and was instrumental in moving the Illinois capital to Springfield, where, during the 1840s, he developed a reputation as an honest and conscientious attorney. As a Whig member of Congress from 1846 to 1848, Lincoln, in speeches in the House, spoke with forceful logic and even self-deprecating humor against what appeared to be a contrived war with Mexico, instigated by President Polk, and in favor of the presidential candidacy of Zachary Taylor, a fellow Whig.

Lincoln returned to private law practice in Springfield in 1849. The Kansas-Nebraska Act, which permitted slavery in U.S. territories and negated the Missouri Compromise, was adopted in 1854; from this time onward the slavery question was the foremost issue in the country and in Lincoln's renewed political life.

Stephen A. Douglas, senator from Illinois, was responsible for the Kansas-Nebraska Act and was the focus of Lincoln's abolitionist rhetoric. Lincoln became his state's most prominent leader in the new Republican party, and in 1858 he was nominated as the party's candidate for U.S. senator to run against Douglas—resulting in the famous series of seven Lincoln-Douglas debates held in various Illinois cities. Lincoln lost that contest, but he continued to gain in stature as the country's foremost antislavery political figure and, again facing Douglas, won the 1860 presidential election.

In his inaugural address President Lincoln appealed for the preservation of the Union; nevertheless, the Southern states seceded to form the Confederacy in February 1861. The Civil War began with the South's attack on Fort Sumter on April 12, 1861. The war went badly for the Union until 1863, when the South suffered major defeats at Vicksburg and Gettysburg. Lincoln declared slavery dead in his Emancipation Proclamation, issued on January 1, 1863. Eleven months later, he delivered his famous Gettysburg Address at a dedication ceremony for a national cemetery at the Pennsylvania battlefield.

Lincoln appointed Ulysses S. Grant commander of the Union army in March 1864 and was reelected president eight months later. Within a few days of General Robert E. Lee's surrender to Grant at Appomattox Court House, Virginia, on April 9, 1865, Abraham Lincoln, sixteenth president of the United States, was assassinated.

The Essential Abraham Lincoln contains a selection of early addresses, personal and official letters, and presidential messages and proclamations that show the Great Emancipator's intimate responses to the events of a turbulent era—from his days as a modest Illinois politician and lawyer to his service as a U.S. president forced to lead a government and army at war, yet able to produce such enduring documents as the Emancipation Proclamation, the Gettysburg Address, and the two inaugural speeches.

Lincoln's powerful social conscience and his sense of morality and honesty are clearly conveyed in this collection; his writings and speeches are marked by good humor, strength of conviction, and, always, a gentlemanly quality. Most impressive is the clarity of his thinking and his ability to cover every aspect of a subject with a full command of facts and then logically refute all arguments against his own position. The apogee of these skills is found in the renowned Senate-campaign debates with Stephen Douglas. While these qualities are also present in his addresses on temperance, the Mexican War, the presidential candidacy of Zachary Taylor, and the life and character of Henry Clay, it was the issue of slavery—at the forefront of the years of verbal battle with Douglas—that kindled Lincoln's moral fire and elicited his supreme rhetorical power.

Lincoln's election in 1860 caused the Southern states to leave the Union and create their own confederacy. The progress of the Civil War can be followed with a startling closeup view through the presidential letters, telegrams, addresses, proclamations, and messages from these years of national anguish. With the surrender of General Lee's army at Appomattox in April 1865, Lincoln was finally free to concentrate on peacetime concerns, the foremost among these being national unity. His final public address in Washington, D.C., treating postwar reconstruction, provides a hint of what might have been had he lived to complete his second term as president.

The selections in *The Essential Abraham Lincoln* have been culled from the eight-volume 1906 edition of Lincoln's works edited by Arthur Brooks Lapsley. Lincoln's papers were collected after his death in *The Complete Works of Abraham Lincoln* (two volumes, 1894; twelve volumes, 1905), edited by John G. Nicolay and John Hay, both of whom had been secretaries to Lincoln during his presidency. The structural editing and changes in punctuation and spelling made in the Nicolay/ Hay collection—prepared with the cooperation of the president's son, Robert Todd Lincoln—and in the Lapsley set have been retained in the present book.

In most cases, the addresses and writings are presented in their complete versions. Lincoln's speeches and replies in the

Lincoln-Douglas debates, for example, would comprise a book in themselves if they were printed in full. Only a few other speeches have warranted trimming: the two annual messages to Congress, which tend to go into financial matters rather comprehensively; the 1854 speech on the Kansas-Nebraska Act at Peoria, Illinois, in which Lincoln actually warns the audience beforehand that his address will take at least as long as Stephen Douglas's—who had just spoken for three hours—and advises them to break for dinner first; the two speeches delivered in Congress; the speech at New Haven, Connecticut; and the Henry Clay eulogy. The rest of Lincoln's letters, telegrams, messages, documents, and addresses—based on the authoritative versions of Nicolay, Hay, and Lapsley—are given in their entirety.

JOHN GABRIEL HUNT

ADDRESS TO THE PEOPLE
OF SANGAMON COUNTY

March 9, 1832

Fellow Citizens: Having become a candidate for the honorable office of one of your representatives in the next General Assembly of this state, in accordance with an established custom and the principles of true republicanism it becomes my duty to make known to you, the people whom I propose to represent, my sentiments with regard to local affairs.

Time and experience have verified to a demonstration the public utility of internal improvements. That the poorest and most thinly populated countries would be greatly benefited by the opening of good roads, and in the clearing of navigable streams within their limits, is what no person will deny. Yet it is folly to undertake works of this or any other kind without first knowing that we are able to finish them—as half-finished work generally proves to be labor lost. There cannot justly be any objection to having railroads and canals, any more than to other good things, provided they cost nothing. The only objection is to paying for them; and the objection arises from the want of ability to pay.

With respect to the county of Sangamon, some more easy means of communication than it now possesses, for the purpose of facilitating the task of exporting the surplus products of its fertile soil, and importing necessary articles from abroad, are indispensably necessary. A meeting has been held of the citizens of Jacksonville and the adjacent country, for the purpose of deliberating and inquiring into the expediency of constructing a railroad from some eligible point on the Illinois River, through the town of Jacksonville, in Morgan County, to the town of Springfield, in Sangamon County. This is, indeed, a very desirable object. No other improvement that reason will justify us in hoping for can equal in utility the railroad. It is a never-failing source of communication between places of business remotely situated from each other. Upon the railroad the regular progress of commercial intercourse is not interrupted by either high or low water, or freezing weather, which are the principal difficulties that render our future hopes of water communication precarious and uncertain.

Yet, however desirable an object the construction of a railroad through our country may be, however high our imaginations may be heated at thoughts of it, there is always a heart-appalling shock accompanying the amount of its cost, which forces us to shrink from our pleasing anticipations. The probable cost of this contemplated railroad is estimated at $290,000; the bare statement of which, in my opinion, is sufficient to justify the belief that the improvement of the Sangamon River is an object much better suited to our infant resources.

Respecting this view, I think I may say, without the fear of being contradicted, that its navigation may be rendered completely practicable as high as the mouth of the South Fork, or probably higher, to vessels of from twenty-five to thirty tons burden, for at least one half of all common years, and to vessels of much greater burden a part of the time. From my peculiar circumstances, it is probable that for the last twelve months I have given as particular attention to the stage of the water in this river as any other person in the country. In the month of March 1831, in company with others, I commenced the building of a flatboat on the Sangamon, and finished and took her out in the course of the spring. Since that time I have been concerned in the mill at New Salem. These circumstances are sufficient evidence that I have not been very inattentive to the stages of the water.

The time at which we crossed the mill-dam being in the last days of April, the water was lower than it had been since the breaking of winter in February, or than it was for several weeks after. The principal difficulties we encountered in descending the river were from the drifted timber, which obstructions all know are not difficult to be removed. Knowing almost precisely the height of water at that time, I believe I am safe in saying that it has as often been higher as lower since.

From this view of the subject it appears that my calculations with regard to the navigation of the Sangamon cannot but be founded in reason; but, whatever may be its natural advantages, certain it is that it never can be practically useful to any great extent without being greatly improved by art. The drifted timber, as I have before mentioned, is the most formidable barrier to this object. Of all parts of this river, none will require so much labor in proportion to make it navigable as the last thirty or thirty-five miles; and going with the meanderings of the channel, when we are this distance above its mouth we are only between twelve and eighteen miles above Beardstown in something near a straight direction; and this route is upon such low ground as to retain water in many places during the season, and in all parts such as to draw two thirds or three fourths of the river water at all high stages.

This route is on prairie-land the whole distance, so that it appears to me, by removing the turf a sufficient width, and damming up the old channel, the whole river in a short time would wash its way through, thereby curtailing the distance and increasing the velocity of the current very considerably, while there would be no timber on the banks to obstruct its navigation in future; and being nearly straight, the timber which might float in at the head would be apt to go clear through. There are also many places above this where the river, in its zigzag course, forms such complete peninsulas as to be easier to cut at the necks than to remove the obstructions from the bends, which, if done, would also lessen the distance.

What the cost of this work would be, I am unable to say. It is probable, however, that it would not be greater than is common to streams of the same length. Finally, I believe the improvement of the Sangamon River to be vastly important and highly desirable to the people of the county; and, if elected, any measure in the legislature having this for its object, which may appear judicious, will meet my approbation and receive my support.

It appears that the practice of loaning money at exorbitant rates of interest has already been opened as a field for discussion; so I suppose I may enter upon it without claiming the honor or risking the danger which may await its first explorer. It seems as though we are never to have an end to this baneful and corroding system, acting almost as prejudicially to the general interests of the community as a direct tax of several thousand dollars annually laid on each county for the benefit of a few individuals only, unless there be a law made fixing the limits of usury. A law for this purpose, I am of opinion, may be made without materially injuring any class of people. In cases of extreme necessity, there could always be means found to cheat the law; while in all other cases it would have its intended effect. I would favor the passage of a law on this subject which might not be very easily evaded. Let it be such that the labor and difficulty of evading it could only be justified in cases of greatest necessity.

Upon the subject of education, not presuming to dictate any plan or system respecting it, I can only say that I view it as the most important subject which we as a people can be engaged in. That every man may receive at least a moderate education, and thereby be enabled to read the histories of his own and other countries, by which he may duly appreciate the value of our free institutions, appears to be an object of vital importance, even on this account alone, to say nothing of the advantages and satisfaction to be derived from all being able to read the Scriptures, and other works both of a religious and moral nature, for themselves.

For my part, I desire to see the time when education—and by its means, morality, sobriety, enterprise, and industry—shall become much more general than at present, and should be gratified to have it in my power to contribute something to the advancement of any measure which might have a tendency to accelerate that happy period.

With regard to existing laws, some alterations are thought to be necessary. Many respectable men have suggested that our estray laws, the law respecting the issuing of executions, the road law, and some others, are deficient in their present form, and require alterations. But, considering the great probability that the framers of those laws were wiser than myself, I should prefer not meddling with them, unless they were first attacked by others; in which case I should feel it both a privilege and a duty to take that stand which, in my view, might tend most to the advancement of justice.

But, fellow citizens, I shall conclude. Considering the great degree of modesty which should always attend youth, it is probable I have already been more presuming than becomes me. However, upon the subjects of which I have treated, I have spoken as I have thought. I may be wrong in regard to any or all of them; but, holding it a sound maxim that it is better only sometimes to be right than at all times to be wrong, so soon as I discover my opinions to be erroneous, I shall be ready to renounce them.

Every man is said to have his peculiar ambition. Whether it be true or not, I can say, for one, that I have no other so great as that of being truly esteemed of my fellow men, by rendering myself worthy of their esteem. How far I shall succeed in gratifying this ambition is yet to be developed. I am young, and unknown to many of you. I was born, and have ever remained, in the most humble walks of life. I have no wealthy or popular relations or friends to recommend me. My case is thrown exclusively upon the independent voters of the county; and, if elected, they will have conferred a favor upon me for which I shall be unremitting in my labors to compensate. But, if the good people in their wisdom shall see fit to keep me in the background, I have been too familiar with disappointments to be very much chagrined.

Letter to the Editor of the Sangamon Journal

New Salem, June 13, 1836

To the Editor of the *Journal:*

In your paper of last Saturday I see a communication, over the signature of "Many Voters," in which the candidates who are announced in the *Journal* are called upon to "show their hands." Agreed. Here's mine.

I go for all sharing the privileges of the government who assist in bearing its burdens. Consequently, I go for admitting all whites to the right of suffrage who pay taxes or bear arms (by no means excluding females).

If elected, I shall consider the whole people of Sangamon my constituents, as well those that oppose as those that support me.

While acting as their representative, I shall be governed by their will on all subjects upon which I have the means of knowing what their will is; and upon all others I shall do what my own judgment teaches me will best advance their interests. Whether elected or not, I go for distributing the proceeds of the sales of the public lands to the several states, to enable our state, in common with others, to dig canals and construct railroads without borrowing money and paying the interest on it.

If alive on the first Monday in November, I shall vote for Hugh L. White for president.

Very respectfully,
A. Lincoln

SPEECH BEFORE THE YOUNG MEN'S LYCEUM OF SPRINGFIELD, ILLINOIS

January 27, 1837

As a subject for the remarks of the evening, "The Perpetuation of our Political Institutions" is selected.

In the great journal of things happening under the sun, we, the American people, find our account running under date of the nineteenth century of the Christian era. We find ourselves in the peaceful possession of the fairest portion of the earth as regards extent of territory, fertility of soil, and salubrity of climate. We find ourselves under the government of a system of political institutions conducing more essentially to the ends of civil and religious liberty than any of which the history of former times tells us. We, when mounting the stage of existence, found ourselves the legal inheritors of these fundamental blessings. We toiled not in the acquirement or establishment of them; they are a legacy bequeathed us by a once hardy, brave, and patriotic, but now lamented and departed, race of ancestors. Theirs was the task (and nobly they performed it) to possess themselves, and through themselves us, of this goodly land, and to uprear upon its hills and its valleys a political edifice of liberty and equal rights; 'tis ours only to transmit these—the former unprofaned by the foot of an invader, the latter undecayed by the lapse of time and untorn by usurpation—to the latest generation that fate shall permit the world to know. This task of gratitude to our fathers, justice to ourselves, duty to posterity, and love for our species in general, imperatively requires us faithfully to perform.

How then shall we perform it? At what point shall we expect the approach of danger? By what means shall we fortify against it? Shall we expect some transatlantic military giant to step the ocean and crush us at a blow? Never! All the armies of Europe, Asia, and Africa combined, with all the treasure of the earth (our own excepted) in their military chest, with a Bonaparte for a commander, could not by force take a drink from the Ohio or make a track on the Blue Ridge in a trial of a thousand years.

At what point then is the approach of danger to be expected? I answer, If it ever reach us it must spring up amongst us; it cannot come from abroad. If destruction be our lot we must ourselves be its author and finisher. As a nation of freemen we must live through all time, or die by suicide.

I hope I am overwary; but if I am not, there is even now something of ill omen amongst us. I mean the increasing disregard for law which pervades the country—the growing disposition to substitute the wild and furious passions in lieu of the sober judgment of courts, and the worse than savage mobs for the executive ministers of justice. This disposition is awfully fearful in any community; and that it now exists in ours, though grating to our feelings to admit, it would be a violation of truth and an insult to our intelligence to deny. Accounts of outrages committed by mobs form the everyday news of the times. They have pervaded the country from New England to Louisiana; they are neither peculiar to the eternal snows of the former nor the burning suns of the latter; they are not the creature of climate, neither are they confined to the slaveholding or the nonslaveholding states. Alike they spring up among the pleasure-hunting masters of Southern slaves, and the order-loving citizens of the land of steady habits. Whatever then their cause may be, it is common to the whole country.

It would be tedious as well as useless to recount the horrors of all of them. Those happening in the state of Mississippi and at St. Louis are perhaps the most dangerous in example and revolting to humanity. In the Mississippi case they first commenced by hanging the regular gamblers—a set of men certainly not following for a livelihood a very useful or very honest occupation, but one which, so far from being forbidden by the laws, was actually licensed by an act of the legislature passed but a single year before. Next, Negroes suspected of conspiring to raise an insurrection were caught up and hanged in all parts of the state; then, white men supposed to be leagued with the Negroes; and finally, strangers from neighboring states, going thither on business, were in many instances subjected to the same fate. Thus went on this process of hanging, from gamblers to Negroes, from Negroes to white citizens, and from these to strangers, till dead men were seen literally dangling from the boughs of trees upon every roadside, and in numbers almost sufficient to rival the native Spanish moss of the country as a drapery of the forest.

Turn then to that horror-striking scene at St. Louis. A single victim only was sacrificed there. This story is very short, and is perhaps the most highly tragic of anything of its length that has ever been witnessed in real life. A mulatto man by the name of McIntosh was seized in the street, dragged to the suburbs of the city, chained to a tree, and actually burned to death; and all within a single hour from the time he had been a freeman attending to his own business and at peace with the world.

Such are the effects of mob law, and such are the scenes becoming more and more frequent in this land so lately famed for love of law and order, and the stories of which have even now grown too familiar to attract anything more than an idle remark.

But you are perhaps ready to ask, "What has this to do with the perpetuation of our political institutions?" I answer, It has much to do with it. Its direct consequences are, comparatively speaking, but a small evil, and much of its danger consists in the proneness of our minds to regard its direct as its only consequences. Abstractly considered, the hanging of the gamblers at Vicksburg was of but little consequence. They constitute a portion of population that is worse than useless in any community; and their death, if no pernicious example be set by it, is never matter of reasonable regret with anyone. If they were annually swept from the stage of existence by the plague or smallpox, honest men would perhaps be much profited by the operation. Similar too is the correct reasoning in regard to the burning of the Negro at St. Louis. He had forfeited his life by the perpetration of an outrageous murder upon one of the most worthy and respectable citizens of the city, and had he not died as he did, he must have died by the sentence of the law in a very short time afterwards. As to him alone, it was as well the way it was as it could otherwise have been. But the example in either case was fearful. When men take it in their heads today to hang gamblers or burn murderers, they should recollect that in the confusion usually attending such transactions they will be as likely to hang or burn someone who is neither a gambler nor a murderer as one who is, and that, acting upon the example they set, the mob of tomorrow may, and probably will, hang or burn some of them by the very same mistake. And not only so: the innocent, those who have ever set their faces against violations of law in every shape, alike with the guilty fall victims to the ravages of mob law; and thus it goes on, step by step, till all the walls erected for the defense of the persons and property of individuals are trodden down and disregarded. But all this, even, is not the full extent of the evil. By such examples, by instances of the perpetrators of such acts going unpunished, the lawless in spirit are encouraged to become lawless in practice; and having been used to no restraint but dread of punishment, they thus become absolutely unrestrained. Having ever regarded government as their deadliest bane, they make a jubilee of the suspension of its operations, and pray for nothing so much as its total annihilation. While, on the other hand, good men, men who love tranquillity, who desire to abide by the laws and enjoy their benefits, who would gladly spill their blood in the defense of their country, seeing their property destroyed, their families insulted, and their lives endangered, their persons injured, and seeing nothing in prospect that forebodes a change for the better, become tired of and disgusted with a government that offers them no protection, and are not much averse to a change in which they imagine they have nothing to lose.

Thus, then, by the operation of this mobocratic spirit which all must admit is now abroad in the land, the strongest bulwark of any government, and particularly of those constituted like ours, may effectually be broken down and destroyed—I mean the attachment of the people. Whenever this effect shall be produced among us—whenever the vicious portion of the population shall be permitted to gather in bands of hundreds and thousands, and burn churches, ravage and rob provision stores, throw printing presses into rivers, shoot editors, and hang and burn obnoxious persons at pleasure and with impunity—depend on it, this government cannot last. By such things the feelings of the best citizens will become more or less alienated from it, and thus it will be left without friends, or with too few, and those few too weak to make their friendship effectual. At such a time, and under such circumstances, men of sufficient talent and ambition will not be wanting to seize the opportunity, strike the blow, and overturn that fair fabric which for the last half century has been the fondest hope of the lovers of freedom throughout the world.

I know the American people are much attached to their government; I know they would suffer much for its sake; I know they would endure evils long and patiently before they would ever think of exchanging it for another—yet, notwithstanding all this, if the laws be continually despised and disregarded, if their rights to be secure in their persons and property are held by no better tenure than the caprice of a mob, the alienation of their affections from the government is the natural consequence; and to that, sooner or later, it must come.

Here, then, is one point at which danger may be expected. The question recurs, How shall we fortify against it? The answer is simple. Let every American, every lover of liberty, every well-wisher to his posterity swear by the blood of the Revolution never to violate in the least particular the laws of the country, and never to tolerate their violation by others. As the patriots of seventy-six did to the support of the Declaration of Independence, so to the support of the Constitution and laws let every American pledge his life, his property, and his sacred honor. Let every man remember that to violate the law is to trample on the blood of his father, and to tear the charter of his own and his children's liberty. Let reverence for the laws be breathed by every American mother to the lisping babe that prattles on her lap; let it be taught in schools, in seminaries, and in colleges; let it be written in primers, spellingbooks, and in almanacs; let it be preached from the pulpit, proclaimed in legislative halls, and enforced in courts of justice. And, in short, let it become the political religion of the nation; and let the old and the young, the rich and the poor, the grave and the gay of all sexes and tongues and colors and conditions, sacrifice unceasingly upon its altars.

While ever a state of feeling such as this shall universally or even very generally prevail throughout the nation, vain will be every effort, and fruitless every attempt, to subvert our national freedom.

When I so pressingly urge a strict observance of all the laws, let me not be understood as saying there are no bad laws, or that grievances may not arise for the redress of which no legal provisions have been made. I mean to say no such thing. But I do mean to say that although bad laws, if they exist, should be repealed as soon as possible, still, while they continue in force, for the sake of example they should be religiously observed. So also in unprovided cases. If such arise, let proper legal provisions be made for them with the least possible delay, but till then let them, if not too intolerable, be borne with.

There is no grievance that is a fit object of redress by mob law. In any case that may arise, as, for instance, the promulgation of abolitionism, one of two positions is necessarily true—

that is, the thing is right within itself, and therefore deserves the protection of all law and all good citizens, or it is wrong, and therefore proper to be prohibited by legal enactments; and in neither case is the interposition of mob law either necessary, justifiable, or excusable.

But it may be asked, Why suppose danger to our political institutions? Have we not preserved them for more than fifty years? And why may we not for fifty times as long?

We hope there is no sufficient reason. We hope all danger may be overcome; but to conclude that no danger may ever arise would itself be extremely dangerous. There are now, and will hereafter be, many causes, dangerous in their tendency, which have not existed heretofore, and which are not too insignificant to merit attention. That our government should have been maintained in its original form, from its establishment until now, is not much to be wondered at. It had many props to support it through that period, which now are decayed and crumbled away. Through that period it was felt by all to be an undecided experiment; now it is understood to be a successful one. Then, all that sought celebrity and fame and distinction expected to find them in the success of that experiment. Their all was staked upon it; their destiny was inseparably linked with it. Their ambition aspired to display before an admiring world a practical demonstration of the truth of a proposition which had hitherto been considered at best no better than problematical—namely, the capability of a people to govern themselves. If they succeeded they were to be immortalized; their names were to be transferred to counties, and cities, and rivers, and mountains; and to be revered and sung, toasted through all time. If they failed, they were to be called knaves, and fools, and fanatics for a fleeting hour; then to sink and be forgotten.

They succeeded. The experiment is successful, and thousands have won their deathless names in making it so. But the game is caught; and I believe it is true that with the catching end the pleasures of the chase. This field of glory is harvested, and the crop is already appropriated. But new reapers will arise, and they too will seek a field. It is to deny what the history of the world tells us is true, to suppose that men of ambition and talents will not continue to spring up amongst us. And when they do, they will as naturally seek the gratification of their ruling passion as others have done before them. The question then is, Can that gratification be found in supporting and maintaining an edifice that has been erected by others? Most certainly it cannot. Many great and good men, sufficiently qualified for any task they should undertake, may ever be found whose ambition would aspire to nothing beyond a seat in Congress, a gubernatorial or a presidential chair; but such belong not to the family of the lion, or the tribe of the eagle. What! think you these places would satisfy an Alexander, a Caesar, or a Napoleon? Never! Towering genius disdains a beaten path. It seeks regions hitherto unexplored. It sees no distinction in adding story to story upon the monuments of fame erected to the memory of others. It denies that it is glory enough to serve under any chief. It scorns to tread in the footsteps of any predecessor, however illustrious. It thirsts and burns for distinction; and if possible, it will have it, whether at the expense of emancipating slaves or enslaving freemen. Is it unreasonable, then, to expect that some man possessed of the loftiest genius, coupled with ambition sufficient to push it to its utmost stretch, will at some time spring up among us? And when such an one does it will require the people to be united with each other, attached to the government and laws, and generally intelligent, to successfully frustrate his designs.

Distinction will be his paramount object, and although he would as willingly, perhaps more so, acquire it by doing good as harm, yet, that opportunity being past, and nothing left to be done in the way of building up, he would set boldly to the task of pulling down.

Here then is a probable case, highly dangerous, and such an one as could not have well existed heretofore.

Another reason which once was, but which, to the same extent, is now no more, has done much in maintaining our institutions thus far. I mean the powerful influence which the interesting scenes of the Revolution had upon the passions of the people as distinguished from their judgment. By this influence, the jealousy, envy, and avarice incident to our nature, and so common to a state of peace, prosperity, and conscious strength, were for the time in a great measure smothered and rendered inactive, while the deep-rooted principles of hate, and the powerful motive of revenge, instead of being turned against each other, were directed exclusively against the British nation. And thus, from the force of circumstances, the basest principles of our nature were either made to lie dormant, or to become the active agents in the advancement of the noblest of causes—that of establishing and maintaining civil and religious liberty.

But this state of feeling must fade, is fading, has faded, with the circumstances that produced it.

I do not mean to say that the scenes of the Revolution are now or ever will be entirely forgotten, but that, like everything else, they must fade upon the memory of the world, and grow more and more dim by the lapse of time. In history, we hope, they will be read of, and recounted, so long as the Bible shall be read; but even granting that they will, their influence cannot be what it heretofore has been. Even then they cannot be so universally known nor so vividly felt as they were by the generation just gone to rest. At the close of that struggle, nearly every adult male had been a participator in some of its scenes. The consequence was that of those scenes, in the form of a husband, a father, a son, or a brother, a living history was to be found in every family—a history bearing the indubitable testimonies of its own authenticity, in the limbs mangled, in the scars of wounds received, in the midst of the very scenes related—a history, too, that could be read and understood alike by all, the wise and the ignorant, the learned and the unlearned. But those histories are gone. They can be read no more forever. They were a fortress of strength; but what invading foeman could never do the silent artillery of time has done—the leveling of its walls. They are gone. They were a forest of giant oaks; but the all-restless hurricane has swept over them, and left only here and there a lonely trunk, despoiled of its verdure, shorn of its foliage, unshading and unshaded, to murmur in a few more gentle breezes, and to combat with its mutilated limbs a few more ruder storms, then to sink and be no more.

They were pillars of the temple of liberty; and now that they have crumbled away that temple must fall unless we, their descendants, supply their places with other pillars, hewn from the solid quarry of sober reason. Passion has helped us, but can do so no more. It will in future be our enemy. Reason—cold, calculating, unimpassioned reason—must furnish all the materials for our future support and defense. Let those materials be moulded into general intelligence, sound morality, and in particular, a reverence for the Constitution and laws; and that we improved to the last, that we remained free to the last, that we revered his name to the last, that during his long sleep we permitted no hostile foot to pass over or desecrate his resting place, shall be that which to learn the last trump shall awaken our Washington.

Upon these let the proud fabric of freedom rest, as the rock of its basis; and as truly as has been said of the only greater institution, "the gates of hell shall not prevail against it."

LETTER TO
MARY S. OWENS

Friend Mary:

I have commenced two letters to send you before this, both of which displeased me before I got half done, and so I tore them up. The first I thought was not serious enough, and the second was on the other extreme. I shall send this, turn out as it may.

This thing of living in Springfield is rather a dull business, after all; at least it is so to me. I am quite as lonesome here as I ever was anywhere in my life. I have been spoken to by but one woman since I have been here, and should not have been by her if she could have avoided it. I've never been to church yet, and probably shall not be soon. I stay away because I am conscious I should not know how to behave myself.

I am often thinking of what we said about your coming to live at Springfield. I am afraid you would not be satisfied. There is a great deal of flourishing about in carriages here, which it would be your doom to see without sharing it. You would have to be poor, without the means of hiding your poverty. Do you believe you could bear that patiently? Whatever woman may cast her lot with mine, should any ever do so, it is my intention to do all in my power to make her happy and contented; and there is nothing I can imagine that would make me more unhappy than to fail in the effort. I know I should be much happier with you than the way I am, provided I saw no signs of discontent in you. What you have said to me may have been in the way of jest, or I may have misunderstood you. If so, then let it be forgotten; if otherwise, I much wish you would think seriously before you decide. What I have said I will most positively abide by, provided you wish it. My opinion is that you had better not do it. You have not been accustomed to hardship, and it may be more severe than you now imagine. I know you are capable of thinking correctly on any subject, and if you deliberate maturely upon this subject before you decide, then I am willing to abide your decision.

You must write me a good long letter after you get this. You have nothing else to do, and though it might not seem interesting to you after you had written it, it would be a good deal of company to me in this "busy wilderness." Tell your sister I don't want to hear any more about selling out and moving. That gives me the "hypo" whenever I think of it.

Yours, etc.,
LINCOLN

LETTER TO
JOSHUA F. SPEED

Springfield, June 19, 1841

Dear Speed:

We have had the highest state of excitement here for a week past that our community has ever witnessed; and, although the public feeling is somewhat allayed, the curious affair which aroused it is very far from being even yet cleared of mystery. It would take a quire of paper to give you anything like a full account of it, and I therefore only propose a brief outline. The chief personages in the drama are Archibald Fisher, supposed to be murdered, and Archibald Trailor, Henry Trailor, and William Trailor, supposed to have murdered him. The three Trailors are brothers: the first, Arch., as you know, lives in town; the second, Henry, in Clary's Grove; and the third, William, in Warren County; and Fisher, the supposed murdered, being without a family, had made his home with William. On Saturday evening, being the 29th of May, Fisher and William came to Henry's in a one-horse dearborn, and there stayed over Sunday; and on Monday all three came to Springfield (Henry on horseback) and joined Archibald at Myers's, the Dutch carpenter. That evening at supper Fisher was missing, and so next morning some ineffectual search was made for him; and on Tuesday, at one o'clock P.M., William and Henry started home without him. In a day or two Henry and one or two of his Clary-Grove neighbors came back for him again, and advertised his disappearance in the papers. The knowledge of the matter thus far had not been general, and here it dropped entirely, till about the 10th instant, when Keys received a letter from the postmaster in Warren County, that William had arrived at home, and was telling a very mysterious and improbable story about the disappearance of Fisher, which induced the community there to sup-

20

pose he had been disposed of unfairly. Keys made this letter public, which immediately set the whole town and adjoining county agog. And so it has continued until yesterday. The mass of the people commenced a systematic search for the dead body, while Wickersham was dispatched to arrest Henry Trailor at the Grove, and Jim Maxcy to Warren to arrest William. On Monday last, Henry was brought in, and showed an evident inclination to insinuate that he knew Fisher to be dead, and that Arch. and William had killed him. He said he guessed the body could be found in Spring Creek, between the Beardstown road and Hickox's mill. Away the people swept like a herd of buffalo, and cut down Hickox's mill-dam *nolens volens,* to draw the water out of the pond, and then went up and down and down and up the creek, fishing and raking, and raking and ducking and diving for two days, and, after all, no dead body found.

In the meantime a sort of scuffling-ground had been found in the brush in the angle, or point, where the road leading into the woods past the brewery and the one leading in past the brickyard meet. From the scuffle-ground was the sign of something about the size of a man having been dragged to the edge of the thicket, where it joined the track of some small-wheeled carriage drawn by one horse, as shown by the road tracks. The carriage track led off toward Spring Creek. Near this drag-trail Dr. Merryman found two hairs, which, after a long scientific examination, he pronounced to be triangular human hairs, which term, he says, includes within it the whiskers, the hair growing under the arms and on other parts of the body; and he judged that these two were of the whiskers, because the ends were cut, showing that they had flourished in the neighborhood of the razor's operations.

On Thursday last Jim Maxcy brought in William Trailor from Warren. On the same day Arch. was arrested and put in jail. Yesterday (Friday) William was put upon his examining trial before May and Lovely. Archibald and Henry were both present. Lamborn prosecuted, and Logan, Baker, and your humble servant defended. A great many witnesses were introduced and examined, but I shall only mention those whose testimony seemed most important. The first of these was Captain Ransdell. He swore that when William and Henry left Springfield for home on Tuesday before mentioned they did not take the direct route—which, you know, leads by the butcher shop—but that they followed the street north until they got opposite, or nearly opposite, May's new house, after which he could not see them from where he stood; and it was afterwards proved that in about an hour after they started, they came into the street by the butcher shop from toward the brickyard. Dr. Merryman and others swore to what is stated about the scuffle-ground, drag-trail, whiskers, and carriage tracks. Henry was then introduced by the prosecution. He swore that when they started for home they went out north, as Ransdell stated, and turned down west by the brickyard into the woods, and there met Archibald; that they proceeded a small distance farther, when he was placed as a sentinel to watch for and announce the approach of anyone that might happen that way; that William and Arch. took the dearborn out of the road a small distance to the edge of the thicket, where they stopped, and he saw them lift the body of a man into it; that they then moved off with the carriage in the direction of Hickox's mill, and he loitered about for something like an hour, when William returned with the carriage, but without Arch., and said they had put him in a safe place; that they went somehow—he did not know exactly how—into the road close to the brewery, and proceeded on to Clary's Grove. He also stated that some time during the day William told him that he and Arch. had killed Fisher the evening before; that the way they did it was by him (William) knocking him down with a club, and Arch. then choking him to death.

An old man from Warren, called Dr. Gilmore, was then introduced on the part of the defense. He swore that he had known Fisher for several years; that Fisher had resided at his house a long time at each of two different spells—once while he built a barn for him, and once while he was doctored for some chronic disease; that two or three years ago Fisher had a serious hurt in his head by the bursting of a gun, since which he had been subject to continued bad health and occasional aberration of mind. He also stated that on last Tuesday, being the same day that Maxcy arrested William Trailor, he (the doctor) was from home in the early part of the day, and on his return, about eleven o'clock, found Fisher at his house in bed, and apparently very unwell; that he asked him how he came from Springfield; that Fisher said he had come by Peoria, and also told of several other places he had been at more in the direction of Peoria, which showed that he at the time of speaking did not know where he had been wandering about in a state of derangement. He further stated that in about two hours he received a note from one of Trailor's friends, advising him of his arrest, and requesting him to go on to Springfield as a witness, to testify as to the state of Fisher's health in former times; that he immediately set off, calling up two of his neighbors as company, and, riding all evening and all night, overtook Maxcy and William at Lewiston in Fulton County; that Maxcy refusing to discharge Trailor upon his statement, his two neighbors returned and he came on to Springfield. Some question being made as to whether the doctor's story was not a fabrication, several acquaintances of his (among whom was the same postmaster who wrote Keys, as before mentioned) were introduced as sort of compurgators, who swore that they knew the doctor to be of good character for truth and veracity, and generally of good character in every way.

Here the testimony ended, and the Trailors were discharged, Arch. and William expressing both in word and manner their entire confidence that Fisher would be found alive at the doctor's by Galloway, Mallory, and Myers, who a day before had been despatched for that purpose; while Henry still protested that no power on earth could ever show Fisher alive. Thus stands this curious affair. When the doctor's story was first made public, it was amusing to scan and contemplate the countenances and hear the remarks of those who had been actively in search for the dead body: some looked quizzical, some melancholy, and some furiously angry. Porter, who had been very active, swore he always knew the man was not dead, and that he had not stirred an inch to hunt for him; Langford, who had taken the lead in cutting down Hickox's mill-dam, and wanted to hang Hickox for objecting, looked most awfully woebegone: he seemed the "victim of unrequited affection," as represented in the comic almanacs we used to laugh over; and Hart, the little drayman that hauled Molly home once, said it was too *damned* bad to have so much trouble, and no hanging after all.

I commenced this letter on yesterday, since which I received yours of the 13th. I stick to my promise to come to Louisville. Nothing new here except what I have written. I have not seen ——— since my last trip, and I am going out there as soon as I mail this letter.

Yours forever,
LINCOLN

Speech Before the Springfield Washingtonian Temperance Society

February 22, 1842

Although the temperance cause has been in progress for near twenty years, it is apparent to all that it is just now being crowned with a degree of success hitherto unparalleled.

The list of its friends is daily swelled by the additions of fifties, of hundreds, and of thousands. The cause itself seems suddenly transformed from a cold abstract theory to a living, breathing, active, and powerful chieftain, going forth "conquering and to conquer." The citadels of his great adversary are daily being stormed and dismantled; his temple and his altars, where the rites of his idolatrous worship have long been performed, and where human sacrifices have long been wont to be made, are daily desecrated and deserted. The triumph of the conqueror's fame is sounding from hill to hill, from sea to sea, and from land to land, and calling millions to his standard at a blast.

For this new and splendid success we heartily rejoice. That that success is so much greater now than heretofore is doubtless owing to rational causes; and if we would have it continue, we shall do well to inquire what those causes are.

The warfare heretofore waged against the demon intemperance has somehow or other been erroneous. Either the champions engaged or the tactics they adopted have not been the most proper. These champions for the most part have been preachers, lawyers, and hired agents. Between these and the mass of mankind there is a want of approachability, if the term be admissible, partially, at least, fatal to their success. They are supposed to have no sympathy of feeling or interest with those very persons whom it is their object to convince and persuade.

And again, it is so common and so easy to ascribe motives to men of these classes other than those they profess to act upon. The preacher, it is said, advocates temperance because he is a fanatic, and desires a union of the church and state; the lawyer from his pride and vanity of hearing himself speak; and the hired agent for his salary. But when one who has long been known as a victim of intemperance bursts the fetters that have bound him, and appears before his neighbors "clothed and in his right mind," a redeemed specimen of long-lost humanity, and stands up, with tears of joy trembling in his eyes, to tell of the miseries once endured, now to be endured no more forever; of his once naked and starving children, now clad and fed comfortably; of a wife long weighed down with woe, weeping, and a broken heart, now restored to health, happiness, and a renewed affection; and how easily it is all done, once it is resolved to be done; how simple his language!—there is a logic and an eloquence in it that few with human feelings can resist. They cannot say that he desires a union of church and state, for he is not a church member; they cannot say he is vain of hearing himself speak, for his whole demeanor shows he would gladly avoid speaking at all; they cannot say he speaks for pay, for he receives none, and asks for none. Nor can his sincerity in any way be doubted, or his sympathy for those he would persuade to imitate his example be denied.

In my judgment, it is to the battles of this new class of champions that our late success is greatly, perhaps chiefly, owing. But, had the old-school champions themselves been of the most wise selecting, was their system of tactics the most judicious? It seems to me it was not. Too much denunciation against dram-sellers and dram-drinkers was indulged in. This I think was both impolitic and unjust. It was impolitic, because it is not much in the nature of man to be driven to anything; still

less to be driven about that which is exclusively his own business; and least of all where such driving is to be submitted to at
the expense of pecuniary interest or burning appetite. When the
dram-seller and -drinker were incessantly told—not in accents
of entreaty and persuasion, diffidently addressed by erring man
to an erring brother, but in the thundering tones of anathema
and denunciation with which the lordly judge often groups
together all the crimes of the felon's life, and thrusts them in his
face just ere he passes sentence of death upon him—that they
were the authors of all the vice and misery and crime in the land;
that they were the manufacturers and material of all the thieves
and robbers and murderers that infest the earth; that their
houses were the workshops of the devil; and that their persons
should be shunned by all the good and virtuous, as moral pesti-
lences—I say, when they were told all this, and in this way, it
is not wonderful that they were slow to acknowledge the truth
of such denunciations, and to join the ranks of their denouncers
in a hue and cry against themselves.

To have expected them to do otherwise than they did—to
have expected them not to meet denunciation with denunciation, crimination with crimination, and anathema with anathema—was to expect a reversal of human nature, which is God's
decree and can never be reversed.

When the conduct of men is designed to be influenced,
persuasion, kind, unassuming persuasion, should ever be
adopted. It is an old and a true maxim that "a drop of honey
catches more flies than a gallon of gall." So with men. If you
would win a man to your cause, first convince him that you are
his sincere friend. Therein is a drop of honey that catches his
heart, which, say what he will, is the great high road to his
reason, and which, when once gained, you will find but little
trouble in convincing his judgment of the justice of your cause,
if indeed that cause really be a just one. On the contrary, assume
to dictate to his judgment, or to command his action, or to mark
him as one to be shunned and despised, and he will retreat
within himself, close all the avenues to his head and his heart;

and though your cause be naked truth itself, transformed to the heaviest lance, harder than steel, and sharper than steel can be made, and though you throw it with more than herculean force and precision, you shall be no more able to pierce him than to penetrate the hard shell of a tortoise with a rye straw. Such is man, and so must he be understood by those who would lead him, even to his own best interests.

On this point the Washingtonians greatly excel the temperance advocates of former times. Those whom they desire to convince and persuade are their old friends and companions. They know they are not demons, nor even the worst of men; they know that generally they are kind, generous, and charitable even beyond the example of their more staid and sober neighbors. They are practical philanthropists; and they glow with a generous and brotherly zeal that mere theorizers are incapable of feeling. Benevolence and charity possess their hearts entirely; and out of the abundance of their hearts their tongues give utterance: "Love through all their actions runs, and all their words are mild." In this spirit they speak and act, and in the same they are heard and regarded. And when such is the temper of the advocate, and such of the audience, no good cause can be unsuccessful. But I have said that denunciations against dram-sellers and dram-drinkers are unjust, as well as impolitic. Let us see.

I have not inquired at what period of time the use of intoxicating liquors commenced; nor is it important to know. It is sufficient that, to all of us who now inhabit the world, the practice of drinking them is just as old as the world itself—that is, we have seen the one just as long as we have seen the other. When all such of us as have now reached the years of maturity first opened our eyes upon the stage of existence, we found intoxicating liquor recognized by everybody, used by everybody, repudiated by nobody. It commonly entered into the first draught of the infant and the last draught of the dying man. From the sideboard of the parson down to the ragged pocket of the houseless loafer, it was constantly found. Physicians prescribed it in this, that, and the other disease; government provided it for soldiers and sailors; and to have a rolling or raising, a husking or "hoedown," anywhere about without it was positively insufferable.

So, too, it was everywhere a respectable article of manufacture and merchandise. The making of it was regarded as an honorable livelihood, and he who could make most was the most enterprising and respectable. Large and small manufactories of it were everywhere erected, in which all the earthly goods of their owners were invested. Wagons drew it from town to town; boats bore it from clime to clime, and the winds wafted it from nation to nation; and merchants bought and sold it, by wholesale and retail, with precisely the same feelings on the part of the seller, buyer, and bystander as are felt at the selling and buying of ploughs, beef, bacon, or any other of the real necessaries of life. Universal public opinion not only tolerated but recognized and adopted its use.

It is true that even then it was known and acknowledged that many were greatly injured by it; but none seemed to think the injury arose from the use of a bad thing, but from the abuse of a very good thing. The victims of it were to be pitied and compassionated, just as are the heirs of consumption and other hereditary diseases. Their failing was treated as a misfortune, and not as a crime, or even as a disgrace. If, then, what I have been saying is true, is it wonderful that some should think and act now as all thought and acted twenty years ago? And is it just to assail, condemn, or despise them for doing so? The universal sense of mankind on any subject is an argument, or at least an influence, not easily overcome. The success of the argument in favor of the existence of an overruling Providence mainly depends upon that sense; and men ought not in justice to be denounced for yielding to it in any case, or giving it up slowly, especially when they are backed by interest, fixed habits, or burning appetites.

Another error, as it seems to me, into which the old reformers fell, was the position that all habitual drunkards were utterly incorrigible, and therefore must be turned adrift and damned without remedy in order that the grace of temperance might abound, to the temperate then, and to all mankind some hundreds of years thereafter. There is in this something so repugnant to humanity, so uncharitable, so cold-blooded and feelingless, that it never did nor ever can enlist the enthusiasm of a popular cause. We could not love the man who taught it— we could not hear him with patience. The heart could not throw open its portals to it, the generous man could not adopt it—it could not mix with his blood. It looked so fiendishly selfish, so like throwing fathers and brothers overboard to lighten the boat for our security, that the noble-minded shrank from the manifest meanness of the thing. And besides this, the benefits of a reformation to be effected by such a system were too remote in point of time to warmly engage many in its behalf. Few can be induced to labor exclusively for posterity, and none will do it enthusiastically. Posterity has done nothing for us; and, theorize on it as we may, practically we shall do very little for it, unless we are made to think we are at the same time doing something for ourselves.

What an ignorance of human nature does it exhibit to ask or to expect a whole community to rise up and labor for the temporal happiness of others, after themselves shall be consigned to the dust, a majority of which community take no pains whatever to secure their own eternal welfare at no more distant day! Great distance in either time or space has wonderful power to lull and render quiescent the human mind. Pleasures to be enjoyed, or pains to be endured, after we shall be dead and gone are but little regarded even in our own cases, and much less in the cases of others. Still, in addition to this there is something so ludicrous in promises of good or threats of evil a great way off as to render the whole subject with which they are connected easily turned into ridicule. "Better lay down that spade you are stealing, Paddy; if you don't you'll pay for it at the day of judgment." "Be the powers, if ye'll credit me so long I'll take another jist."

By the Washingtonians this system of consigning the habitual drunkard to hopeless ruin is repudiated. They adopt a more enlarged philanthropy; they go for present as well as future good. They labor for all now living, as well as hereafter to live. They teach hope to all—despair to none. As applying to their cause, they deny the doctrine of unpardonable sin; as in Christianity it is taught, so in this they teach: "While the lamp holds out to burn, The vilest sinner may return." And, what is a matter of more profound congratulation, they, by experiment upon experiment and example upon example, prove the maxim to be no less true in the one case than in the other. On every hand we behold those who but yesterday were the chief of sinners, now the chief apostles of the cause. Drunken devils are cast out by ones, by sevens, by legions; and their unfortunate victims, like the poor possessed who were redeemed from their long and lonely wanderings in the tombs, are publishing to the ends of the earth how great things have been done for them.

To these new champions and this new system of tactics our late success is mainly owing, and to them we must mainly look for the final consummation. The ball is now rolling gloriously on, and none are so able as they to increase its speed and its bulk, to add to its momentum and its magnitude—even though unlearned in letters, for this task none are so well educated. To fit them for this work they have been taught in the true school. They have been in that gulf from which they would teach others the means of escape. They have passed that prison wall which others have long declared impassable; and who that has not shall dare to weigh opinions with them as to the mode of passing?

But if it be true, as I have insisted, that those who have suffered by intemperance personally, and have reformed, are the most powerful and efficient instruments to push the reformation to ultimate success, it does not follow that those who have not suffered have no part left them to perform. Whether or not the world would be vastly benefited by a total and final banishment from it of all intoxicating drinks seems to me not now an open question. Three fourths of mankind confess the affirmative with their tongues, and, I believe, all the rest acknowledge it in their hearts.

Ought any, then, to refuse their aid in doing what good the good of the whole demands? Shall he who cannot do much be for that reason excused if he do nothing? "But," says one, "what good can I do by signing the pledge? I never drank, even without signing." This question has already been asked and answered more than a million of times. Let it be answered once more. For the man suddenly or in any other way to break off from the use of drams, who has indulged in them for a long course of years and until his appetite for them has grown ten- or a hundredfold stronger and more craving than any natural appetite can be, requires a most powerful moral effort. In such an undertaking he needs every moral support and influence that can possibly be brought to his aid and thrown around him. And not only so, but every moral prop should be taken from whatever argument might rise in his mind to lure him to his backsliding. When he casts his eyes around him, he should be able to see all that he respects, all that he admires, all that he loves, kindly and anxiously pointing him onward, and none beckoning him back to his former miserable "wallowing in the mire."

But it is said by some that men will think and act for themselves; that none will disuse spirits or anything else because his neighbors do; and that moral influence is not that powerful engine contended for. Let us examine this. Let me ask the man who could maintain this position most stiffly, what compensation he will accept to go to church some Sunday and sit during the sermon with his wife's bonnet upon his head? Not a trifle, I'll venture. And why not? There would be nothing irreligious in it, nothing immoral, nothing uncomfortable—then why not? Is it not because there would be something egregiously unfashionable in it? Then it is the influence of fashion; and what is the influence of fashion but the influence that other people's actions have on our actions—the strong inclination each of us feels to do as we see all our neighbors do? Nor is the influence of fashion confined to any particular thing or class of things; it is just as strong on one subject as another. Let us make it as unfashionable to withhold our names from the temperance cause as for husbands to wear their wives' bonnets to church, and instances will be just as rare in the one case as the other.

"But," say some, "we are no drunkards, and we shall not acknowledge ourselves such by joining a reformed-drunkards' society, whatever our influence might be." Surely no Christian will adhere to this objection. If they believe as they profess, that Omnipotence condescended to take on himself the form of sinful man, and as such to die an ignominious death for their sakes, surely they will not refuse submission to the infinitely lesser condescension, for the temporal, and perhaps eternal, salvation of a large, erring, and unfortunate class of their fellow creatures. Nor is the condescension very great.

In my judgment such of us as have never fallen victims have been spared more by the absence of appetite than from any mental or moral superiority over those who have. Indeed, I believe if we take habitual drunkards as a class, their heads and their hearts will bear an advantageous comparison with those of any other class. There seems ever to have been a proneness in the brilliant and warm-blooded to fall into this vice—the demon of intemperance ever seems to have delighted in sucking the blood of genius and of generosity. What one of us but can call to mind some relative, more promising in youth than all his fellows, who has fallen a sacrifice to his rapacity? He ever seems to have gone forth like the Egyptian angel of death, commissioned to slay, if not the first, the fairest born of every family. Shall he now be arrested in his desolating career? In that arrest all can give aid that will; and who shall be excused that can and will not? Far around as human breath has ever blown he keeps our fathers, our brothers, our sons, and our friends prostrate in the chains of moral death. To all the living everywhere we cry, "Come sound the moral trump, that these may rise and stand up an exceeding great army." "Come from the four winds, Oh breath! and breathe upon these slain that they may live." If the relative grandeur of revolutions shall be estimated by the great amount of human misery they alleviate, and the small amount they inflict, then indeed will this be the grandest the world shall ever have seen.

Of our political revolution of '76 we are all justly proud. It has given us a degree of political freedom far exceeding that of any other nation of the earth. In it the world has found a solution of the long-mooted problem as to the capability of man to govern himself. In it was the germ which has vegetated, and still is to grow and expand into the universal liberty of mankind. But, with all these glorious results, past, present, and to come, it had its evils too. It breathed forth famine, swam in blood, and rode in fire; and long, long after, the orphan's cry and the widow's wail continued to break the sad silence that ensued. These were the price, the inevitable price, paid for the blessings it bought.

Turn now to the temperance revolution. In it we shall find a stronger bondage broken, a viler slavery manumitted, a greater tyrant deposed; in it, more of want supplied, more disease healed, more sorrow assuaged. By it no orphans starving, no widows weeping. By it none wounded in feeling, none injured in interest; even the dram-maker and dram-seller will have glided into other occupations so gradually as never to have felt the change, and will stand ready to join all others in the universal song of gladness. And what a noble ally this to the cause of political freedom; with such an aid its march cannot fail to be on and on, till every son of earth shall drink in rich fruition the sorrow-quenching draughts of perfect liberty. Happy day when —all appetites controlled, all poisons subdued, all matter subjected—mind, all-conquering mind, shall live and move, the monarch of the world. Glorious consummation! Hail, fall of fury! Reign of reason, all hail!

And when the victory shall be complete—when there shall be neither a slave nor a drunkard on the earth—how proud the title of that land which may truly claim to be the birthplace and the cradle of both those revolutions that shall have ended in that victory. How nobly distinguished that people who shall have planted and nurtured to maturity both the political and moral freedom of their species.

This is the 110th anniversary of the birthday of Washington; we are met to celebrate this day. Washington is the mightiest name of earth—long since mightiest in the cause of civil liberty, still mightiest in moral reformation. On that name no eulogy is expected. It cannot be. To add brightness to the sun or glory to the name of Washington is alike impossible. Let none attempt it. In solemn awe pronounce the name, and in its naked deathless splendor leave it shining on.

LETTER TO
JOSHUA F. SPEED

Springfield, October [4?], 1842

Dear Speed:

You have heard of my duel with Shields, and I have now to inform you that the dueling business still rages in this city. Day before yesterday Shields challenged Butler, who accepted, and proposed fighting next morning at sunrise in Bob Allen's meadow, one hundred yards' distance, with rifles. To this Whitesides, Shields's second, said no, because of the law. Thus ended duel no. 2. Yesterday Whitesides chose to consider himself insulted by Dr. Merryman, so sent him a kind of quasi-challenge, inviting him to meet him at the Planter's House in St. Louis on the next Friday, to settle their difficulty. Merryman made me his friend, and sent Whitesides a note, inquiring to know if he meant his note as a challenge, and if so, that he would, according to the law in such case made and provided, prescribe the terms of the meeting. Whitesides returned for answer that if Merryman would meet him at the Planter's House as desired, he would challenge him. Merryman replied in a note that he denied Whitesides's right to dictate time and place, but that he (Merryman) would waive the question of time, and meet him at Louisiana, Missouri. Upon my presenting this note to Whitesides and stating verbally its contents, he declined receiving it, saying he had business in St. Louis, and it was as near as Louisiana. Merryman then directed me to notify Whitesides that he should publish the correspondence between them, with such comments as he thought fit. This I did. Thus it stood at bedtime last night. This morning Whitesides, by his friend Shields, is praying for a new trial, on the ground that he was mistaken in Merryman's proposition to meet him at Louisiana, Missouri, thinking it was the state of Louisiana. This Merryman hoots at, and is preparing his publication; while the town is in a ferment, and a street fight somewhat anticipated.

But I began this letter not for what I have been writing, but to say something on that subject which you know to be of such infinite solicitude to me. The immense sufferings you endured from the first days of September till the middle of February you never tried to conceal from me, and I well understood. You have now been the husband of a lovely woman nearly eight months. That you are happier now than the day you married her I well know, for without you could not be living. But I have your word for it, too, and the returning elasticity of spirits which is manifested in your letters. But I want to ask a close question: "Are you now in feeling as well as judgment glad that you are married as you are?" From anybody but me this would be an impudent question, not to be tolerated; but I know you will pardon it in me. Please answer it quickly, as I am impatient to know. I have sent my love to your Fanny so often, I fear she is getting tired of it. However, I venture to tender it again.

Yours forever,
LINCOLN

LETTER TO
WILLIAMSON DURLEY

Springfield, October 3, 1845

Friend Durley:

When I saw you at home, it was agreed that I should write to you and your brother Madison. Until I then saw you I was not aware of your being what is generally called an abolitionist, or, as you call yourself, a Liberty man, though I well knew there were many such in your country.

I was glad to hear that you intended to attempt to bring about, at the next election in Putnam, a union of the Whigs proper and such of the Liberty men as are Whigs in principle on all questions save only that of slavery. So far as I can perceive, by such union neither party need yield anything on *the* point in difference between them. If the Whig abolitionists of New York had voted with us last fall, Mr. Clay would now be president, Whig principles in the ascendant, and Texas not annexed; whereas, by the division, all that either had at stake in the contest was lost. And, indeed, it was extremely probable, beforehand, that such would be the result. As I always understood, the Liberty men deprecated the annexation of Texas extremely; and this being so, why they should refuse to cast their votes as to prevent it, even to me seemed wonderful. What was their process of reasoning, I can only judge from what a single one of them told me. It was this: "We are not to do evil that good may come." This general proposition is doubtless correct; but did it apply? If by your votes you could have prevented the *extension,* etc., of slavery would it not have been *good,* and not *evil,* so to have used your votes, even though it involved the casting of them for a slaveholder? By the *fruit* the tree is to be known. An *evil* tree cannot bring forth *good* fruit. If the fruit of electing Mr. Clay would have been to prevent the

38

extension of slavery, could the act of electing have been evil? But I will not argue further. I perhaps ought to say that individually I never was much interested in the Texas question. I never could see much good to come of annexation, inasmuch as they were already a free republican people on our own model. On the other hand, I never could very clearly see how the annexation would augment the evil of slavery. It always seemed to me that slaves would be taken there in about equal numbers, with or without annexation. And if more *were* taken because of annexation, still there would be just so many the fewer left where they were taken from. It is possibly true, to some extent, that, with annexation, some slaves may be sent to Texas and continued in slavery that otherwise might have been liberated. To whatever extent this may be true, I think annexation an evil. I hold it to be a paramount duty of us in the free states, due to the Union of the States, and perhaps to liberty itself (paradox though it may seem), to let the slavery of the other states alone; while, on the other hand, I hold it to be equally clear that we should never knowingly lend ourselves, directly or indirectly, to prevent that slavery from dying a natural death—to find new places for it to live in when it can no longer exist in the old. Of course I am not now considering what would be our duty in cases of insurrection among the slaves. To recur to the Texas question, I understand the Liberty men to have viewed annexation as a much greater evil than ever I did; and I would like to convince you, if I could, that they could have prevented it, if they had chosen. I intend this letter for you and Madison together; and if you and he or either shall think fit to drop me a line, I shall be pleased.

Yours with respect,
A. LINCOLN

SPEECH IN THE U.S. HOUSE OF REPRESENTATIVES

WAR WITH MEXICO

January 12, 1848

Mr. Chairman: Some if not all the gentlemen on the other side of the House who have addressed the committee within the last two days have spoken rather complainingly, if I have rightly understood them, of the vote given a week or ten days ago declaring that the war with Mexico was unnecessarily and unconstitutionally commenced by the president. I admit that such a vote should not be given in mere party wantonness, and that the one given is justly censurable if it have no other or better foundation. I am one of those who joined in that vote; and I did so under my best impression of the truth of the case. How I got this impression, and how it may possibly be remedied, I will now try to show.

When the war began, it was my opinion that all those who because of knowing too little, or because of knowing too much, could not conscientiously approve the conduct of the president in the beginning of it should nevertheless, as good citizens and patriots, remain silent on that point, at least till the war should be ended. Some leading Democrats, including ex-president Van Buren, have taken this same view, as I understand them; and I adhered to it and acted upon it, until since I took my seat here; and I think I should still adhere to it were it not that the president and his friends will not allow it to be so. Besides the continual effort of the president to argue every silent vote given for supplies into an endorsement of the justice and wisdom of his conduct; besides that singularly candid paragraph in his late message in which he tells us that Congress with great unanimity had declared that "by the act of the Republic of Mexico, a state of war exists between that government and the United States," when the same journals that informed him of this also informed him that when that declaration stood disconnected from the question of supplies sixty-seven in the House, and not fourteen merely, voted against it; besides this open attempt to prove by telling the truth what he could not prove by telling the whole truth—demanding of all who will not submit to be misrepresented, in justice to themselves, to speak out—besides all this, one of my colleagues [Mr. Richardson] at a very early day in the session brought in a set of resolutions expressly endorsing the original justice of the war on the part of the president. Upon these resolutions when they shall be put on their passage I shall be compelled to vote; so that I cannot be silent if I would. Seeing this, I went about preparing myself to give the vote understandingly when it should come. I carefully examined the president's message, to ascertain what he himself had said and proved upon the point. The result of this examination was to make the impression that, taking for true all the president states as facts, he falls far short of proving his justification; and that the president would have gone further with his proof if it had not been for the small matter that the truth would not permit him. Under the impression thus made I gave the vote before mentioned. I propose now to give concisely the process of the examination I made, and how I reached the conclusion I did.

The president, in his first war message of May 1846, declares that the soil was ours on which hostilities were commenced by Mexico, and he repeats that declaration almost in the same language in each successive annual message, thus showing that he deems that point a highly essential one. In the importance of that point I entirely agree with the president. To my judgment it is the very point upon which he should be justified, or condemned. In his message of December 1846, it seems to have occurred to him, as is certainly true, that title—

ownership—to soil or anything else is not a simple fact, but is a conclusion following on one or more simple facts; and that it was incumbent upon him to present the facts from which he concluded the soil was ours on which the first blood of the war was shed.

Accordingly, a little below the middle of page twelve in the message last referred to he enters upon that task; forming an issue and introducing testimony, extending the whole to a little below the middle of page fourteen. Now, I propose to try to show that the whole of this—issue and evidence—is from beginning to end the sheerest deception. The issue, as he presents it, is in these words: "But there are those who, conceding all this to be true, assume the ground that the true western boundary of Texas is the Nueces, instead of the Rio Grande; and that, therefore, in marching our army to the east bank of the latter river, we passed the Texas line and invaded the territory of Mexico." Now this issue is made up of two affirmatives and no negative. The main deception of it is that it assumes as true that one river or the other is necessarily the boundary; and cheats the superficial thinker entirely out of the idea that possibly the boundary is somewhere between the two, and not actually at either. A further deception is that it will let in evidence which a true issue would exclude. A true issue made by the president would be about as follows: "I say the soil was ours, on which the first blood was shed; there are those who say it was not."

I now proceed to examine the president's evidence as applicable to such an issue. When that evidence is analyzed, it is all included in the following propositions:

1. That the Rio Grande was the western boundary of Louisiana as we purchased it of France in 1803.
2. That the Republic of Texas always claimed the Rio Grande as her eastern boundary.
3. That by various acts she had claimed it on paper.
4. That Santa Anna in his treaty with Texas recognized the Rio Grande as her boundary.

5. That Texas before, and the United States after, annexation had exercised jurisdiction beyond the Nueces—between the two rivers.

6. That our Congress understood the boundary of Texas to extend beyond the Nueces.

Now for each of these in its turn. His first item is that the Rio Grande was the western boundary of Louisiana, as we purchased it of France in 1803; and seeming to expect this to be disputed, he argues over the amount of nearly a page to prove it true, at the end of which he lets us know that by the treaty of 1819 we sold to Spain the whole country from the Rio Grande eastward to the Sabine. Now, admitting for the present that the Rio Grande was the boundary of Louisiana, what under heaven had that to do with the present boundary between us and Mexico? How, Mr. Chairman, the line that once divided your land from mine can still be the boundary between us after I have sold my land to you is to me beyond all comprehension. And how any man, with an honest purpose only of proving the truth, could ever have thought of introducing such a fact to prove such an issue is equally incomprehensible.

His next piece of evidence is that "the Republic of Texas always claimed this river [Rio Grande] as her western boundary." That is not true, in fact. Texas has claimed it, but she has not always claimed it. There is at least one distinguished exception. Her state constitution—the republic's most solemn and well-considered act, that which may, without impropriety, be called her last will and testament, revoking all others—makes no such claim. But suppose she had always claimed it. Has not Mexico always claimed the contrary? So that there is but claim against claim, leaving nothing proved until we get back of the claims and find which has the better foundation. Though not in the order in which the president presents his evidence, I now consider that class of his statements which are in substance nothing more than that Texas has, by various acts of her Convention and Congress, claimed the Rio Grande as her boundary, on paper. I mean here what he says about the fixing of the Rio Grande as her boundary in her old constitution (not her state constitution), about forming congressional districts, counties, etc.

Now all of this is but naked claim; and what I have already said about claims is strictly applicable to this. If I should claim your land by word of mouth, that certainly would not make it mine; and if I were to claim it by a deed which I had made myself, and with which you had had nothing to do, the claim would be quite the same in substance—or rather, in utter nothingness. I next consider the president's statement that Santa Anna in his treaty with Texas recognized the Rio Grande as the western boundary of Texas. Besides the position so often taken, that Santa Anna while a prisoner of war, a captive, could not bind Mexico by a treaty, which I deem conclusive—besides this, I wish to say something in relation to this treaty, so called by the president, with Santa Anna. If any man would like to be amused by a sight of that little thing which the president calls by that big name, he can have it by turning to *Niles's Register,* volume 1, page 336. And if any one should suppose that *Niles's Register* is a curious repository of so mighty a document as a solemn treaty between nations, I can only say that I learned to a tolerable degree of certainty, by inquiry at the State Department, that the president himself never saw it anywhere else.

By the way, I believe I should not err if I were to declare that during the first ten years of the existence of that document it was never by anybody called a treaty—that it was never so called till the president, in his extremity, attempted by so calling it to wring something from it in justification of himself in connection with the Mexican War. It has none of the distinguishing features of a treaty. It does not call itself a treaty. Santa Anna does not therein assume to bind Mexico; he assumes only to act as the president-commander-in-chief of the Mexican army and navy; stipulates that the then present hostilities should cease, and that he would not himself take up arms, nor influence the Mexican people to take up arms, against Texas during the existence of the war of independence. He did not recognize the independence of Texas; he did not assume to put an end to the war, but clearly indicated his expectation of its continuance; he did not say one word about boundary, and, most probably, never thought of it. It is stipulated therein that the Mexican forces should evacuate the territory of Texas, passing to the other side of the Rio Grande; and in another article it is stipulated that, to prevent collisions between the armies, the Texas army should not approach nearer than within five leagues—of what is not said, but clearly, from the object stated, it is of the Rio Grande. Now, if this is a treaty recognizing the Rio Grande as the boundary of Texas, it contains the singular feature of stipulating that Texas shall not go within five leagues of her own boundary.

Next comes the evidence of Texas before annexation, and the United States afterwards, exercising jurisdiction beyond the Nueces and between the two rivers. This actual exercise of jurisdiction is the very class or quality of evidence we want. It is excellent so far as it goes; but does it go far enough? He tells us it went beyond the Nueces, but he does not tell us it went to the Rio Grande. He tells us jurisdiction was exercised between the two rivers, but he does not tell us it was exercised over all the territory between them. Some simple-minded people think it is possible to cross one river and go beyond it without going all the way to the next, that jurisdiction may be exercised between two rivers without covering all the country between them. I know a man, not very unlike myself, who exercises jurisdiction over a piece of land between the Wabash and the Mississippi; and yet so far is this from being all there is between those rivers that it is just 152 feet long by 50 feet wide, and no part of it much within a hundred miles of either. He has a neighbor between him and the Mississippi—that is, just across the street, in that direction—whom I am sure he could neither persuade nor force to give up his habitation; but which nevertheless he could certainly annex, if it were to be done by merely standing on his own side of the street and claiming it, or even sitting down and writing a deed for it.

But next the president tells us the Congress of the United States understood the state of Texas they admitted into the Union to extend beyond the Nueces. Well, I suppose they did. I certainly so understood it. But how far beyond? That Congress did not understand it to extend clear to the Rio Grande is quite certain, by the fact of their joint resolutions for admission expressly leaving all questions of boundary to future adjustment. And it may be added that Texas herself is proven to have had the same understanding of it that our Congress had, by the fact of the exact conformity of her new constitution to those resolutions.

I am now through the whole of the president's evidence; and it is a singular fact that if anyone should declare the president sent the army into the midst of a settlement of Mexican people who had never submitted, by consent or by force, to the authority of Texas or of the United States, and that there and thereby the first blood of the war was shed, there is not one word in all the president has said which would either admit or deny the declaration. . . .

How like the half-insane mumbling of a fever dream is the whole war part of his late message! At one time telling us that Mexico has nothing whatever that we can get but territory; at another showing us how we can support the war by levying contributions on Mexico. At one time urging the national honor, the security of the future, the prevention of foreign interference, and even the good of Mexico herself as among the objects of the war; at another telling us that "to reject indemnity, by refusing to accept a cession of territory, would be to abandon all our just demands, and to wage the war, bearing all its expenses, without a purpose or definite object." So then this national honor, security of the future, and everything but territorial indemnity may be considered the no-purposes and indefinite objects of the war! But, having it now settled that territorial indemnity is the only object, we are urged to seize, by legislation here, all that he was content to take a few months ago, and the whole province of Lower California to boot, and to still carry on the war—to take all we are fighting for, and still fight on. Again, the president is resolved under all circumstances to have full territorial indemnity for the expenses of the war; but he forgets to tell us how we are to get the excess after those expenses shall have surpassed the value of the whole of the Mexican territory. So again, he insists that the separate national existence of Mexico shall be maintained; but he does not tell us how this can be done, after we shall have taken all her territory.

Lest the questions I have suggested be considered speculative merely, let me be indulged a moment in trying to show they are not. The war has gone on some twenty months; for the expenses of which, together with an inconsiderable old score, the president now claims about one half of the Mexican territory, and that by far the better half, so far as concerns our ability to make anything out of it. It is comparatively uninhabited; so that we could establish land offices in it, and raise some money in that way. But the other half is already inhabited, as I understand it, tolerably densely for the nature of the country, and all its lands, or all that are valuable, already appropriated as private property. How then are we to make anything out of these lands with this encumbrance on them? or how remove the encumbrance? I suppose no one would say we should kill the people, or drive them out, or make slaves of them, or confiscate their property. How, then, can we make much out of this part of the territory? If the prosecution of the war has in expenses already equalled the better half of the country, how long its future prosecution will be in equalling the less valuable half is not a speculative, but a practical, question, pressing closely upon us. And yet it is a question which the president seems never to have thought of.

As to the mode of terminating the war and securing peace, the president is equally wandering and indefinite. First, it is to be done by a more vigorous prosecution of the war in the vital parts of the enemy's country; and after apparently talking himself tired on this point, the president drops down into a half-despairing tone, and tells us that "with a people distracted and divided by contending factions, and a government subject to constant changes by successive revolutions, the continued success of our arms may fail to secure a satisfactory peace." Then he suggests the propriety of wheedling the Mexican people to desert the counsels of their own leaders, and, trusting in our protestations, to set up a government from which we can secure a satisfactory peace; telling us that "this may become the only mode of obtaining such a peace." But soon he falls into doubt of this too; and then drops back on to the already half-abandoned ground of "more vigorous prosecution." All this shows that the president is in nowise satisfied with his own positions. First he takes up one, and in attempting to argue us into it he argues himself out of it, then seizes another and goes through the same process, and then, confused at being able to think of nothing new, he snatches up the old one again, which he has some time before cast off. His mind, taxed beyond its power, is running hither and thither, like some tortured creature on a burning surface, finding no position on which it can settle down and be at ease.

Again, it is a singular omission in this message that it nowhere intimates when the president expects the war to terminate. At its beginning, General Scott was by this same president driven into disfavor if not disgrace, for intimating that peace could not be conquered in less than three or four months. But now, at the end of about twenty months, during which time our arms have given us the most splendid successes, every department and every part, land and water, officers and privates, regulars and volunteers, doing all that men could do, and hundreds of things which it had ever before been thought men could not do—after all this, this same president gives a long message, without showing us that as to the end he himself has even an imaginary conception. As I have before said, he knows not where he is. He is a bewildered, confounded, and miserably perplexed man. God grant he may be able to show there is not something about his conscience more painful than his mental perplexity.

Speech in the U.S. House of Representatives

General Zachary Taylor as a Presidential Candidate

July 27, 1848

Mr. Speaker, our Democratic friends seem to be in great distress because they think our candidate for the presidency don't suit us. Most of them cannot find out that General Taylor has any principles at all; some, however, have discovered that he has one, but that one is entirely wrong. This one principle is his position on the veto power. The gentleman from Tennessee [Mr. Stanton] who has just taken his seat, indeed, has said there is very little, if any, difference on this question between General Taylor and all the presidents; and he seems to think it sufficient detraction from General Taylor's position on it that it has nothing new in it. But all others whom I have heard speak assail it furiously. A new member from Kentucky [Mr. Clark], of very considerable ability, was in particular concerned about it. He thought it altogether novel and unprecedented for a president or a presidential candidate to think of approving bills whose constitutionality may not be entirely clear to his own mind. He thinks the ark of our safety is gone unless presidents shall always veto such bills as in their judgment may be of doubtful constitutionality. However clear Congress may be on their authority to pass any particular act, the gentleman from Kentucky thinks the president must veto it if he has doubts about it. Now I have neither time nor inclination to argue with the gentleman on the veto power as an original question; but I wish to show

that General Taylor, and not he, agrees with the earlier statesmen on this question.

When the bill chartering the first Bank of the United States
passed Congress, its constitutionality was questioned. Mr.
Madison, then in the House of Representatives, as well as others, had opposed it on that ground. General Washington, as
president, was called on to approve or reject it. He sought and
obtained on the constitutionality question the separate written
opinions of Jefferson, Hamilton, and Edmund Randolph—they
then being respectively secretary of state, secretary of the Treasury, and attorney general. Hamilton's opinion was for the
power; while Randolph's and Jefferson's were both against it.
Mr. Jefferson, after giving his opinion deciding only against the
constitutionality of the bill, closes his letter with the paragraph
which I now read:

> It must be admitted, however, that unless the president's mind,
> on a view of everything which is urged for and against this bill,
> is tolerably clear that it is unauthorized by the Constitution—if
> the pro and con hang so even as to balance his judgment—a just
> respect for the wisdom of the legislature would naturally decide
> the balance in favor of their opinion. It is chiefly for cases where
> they are clearly misled by error, ambition, or interest, that the
> Constitution has placed a check in the negative of the president.
>
> THOMAS JEFFERSON
>
> February 15, 1791

General Taylor's opinion, as expressed in his Allison letter, is as
I now read:

> The power given by the veto is a high conservative power; but,
> in my opinion, should never be exercised except in cases of clear
> violation of the Constitution, or manifest haste and want of
> consideration by Congress.

It is here seen that, in Mr. Jefferson's opinion, if on the
constitutionality of any given bill the president doubts, he is not
to veto it, as the gentleman from Kentucky would have him do,

but is to defer to Congress and approve it. And if we compare the opinion of Jefferson and Taylor, as expressed in these paragraphs, we shall find them more exactly alike than we can often find any two expressions having any literal difference. None but interested faultfinders, I think, can discover any substantial variation.

But gentlemen on the other side are unanimously agreed that General Taylor has no other principles. They are in utter darkness as to his opinions on any of the questions of policy which occupy the public attention. But is there any doubt as to what he will do on the prominent questions if elected? Not the least. It is not possible to know what he will or would do in every imaginable case, because many questions have passed away, and others doubtless will arise which none of us have yet thought of; but on the prominent questions of currency, tariff, internal improvements, and Wilmot Proviso, General Taylor's course is at least as well defined as is General Cass's. Why, in their eagerness to get at General Taylor, several Democratic members here have desired to know whether, in case of his election, a bankrupt law is to be established. Can they tell us General Cass's opinion on this question? [A voice: "He is against it."] Aye, how do you know he is? There is nothing about it in the platform, nor elsewhere, that I have seen. If the gentleman knows of anything which I do not know he can show it. But to return. General Taylor, in his Allison letter, says:

> Upon the subject of the tariff, the currency, the improvement of our great highways, rivers, lakes, and harbors, the will of the people, as expressed through their representatives in Congress, ought to be respected and carried out by the executive.

Now this is the whole matter. In substance, it is this: The people say to General Taylor, "If you are elected, shall we have a national bank?" He answers, "Your will, gentlemen, not mine." "What about the tariff?" "Say yourselves." "Shall our rivers and harbors be improved?" "Just as you please. If you desire a bank, an alteration of the tariff, internal improvements, any or all, I will not hinder you. If you do not desire them, I will not attempt to force them on you. Send up your members of Congress from the various districts, with opinions according to your own, and if they are for these measures, or any of them, I shall have nothing to oppose; if they are not for them, I shall not, by any appliances whatever, attempt to dragoon them into their adoption." Now can there be any difficulty in understanding this? To you Democrats it may not seem like principle; but surely you cannot fail to perceive the position plainly enough. The distinction between it and the position of your candidate is broad and obvious, and I admit you have a clear right to show it is wrong if you can; but you have no right to pretend you cannot see it at all. We see it, and to us it appears like principle, and the best sort of principle at that—the principle of allowing the people to do as they please with their own business.

My friend from Indiana [C. B. Smith] has aptly asked, "Are you willing to trust the people?" Some of you answered substantially, "We are willing to trust the people; but the president is as much the representative of the people as Congress." In a certain sense, and to a certain extent, he is the representative of the people. He is elected by them, as well as Congress is; but can he, in the nature of things, know the wants of the people as well as three hundred other men, coming from all the various localities of the nation? If so, where is the propriety of having a Congress? That the Constitution gives the president a negative on legislation, all know; but that this negative should be so combined with platforms and other appliances as to enable him, and in fact almost compel him, to take the whole of legislation into his own hands, is what we object to, is what General Taylor objects to, and is what constitutes the broad distinction between you and us. To thus transfer legislation is clearly to take it from those who understand with minuteness the interests of the people, and give it to one who does not and cannot so well understand it.

I understand your idea that if a presidential candidate avow his opinion upon a given question, or rather upon all questions, and the people, with full knowledge of this, elect him, they thereby distinctly approve all those opinions. By means of it, measures are adopted or rejected contrary to the wishes of the whole of one party, and often nearly half of the other. Three, four, or half a dozen questions are prominent at a given time; the party selects its candidate, and he takes his position on each of these questions. On all but one his positions have already been endorsed at former elections, and his party fully committed to them; but that one is new, and a large portion of them are against it. But what are they to do? The whole was strung together; and they must take all, or reject all. They cannot take what they like, and leave the rest. What they are already committed to being the majority, they shut their eyes, and gulp the whole. Next election, still another is introduced in the same way. If we run our eyes along the line of the past, we shall see that almost if not quite all the articles of the present Democratic creed have been at first forced upon the party in this very way. And just now, and just so, opposition to internal improvements is to be established if General Cass shall be elected. Almost half the Democrats here are for improvements; but they will vote for Cass, and if he succeeds, their vote will have aided in closing the doors against improvements. Now this is a process which we think is wrong. We prefer a candidate who, like General Taylor, will allow the people to have their own way, regardless of his private opinions; and I should think the internal-improvement Democrats, at least, ought to prefer such a candidate. He would force nothing on them which they don't want, and he would allow them to have improvements which their own candidate, if elected, will not.

Mr. Speaker, I have said General Taylor's position is as well defined as is that of General Cass. In saying this, I admit I do not certainly know what he would do on the Wilmot Proviso. I am a Northern man, or rather a western-free-state man, with a constitutency I believe to be, and with personal feelings I know to be, against the extension of slavery. As such, and with what information I have, I hope and believe General Taylor, if

elected, would not veto the proviso. But I do not know it. Yet
if I knew he would, I still would vote for him. I should do so
because, in my judgment, his election alone can defeat General
Cass; and because, should slavery thereby go to the territory we
now have, just so much will certainly happen by the election of
Cass, and in addition a course of policy leading to new wars,
new acquisitions of territory and still further extensions of slavery. One of the two is to be president. Which is preferable? . . .

The gentleman from Georgia [Mr. Iverson] says we have
deserted all our principles, and taken shelter under General
Taylor's military coattail, and he seems to think this is exceedingly degrading. Well, as his faith is, so be it unto him. But can
he remember no other military coattail under which a certain
other party have been sheltering for near a quarter of a century?
Has he no acquaintance with the ample military coattail of
General Jackson? Does he not know that his own party have run
the five last presidential races under that coattail, and that they
are now running the sixth under the same cover? Yes, sir, that
coattail was used not only for General Jackson himself, but has
been clung to, with the grip of death, by every Democratic
candidate since. You have never ventured, and dare not now
venture, from under it. Your campaign papers have constantly
been "Old Hickories," with rude likenesses of the old general
upon them; hickory poles and hickory brooms your never-
ending emblems; Mr. Polk himself was "Young Hickory," or
something so; and even now your campaign paper here is proclaiming that Cass and Butler are of the true "Hickory stripe."
Now, sir, you dare not give it up. Like a horde of hungry ticks
you have stuck to the tail of the Hermitage lion to the end of his
life; and you are still sticking to it, and drawing a loathsome
sustenance from it, after he is dead. A fellow once advertised
that he had made a discovery by which he could make a new
man out of an old one, and have enough of the stuff left to make
a little yellow dog. Just such a discovery has General Jackson's
popularity been to you. You not only twice made president of
him out of it, but you have had enough of the stuff left to make

presidents of several comparatively small men since; and it is your chief reliance now to make still another.

Mr. Speaker, old horses and military coattails, or tails of any sort, are not figures of speech such as I would be the first to introduce into discussions here; but as the gentleman from Georgia has thought fit to introduce them, he and you are welcome to all you have made, or can make by them. If you have any more old horses, trot them out; any more tails, just cock them and come at us. I repeat, I would not introduce this mode of discussion here; but I wish gentlemen on the other side to understand that the use of degrading figures is a game at which they may not find themselves able to take all the winnings. [A voice: "We give it up!"] Aye, you give it up, and well you may; but for a very different reason from that which you would have us understand. The point—the power to hurt—of all figures consists in the truthfulness of their application; and, understanding this, you may well give it up. They are weapons which hit you, but miss us.

But in my hurry I was very near closing this subject of military tails before I was done with it. There is one entire article of the sort I have not discussed yet—I mean the military tail you Democrats are now engaged in dovetailing into the great Michigander. Yes, sir; all his biographies—and they are legion—have him in hand, tying him to a military tail, like so many mischievous boys tying a dog to a bladder of beans. True, the material they have is very limited, but they drive at it might and main. He *in*vaded Canada without resistance, and he *out*-vaded it without pursuit. As he did both under orders, I suppose there was to him neither credit nor discredit in them; but they constitute a large part of the tail. He was not at Hull's surrender, but he was close by; he was volunteer aid to General Harrison on the day of the battle of the Thames; and as you said in 1840 Harrison was picking huckleberries two miles off while the battle was fought, I suppose it is a just conclusion with you to say Cass was aiding Harrison to pick huckleberries. This is about all, except the mooted question of the broken sword.

Some authors say he broke it, some say he threw it away, and some others, who ought to know, say nothing about it. Perhaps it would be a fair historical compromise to say, if he did not break it, he did not do anything else with it.

By the way, Mr. Speaker, did you know I am a military hero? Yes, sir; in the days of the Black Hawk War I fought, bled, and came away. Speaking of General Cass's career reminds me of my own. I was not at Stillman's defeat, but I was about as near it as Cass was to Hull's surrender; and, like him, I saw the place very soon afterward. It is quite certain I did not break my sword, for I had none to break; but I bent a musket pretty badly on one occasion. If Cass broke his sword, the idea is he broke it in desperation; I bent the musket by accident. If General Cass went in advance of me in picking huckleberries, I guess I surpassed him in charges upon the wild onions. If he saw any live, fighting Indians, it was more than I did; but I had a good many bloody struggles with the mosquitoes, and although I never fainted from the loss of blood, I can truly say I was often very hungry. Mr. Speaker, if I should ever conclude to doff whatever our Democratic friends may suppose there is of black-cockade federalism about me, and therefore they shall take me up as their candidate for the presidency, I protest they shall not make fun of me, as they have of General Cass, by attempting to write me into a military hero. . . .

But, as General Taylor is, par excellence, the hero of the Mexican War, and as you Democrats say we Whigs have always opposed the war, you think it must be very awkward and embarrassing for us to go for General Taylor. The declaration that we have always opposed the war is true or false, according as one may understand the term "oppose the war." If to say "the war was unnecessarily and unconstitutionally commenced by the president" be opposing the war, then the Whigs have very generally opposed it. Whenever they have spoken at all, they have said this; and they have said it on what has appeared good reason to them. The marching an army into the midst of a peaceful Mexican settlement, frightening the inhabitants away, leaving their growing crops and other property to destruction, to you may appear a perfectly amiable, peaceful, unprovoking procedure; but it does not appear so to us. So to call such an act, to us appears no other than a naked, impudent absurdity, and we speak of it accordingly. But if, when the war had begun, and had become the cause of the country, the giving of our money and our blood, in common with yours, was support of the war, then it is not true that we have always opposed the war. With few individual exceptions, you have constantly had our votes here for all the necessary supplies. And, more than this, you have had the services, the blood, and the lives of our political brethren in every trial and on every field. The beardless boy and the mature man, the humble and the distinguished—you have had them. Through suffering and death, by disease and in battle they have endured and fought and fell with you. Clay and Webster each gave a son, never to be returned. From the state of my own residence, besides other worthy but less known Whig names, we sent Marshall, Morrison, Baker, and Hardin; they all fought, and one fell, and in the fall of that one we lost our best Whig man. Nor were the Whigs few in number, or laggard in the day of danger. In that fearful, bloody, breathless struggle at Buena Vista, where each man's hard task was to beat back five foes or die himself, of the five high officers who perished, four were Whigs. . . .

Mr. Speaker, I see I have but three minutes left, and this forces me to throw out one whole branch of my subject. A single word on still another. The Democrats are keen enough to frequently remind us that we have some dissensions in our ranks. Our good friend from Baltimore immediately before me [Mr. McLane] expressed some doubt the other day as to which branch of our party General Taylor would ultimately fall into the hands of. That was a new idea to me. I knew we had dissenters, but I did not know they were trying to get our candidate away from us. I would like to say a word to our dissenters, but I have not the time. Some such we certainly have; have you none, gentlemen Democrats? Is it all union and harmony in your ranks? no bickerings? no divisions? If there be doubt as to which of our divisions will get our candidate, is there no doubt as to which of your candidates will get your party? I have heard some things from New York; and if they are true, one might well say of your party there, as a drunken fellow once said when he heard the reading of an indictment for hog-stealing. The clerk read on till he got to and through the words "did steal, take, and carry away ten boars, ten sows, ten shoats, and ten pigs," at which he exclaimed, "Well, by golly, that is the most equally divided gang of hogs I ever did hear of!" If there is any other gang of hogs more equally divided than the Democrats of New York are about this time, I have not heard of it.

LETTER TO
JOHN D. JOHNSTON

Shelbyville, November 4, 1851

Dear Brother:

When I came into Charleston day before yesterday I learned that you are anxious to sell the land where you live, and move to Missouri. I have been thinking of this ever since, and cannot but think such a notion is utterly foolish. What can you do in Missouri better than here? Is the land richer? Can you there, any more than here, raise corn and wheat and oats without work? Will anybody there, any more than here, do your work for you? If you intend to go to work, there is no better place than right where you are; if you do not intend to go to work you cannot get along anywhere. Squirming and crawling about from place to place can do no good. You have raised no crop this year, and what you really want is to sell the land, get the money and spend it. Part with the land you have, and, my life upon it, you will never after own a spot big enough to bury you in. Half you will get for the land you spend in moving to Missouri, and the other half you will eat and drink and wear out, and no foot of land will be bought. Now I feel it is my duty to have no hand in such a piece of foolery. I feel that it is so even on your own account, and particularly on *Mother*'s account. The eastern forty acres I intend to keep for Mother while she lives; if you *will not cultivate it,* it will rent for enough to support her; at least it will rent for something. Her dower in the other two forties she can let you have, and no thanks to me.

Now do not misunderstand this letter. I do not write it in any unkindness. I write it in order, if possible, to get you to *face* the truth, which truth is, you are destitute because you have idled away all your time. Your thousand pretenses for not get-

59

ting along better are all nonsense; they deceive nobody but yourself. *Go to work* is the only cure for your case.

A word for Mother: Chapman tells me he wants you to go and live with him. If I were you I would try it awhile. If you get tired of it (as I think you will not) you can return to your own home. Chapman feels very kindly to you; and I have no doubt he will make your situation very pleasant.

Sincerely yours,
A. LINCOLN

EULOGY ON HENRY CLAY

State House, Springfield, Illinois, July 16, 1852

On the fourth day of July 1776, the people of a few feeble and oppressed colonies of Great Britain, inhabiting a portion of the Atlantic coast of North America, publicly declared their national independence, and made their appeal to the justice of their cause and to the God of battles for the maintenance of that declaration. That people were few in number and without resources, save only their wise heads and stout hearts. Within the first year of that declared independence, and while its maintenance was yet problematical—while the bloody struggle between those resolute rebels and their haughty would-be masters was still waging—of undistinguished parents and in an obscure district of one of those colonies Henry Clay was born. The infant nation and the infant child began the race of life together. For three-quarters of a century they have travelled hand in hand. They have been companions ever. The nation has passed its perils, and it is free, prosperous, and powerful. The child has reached his manhood, his middle age, his old age, and is dead. In all that has concerned the nation the man ever sympathized; and now the nation mourns the man. . . .

While it is customary and proper upon occasions like the present to give a brief sketch of the life of the deceased, in the case of Mr. Clay it is less necessary than most others; for his biography has been written and rewritten and read and reread for the last twenty-five years; so that, with the exception of a few of the latest incidents of his life, all is as well known as it can be. The short sketch which I give is, therefore, merely to maintain the connection of this discourse.

Henry Clay was born on the twelfth day of April 1777, in Hanover County, Virginia. Of his father, who died in the fourth or fifth year of Henry's age, little seems to be known, except that he was a respectable man and a preacher of the Baptist persuasion. Mr. Clay's education to the end of life was comparatively limited. I say "to the end of life," because I have understood that from time to time he added something to his education during the greater part of his whole life. Mr. Clay's lack of a more prefect early education, however it may be regretted generally, teaches at least one profitable lesson: it teaches that in this country one can scarcely be so poor but that, if he will, he can acquire sufficient education to get through the world respectably.

In his twenty-third year Mr. Clay was licensed to practice law, and emigrated to Lexington, Kentucky. Here he commenced and continued the practice till the year 1803, when he was first elected to the Kentucky legislature. By successive elections he was continued in the legislature till the latter part of 1806, when he was elected to fill a vacancy of a single session in the United States Senate. In 1807 he was again elected to the Kentucky House of Representatives, and by that body chosen Speaker. In 1808 he was reelected to the same body. In 1809 he was again chosen to fill a vacancy of two years in the United States Senate. In 1811 he was elected to the United States House of Representatives, and on the first day of taking his seat in that body he was chosen its Speaker. In 1813 he was again elected Speaker.

Early in 1814, being the period of our last British war, Mr. Clay was sent as commissioner, with others, to negotiate a treaty of peace, which treaty was concluded in the latter part of the same year. On his return from Europe he was again elected to the lower branch of Congress, and on taking his seat in December 1815, was called to his old post—the Speaker's chair, a position in which he was retained by successive elections, with one brief intermission, till the inauguration of John Quincy Adams, in March 1825. He was then appointed secretary of state, and occupied that important station till the inauguration of General Jackson, in March 1829. After this he returned to Kentucky, resumed the practice of law, and continued it till the autumn of 1831, when he was by the legislature of Kentucky again placed in the United States Senate. By a reelection he was continued in the Senate till he resigned his seat and retired, in March 1848. In December 1849, he again took his seat in the Senate, which he again resigned only a few months before his death.

By the foregoing it is perceived that the period from the beginning of Mr. Clay's official life in 1803 to the end of 1852 is but one year short of half a century, and that the sum of all the intervals in it will not amount to ten years. But mere duration of time in office constitutes the smallest part of Mr. Clay's history. Throughout that long period he has constantly been the most loved and most implicitly followed by friends, and the most dreaded by opponents, of all living American politicians. In all the great questions which have agitated the country, and particularly in those fearful crises, the Missouri question, the nullification question, and the late slavery question, as connected with the newly acquired territory, involving and endangering the stability of the Union, his has been the leading and most conspicuous part.

In 1824 he was first a candidate for the presidency, and was defeated; and, although he was successively defeated for the same office in 1832 and in 1844, there has never been a moment since 1824 till after 1848 when a very large portion of the American people did not cling to him with an enthusiastic hope and purpose of still elevating him to the presidency. With other men, to be defeated was to be forgotten; but with him defeat was but a trifling incident, neither changing him nor the world's estimate of him. Even those of both political parties who have been preferred to him for the highest office have run far briefer courses than he, and left him still shining high in the heavens of the political world. Jackson, Van Buren, Harrison, Polk, and Taylor all rose after, and set long before him. The spell—the long-enduring spell—with which the souls of men were bound to him is a miracle. Who can compass it? It is probably true he owed his preeminence to no one quality, but to a fortunate combination of several. He was surpassingly eloquent; but many eloquent men fail utterly, and they are not, as a class, generally successful. His judgment was excellent; but many men of good judgment live and die unnoticed. His will was indomitable; but this quality often secures to its owner nothing better than a character for useless obstinacy. These, then, were Mr. Clay's leading qualities. No one of them is very uncommon; but all together are rarely combined in a single individual, and this is probably the reason why such men as Henry Clay are so rare in the world.

Mr. Clay's eloquence did not consist, as many fine specimens of eloquence do, of types and figures, of antithesis and elegant arrangement of words and sentences, but rather of that deeply earnest and impassioned tone and manner which can proceed only from great sincerity, and a thorough conviction in the speaker of the justice and importance of his cause. This it is that truly touches the chords of sympathy; and those who heard Mr. Clay never failed to be moved by it, or ever afterward forgot the impression. All his efforts were made for practical effect. He never spoke merely to be heard. He never delivered a Fourth of July oration, or a eulogy on an occasion like this. As a politician or statesman, no one was so habitually careful to avoid all sectional ground. Whatever he did he did for the whole country. In the construction of his measures, he ever carefully surveyed every part of the field, and duly weighed every conflicting interest. Feeling as he did, and as the truth surely is, that the world's best hope depended on the continued union of these states, he was ever jealous of and watchful for whatever might have the slightest tendency to separate them.

Mr. Clay's predominant sentiment, from first to last, was a deep devotion to the cause of human liberty—a strong sympathy with the oppressed everywhere, and an ardent wish for their elevation. With him this was a primary and all-controlling passion. Subsidiary to this was the conduct of his whole life. He loved his country partly because it was his own country, and mostly because it was a free country; and he burned with a zeal for its advancement, prosperity, and glory, because he saw in such the advancement, prosperity, and glory of human liberty, human right, and human nature. He desired the prosperity of his countrymen; partly because they were his countrymen, but chiefly to show to the world that free men could be prosperous.

That his views and measures were always the wisest needs not to be affirmed; nor should it be on this occasion, where so many thinking differently join in doing honor to his memory. A free people in times of peace and quiet—when pressed by no common danger—naturally divide into parties. At such times the man who is of neither party is not, cannot be, of any consequence. Mr. Clay therefore was of a party. Taking a prominent part, as he did, in all the great political questions of his country for the last half century, the wisdom of his course on many is doubted and denied by a large portion of his countrymen; and of such it is not now proper to speak particularly. But there are many others, about his course upon which there is little or no disagreement amongst intelligent and patriotic Americans. Of these last are the War of 1812, the Missouri question, nullification, and the now recent compromise measures. In 1812 Mr. Clay, though not unknown, was still a young man. Whether we should go to war with Great Britain being the question of the day, a minority opposed the declaration of war by Congress, while the majority, though apparently inclined to war, had for years wavered, and hesitated to act decisively. Meanwhile British aggressions multiplied, and grew more daring and aggravated. By Mr. Clay more than any other man the struggle was brought to a decision in Congress. The question, being now fully before Congress, came up in a variety of ways in rapid succession, on most of which occasions Mr. Clay spoke. Adding to all the logic of which the subject was susceptible that noble inspiration which came to him as it came to no other, he aroused and nerved and inspired his friends, and confounded and bore down all opposition.

Several of his speeches on these occasions were reported and are still extant, but the best of them all never was. During its delivery the reporters forgot their vocation, dropped their pens, and sat enchanted from near the beginning to quite the close. The speech now lives only in the memory of a few old men, and the enthusiasm with which they cherish their recollection of it is absolutely astonishing. The precise language of this speech we shall never know; but we do know—we cannot help knowing —that with deep pathos it pleaded the cause of the injured sailor, that it invoked the genius of the Revolution, that it apostrophized the names of Otis, of Henry, and of Washington, that it appealed to the interests, the pride, the honor, and the glory of the nation, that it shamed and taunted the timidity of friends, that it scorned and scouted and withered the temerity of domestic foes, that it bearded and defied the British lion, and, rising and swelling and maddening in its course, it sounded the onset, till the charge, the shock, the steady struggle, and the glorious victory all passed in vivid review before the entranced hearers.

Important and exciting as was the war question of 1812, it never so alarmed the sagacious statesmen of the country for the safety of the Republic as afterward did the Missouri question. This sprang from that unfortunate source of discord—Negro slavery. When our federal Constitution was adopted, we owned no territory beyond the limits or ownership of the states, except the territory northwest of the River Ohio and east of the Mississippi. What has since been formed into the states of Maine, Kentucky and Tennessee, was, I believe, within the limits of or owned by Massachusetts, Virginia, and North Carolina. As to the Northwestern Territory, provision had been made even before the adoption of the Constitution that slavery should never go there. On the admission of states into the Union, carved from the territory we owned before the Constitution, no question, or at most no considerable question, arose about slavery—those which were within the limits of or owned by the old states following respectively the condition of the parent state, and those within the Northwest Territory following the previously made provision. But in 1803 we purchased Louisiana of the French, and it included with much more what has since been formed into the state of Missouri. With regard to it, nothing had been done to forestall the question of slavery. When, therefore, in 1819, Missouri, having formed a state constitution without excluding slavery, and with slavery already actually existing within its limits, knocked at the door of the Union for admission, almost the entire representation of the nonslaveholding states objected. A fearful and angry struggle instantly followed. This alarmed thinking men more than any previous question, because, unlike all the former, it divided the country by geographical lines. Other questions had their opposing partisans in all localities of the country and in almost every family, so that no division of the Union could follow such without a separation of friends to quite as great an extent as that of opponents. Not so with the Missouri question. On this a geographical line could be traced, which in the main would separate opponents only. This was the danger. . . .

Mr. Clay was in Congress, and, perceiving the danger, at once engaged his whole energies to avert it. It began, as I have said, in 1819; and it did not terminate till 1821. Missouri would not yield the point; and Congress—that is, a majority in Congress—by repeated votes showed a determination not to admit the state unless it should yield. After several failures, and great labor on the part of Mr. Clay to so present the question that a majority could consent to the admission, it was by a vote rejected, and, as all seemed to think, finally. A sullen gloom hung over the nation. All felt that the rejection of Missouri was equivalent to a dissolution of the Union, because those states which already had what Missouri was rejected for refusing to relinquish would go with Missouri. All deprecated and deplored this, but none saw how to avert it. For the judgment of members to be convinced of the necessity of yielding was not the whole difficulty; each had a constituency to meet and to answer to. Mr. Clay, though worn down and exhausted, was appealed to by members to renew his efforts at compromise. He did so, and by some judicious modifications of his plan, coupled with laborious efforts with individual members and his own overmastering eloquence upon that floor, he finally secured the admission of the state. Brightly and captivating as it had previously shown, it was now perceived that his great eloquence was a mere embellishment, or at most but a helping hand to his inventive genius and his devotion to his country in the day of her extreme peril.

After the settlement of the Missouri question, although a portion of the American people have differed with Mr. Clay, and a majority even appear generally to have been opposed to him on questions of ordinary administration, he seems constantly to have been regarded by all as the man for the crisis. Accordingly, in the days of nullification, and more recently in the reappearance of the slavery question connected with our territory newly acquired of Mexico, the task of devising a mode of adjustment seems to have been cast upon Mr. Clay by common consent—and his performance of the task in each case was little else than a literal fulfillment of the public expectation.

Mr. Clay's efforts on behalf of the South Americans, and afterwards on behalf of the Greeks, in the times of their respective struggles for civil liberty, are among the finest on record, upon the noblest of all themes, and bear ample corroboration of what I have said was his ruling passion—a love of liberty and right, unselfishly, and for their own sakes.

Having been led to allude to domestic slavery so frequently already, I am unwilling to close without referring more particularly to Mr. Clay's views and conduct in regard to it. He ever was on principle and in feeling opposed to slavery. The very earliest, and one of the latest, public efforts of his life, separated by a period of more than fifty years, were both made in favor of gradual emancipation. He did not perceive that on a question of human rights the Negroes were to be excepted from the human race. And yet Mr. Clay was the owner of slaves. Cast into life when slavery was already widely spread and deeply seated, he did not perceive, as I think no wise man has perceived, how it could be at once eradicated without producing a greater evil even to the cause of human liberty itself. His feeling and his judgment, therefore, ever led him to oppose both extremes of opinion on the subject. Those who would shiver into fragments the Union of these states, tear to tatters its now venerated Constitution, and even burn the last copy of the Bible, rather than slavery should continue a single hour, together with all their more halting sympathizers, have received, and are receiving, their just execration; and the name and opinions and influence of Mr. Clay are fully and, as I trust, effectually and enduringly arrayed against them. . . .

The American Colonization Society was organized in 1816. Mr. Clay, though not its projector, was one of its earliest members; and he died, as for many preceding years he had been, its president. It was one of the most cherished objects of his direct care and consideration, and the association of his name with it has probably been its very greatest collateral support. He considered it no demerit in the society that it tended to relieve the slaveholders from the troublesome presence of the free Negroes; but this was far from being its whole merit in his estimation. [Clay said:]

> There is a moral fitness in the idea of returning to Africa her children, whose ancestors have been torn from her by the ruthless hand of fraud and violence. Transplanted in a foreign land, they will carry back to their native soil the rich fruits of religion, civilization, law, and liberty. May it not be one of the great designs of the Ruler of the universe, whose ways are often inscrutable by shortsighted mortals, thus to transform an original crime into a signal blessing to that most unfortunate portion of the globe?

This suggestion of the possible ultimate redemption of the African race and African continent was made twenty-five years ago. Every succeeding year has added strength to the hope of its realization. May it indeed be realized. Pharaoh's country was cursed with plagues, and his hosts were lost in the Red Sea, for striving to retain a captive people who had already served them more than four hundred years. May like disasters never befall us! If, as the friends of colonization hope, the present and coming generations of our countrymen shall by any means succeed in freeing our land from the dangerous presence of slavery, and at the same time in restoring a captive people to their long-lost fatherland with bright prospects for the future, and this too so gradually that neither races nor individuals shall have suffered by the change, it will indeed be a glorious consummation. And if to such a consummation the efforts of Mr. Clay shall have contributed, it will be what he most ardently wished, and none of his labors will have been more valuable to his country and his kind.

But Henry Clay is dead. His long and eventful life is closed. Our country is prosperous and powerful; but could it have been quite all it has been, and is, and is to be, without Henry Clay? Such a man the times have demanded, and such in the providence of God was given us. But he is gone. Let us strive to deserve, as far as mortals may, the continued care of Divine Providence, trusting that in future national emergencies He will not fail to provide us the instruments of safety and security.

Speech at Peoria, Illinois

The Kansas-Nebraska Act

October 16, 1854

I do not rise to speak now, if I can stipulate with the audience to meet me here at half past six or at seven o'clock. It is now several minutes past five, and Judge Douglas has spoken over three hours. If you hear me at all, I wish you to hear me through. It will take me as long as it has taken him. That will carry us beyond eight o'clock at night. Now, every one of you who can remain that long can just as well get his supper, meet me at seven, and remain an hour or two later. The judge has already informed you that he is to have an hour to reply to me. I doubt not but you have been a little surprised to learn that I have consented to give one of his high reputation and known ability this advantage of me. Indeed, my consenting to it, though reluctant, was not wholly unselfish, for I suspected, if it were understood that the judge was entirely done, you Democrats would leave and not hear me; but by giving him the close, I felt confident you would stay for the fun of hearing him skin me.

[The audience signified their assent to the arrangement, and adjourned to 7:00 P.M., at which time they reassembled, and Mr. Lincoln spoke substantially as follows.]

The repeal of the Missouri Compromise, and the propriety of its restoration, constitute the subject of what I am about to say. As I desire to present my own connected view of this subject, my remarks will not be specifically an answer to Judge Douglas; yet, as I proceed, the main points he has presented will arise, and will receive such respectful attention as I may be able to give them. I wish further to say that I do not propose to question the patriotism or to assail the motives of any man or class of men, but rather to confine myself strictly to the naked merits of the question. I also wish to be no less than national in all the positions I may take, and whenever I take ground which others have thought, or may think, narrow, sectional, and dangerous to the Union, I hope to give a reason which will appear sufficient, at least to some, why I think differently.

And as this subject is no other than part and parcel of the larger general question of domestic slavery, I wish to make and to keep the distinction between the existing institution and the extension of it so broad and so clear that no honest man can misunderstand me, and no dishonest one successfully misrepresent me.

In order to a clear understanding of what the Missouri Compromise is, a short history of the preceding kindred subjects will perhaps be proper.

When we established our independence, we did not own or claim the country to which this compromise applies. Indeed, strictly speaking, the Confederacy then owned no country at all; the states respectively owned the country within their limits, and some of them owned territory beyond their strict state limits. Virginia thus owned the Northwestern Territory—the country out of which the principal part of Ohio, all Indiana, all Illinois, all Michigan, and all Wisconsin have since been formed. She also owned (perhaps within her then limits) what has since been formed into the state of Kentucky. North Carolina thus owned what is now the state of Tennessee; and South Carolina and Georgia owned, in separate parts, what are now Mississippi and Alabama. Connecticut, I think, owned the little remaining part of Ohio, being the same where they now send Giddings to Congress and beat all creation in making cheese.

These territories, together with the states themselves, constitute all the country over which the Confederacy then claimed any sort of jurisdiction. We were then living under the Articles of Confederation, which were superseded by the Constitution several years afterward. The question of ceding the territories to the general government was set on foot. Mr. Jefferson—the author of the Declaration of Independence, and otherwise a chief actor in the Revolution; then a delegate in Congress; afterwards, twice president; who was, is, and perhaps will continue to be, the most distinguished politician of our history; a Virginian by birth and continued residence, and withal a slaveholder —conceived the idea of taking that occasion to prevent slavery ever going into the Northwestern Territory. He prevailed on the Virginia legislature to adopt his views, and to cede the territory, making the prohibition of slavery therein a condition of the deed. Congress accepted the cession with the condition; and the first ordinance (which the acts of Congress were then called) for the government of the territory provided that slavery should never be permitted therein. This is the famed Ordinance of 1787, so often spoken of.

Thenceforward for sixty-one years, and until, in 1848, the last scrap of this territory came into the Union as the state of Wisconsin, all parties acted in quiet obedience to this ordinance. It is now what Jefferson foresaw and intended—the happy home of teeming millions of free, white, prosperous people, and no slave among them.

Thus, with the author of the Declaration of Independence, the policy of prohibiting slavery in new territory originated. Thus, away back to the Constitution, in the pure, fresh, free breath of the Revolution, the state of Virginia and the national Congress put that policy into practice. Thus, through more than sixty of the best years of the Republic, did that policy steadily work to its great and beneficent end. And thus, in those five states, and in five millions of free, enterprising people, we have before us the rich fruits of this policy.

But now new light breaks upon us. Now Congress declares this ought never to have been, and the like of it must never be again. The sacred right of self-government is grossly violated by it. We even find some men who drew their first breath—and every other breath of their lives—under this very restriction, now live in dread of absolute suffocation if they should be restricted in the "sacred right" of taking slaves to Nebraska. That perfect liberty they sigh for—the liberty of making slaves of other people—Jefferson never thought of, their own fathers never thought of, they never thought of themselves, a year ago. How fortunate for them they did not sooner become sensible of their great misery! Oh, how difficult it is to treat with respect such assaults upon all we have ever really held sacred!

But to return to history. In 1803 we purchased what was then called Louisiana, of France. It included the present states of Louisiana, Arkansas Miss ri, and Iowa; also the territory of Minnesota, and the present bone of contention, Kansas and Nebraska. Slavery already existed among the French at New Orleans, and to some extent at St. Louis. In 1812 Louisiana came into the Union as a slave state, without controversy. In 1818 or 1819, Missouri showed signs of a wish to come in with slavery. This was resisted by Northern members of Congress; and thus began the first great slavery agitation in the nation. This controversy lasted several months, and became very angry and exciting—the House of Representatives voting steadily for the prohibition of slavery in Missouri, and the Senate voting as steadily against it. Threats of the breaking up of the Union were freely made, and the ablest public men of the day became seriously alarmed.

At length a compromise was made, in which, as in all compromises, both sides yielded something. It was a law, passed on the sixth of March 1820, providing that Missouri might come into the Union with slavery, but that in all the remaining part of the territory purchased of France which lies north of thirty-six degrees and thirty minutes north latitude, slavery should never be permitted. This provision of law is the Missouri Compromise. In excluding slavery north of the line, the same language is employed as in the Ordinance of 1787. It directly applied to Iowa, Minnesota, and to the present bone of contention, Kansas and Nebraska. Whether there should or should not be slavery south of that line, nothing was said in the law. But Arkansas constituted the principal remaining part south of the line; and it has since been admitted as a slave state, without serious controversy. More recently, Iowa, north of the line, came in as a free state without controversy. Still later, Minnesota, north of the line, had a territorial organization without controversy. Texas, principally south of the line, and west of Arkansas, though originally within the purchase from France, had, in 1819, been traded off to Spain in our treaty for the acquisition of Florida. It had thus become a part of Mexico. Mexico revolutionized and became independent of Spain. American citizens began settling rapidly with their slaves in the southern part of Texas. Soon they revolutionized against Mexico, and established an independent government of their own, adopting a constitution with slavery, strongly resembling the constitutions of our slave states. By still another rapid move, Texas, claiming a boundary much farther west than when we parted with her in 1819, was brought back to the United States, and admitted into the Union as a slave state. Then there was little or no settlement in the northern part of Texas, a considerable portion of which lay north of the Missouri line; and in the resolutions admitting her into the Union, the Missouri restriction was expressly extended westward across her territory. This was in 1845, only nine years ago.

Thus originated the Missouri Compromise; and thus has it been respected down to 1845. . . .

Our war with Mexico broke out in 1846. When Congress was about adjourning that session, President Polk asked them to place two millions of dollars under his control, to be used by him in the recess, if found practicable and expedient, in negotiating a treaty of peace with Mexico, and acquiring some part of her territory. A bill was duly gotten up for the purpose, and was progressing swimmingly in the House of Representatives, when a member by the name of David Wilmot, a Democrat from Pennsylvania, moved as an amendment, "Provided, that in any territory thus acquired there never shall be slavery."

This is the origin of the far-famed Wilmot Proviso. It created a great flutter; but it stuck like wax, was voted into the bill, and the bill passed with it through the House. The Senate, however, adjourned without final action on it, and so both appropriation and proviso were lost for the time. The war continued, and at the next session the president renewed his request for the appropriation, enlarging the amount, I think, to three millions. Again came the proviso, and defeated the measure. Congress adjourned again, and the war went on. In December 1847, the new Congress assembled. I was in the lower House that term. The Wilmot Proviso, or the principle of it, was constantly coming up in some shape or other, and I think I may venture to say I voted for it at least forty times during the short time I was there. The Senate, however, held it in check, and it never became a law. In the spring of 1848 a treaty of peace was made with Mexico, by which we obtained that portion of her country which now constitutes the territories of New Mexico and Utah and the present state of California. By this treaty the Wilmot Proviso was defeated, in so far as it was intended to be a condition of the acquisition of territory. Its friends, however, were still determined to find some way to restrain slavery from getting into the new country. This new acquisition lay directly west of our old purchase from France, and extended west to the Pacific Ocean, and was so situated that if the Missouri line should be extended straight west, the new country would be divided by such extended line, leaving some north and some south of it. On Judge Douglas's motion, a bill, or provision of a bill, passed the Senate to so extend the Missouri line. The proviso men in the House, including myself, voted it down, because, by implication, it gave up the southern part to slavery, while we were bent on having it all free.

In the fall of 1848 the gold mines were discovered in California. This attracted people to it with unprecedented rapidity, so that on, or soon after, the meeting of the new Congress in December 1849, she already had a population of nearly a hundred thousand, had called a convention, formed a state constitution excluding slavery, and was knocking for admission into the Union. The proviso men, of course, were for letting her in, but the Senate, always true to the other side, would not consent to her admission, and there California stood, kept out of the Union because she would not let slavery into her borders. Under all the circumstances, perhaps, this was not wrong. There were other points of dispute connected with the general question of slavery, which equally needed adjustment. The South clamored for a more efficient Fugitive Slave Law. The North clamored for the abolition of a peculiar species of slave trade in the District of Columbia, in connection with which, in view from the windows of the Capitol, a sort of Negro livery stable, where droves of Negroes were collected, temporarily kept, and finally taken to Southern markets, precisely like droves of horses, had been openly maintained for fifty years. Utah and New Mexico needed territorial governments; and whether slavery should or should not be prohibited within them was another question. The indefinite western boundary of Texas was to be settled. She was a slave state, and consequently the farther west the slavery men could push her boundary, the more slave country they secured; and the farther east the slavery opponents could thrust the boundary back, the less slave ground was secured. Thus this was just as clearly a slavery question as any of the others.

These points all needed adjustment, and they were held up, perhaps wisely, to make them help adjust one another. The Union now, as in 1820, was thought to be in danger, and devotion to the Union rightfully inclined men to yield somewhat in points where nothing else could have so inclined them. A compromise was finally effected. The South got their new fugitive slave law, and the North got California (by far the best part of our acquisition from Mexico) as a free state. The South got a provision that New Mexico and Utah, when admitted as states, may come in with or without slavery as they may then choose; and the North got the slave trade abolished in the District of Columbia. The North got the western boundary of Texas thrown farther back eastward than the South desired; but, in turn, they gave Texas ten millions of dollars with which to pay her old debts. This is the Compromise of 1850.

Preceding the presidential election of 1852, each of the great political parties, Democrats and Whigs, met in convention and adopted resolutions endorsing the Compromise of 1850, as a "finality," a final settlement, so far as these parties could make it so, of all slavery agitation. Previous to this, in 1851, the Illinois legislature had endorsed it.

During this long period of time, Nebraska had remained substantially an uninhabited country, but now emigration to and settlement within it began to take place. It is about one third as large as the present United States, and its importance, so long overlooked, begins to come into view. The restriction of slavery by the Missouri Compromise directly applies to it—in fact was first made, and has since been maintained, expressly for it. In 1853, a bill to give it a territorial government passed the House of Representatives, and, in the hands of Judge Douglas, failed of passing only for want of time. This bill contained no repeal of the Missouri Compromise. Indeed, when it was assailed because it did not contain such repeal, Judge Douglas defended it in its existing form. On January 4, 1854, Judge Douglas introduces a new bill to give Nebraska territorial government. He accompanies this bill with a report, in which last he expressly recommends that the Missouri Compromise shall neither be affirmed nor repealed. Before long the bill is so modified as to make two territories instead of one, calling the southern one Kansas.

Also, about a month after the introduction of the bill, on the Judge's own motion it is so amended as to declare the Missouri Compromise inoperative and void; and, substantially, that the people who go and settle there may establish slavery, or exclude it, as they may see fit. In this shape the bill passed both branches of Congress and became a law.

This is the repeal of the Missouri Compromise. The foregoing history may not be precisely accurate in every particular, but I am sure it is sufficiently so for all the use I shall attempt to make of it, and in it we have before us the chief material enabling us to judge correctly whether the repeal of the Missouri Compromise is right or wrong. I think, and shall try to show, that it is wrong—wrong in its direct effect, letting slavery into Kansas and Nebraska, and wrong in its prospective principle, allowing it to spread to every other part of the wide world where men can be found inclined to take it.

This declared indifference, but, as I must think, covert real zeal, for the spread of slavery, I cannot but hate. I hate it because of the monstrous injustice of slavery itself. I hate it because it deprives our republican example of its just influence in the world; enables the enemies of free institutions with plausibility to taunt us as hypocrites; causes the real friends of freedom to doubt our sincerity; and especially because it forces so many good men among ourselves into an open war with the very fundamental principles of civil liberty, criticizing the Declaration of Independence, and insisting that there is no right principle of action but self-interest.

Before proceeding let me say that I think I have no prejudice against the Southern people. They are just what we would be in their situation. If slavery did not now exist among them, they would not introduce it. If it did now exist among us, we should not instantly give it up. This I believe of the masses North and South. Doubtless there are individuals on both sides who would not hold slaves under any circumstances, and others who would gladly introduce slavery anew if it were out of existence. We know that some Southern men do free their slaves, go North and become tip-top abolitionists, while some Northern ones go South and become most cruel slave-masters.

When Southern people tell us that they are no more responsible for the origin of slavery than we are, I acknowledge the fact. When it is said that the institution exists, and that it is very difficult to get rid of it in any satisfactory way, I can understand and appreciate the saying. I surely will not blame them for not doing what I should not know how to do myself. If all earthly power were given me, I should not know what to do as to the existing institution. My first impulse would be to free all the slaves, and send them to Liberia, to their own native land. But a moment's reflection would convince me that whatever of high hope (as I think there is) there may be in this in the long run, its sudden execution is impossible. If they were all landed there in a day, they would all perish in the next ten days; and there are not surplus shipping and surplus money enough to carry them there in many times ten days. What then? Free them all, and keep them among us as underlings? Is it quite certain that this betters their condition? I think I would not hold one in slavery at any rate, yet the point is not clear enough for me to denounce people upon. What next? Free them, and make them politically and socially our equals? My own feelings will not admit of this, and if mine would, we well know that those of the great mass of whites will not. Whether this feeling accords with justice and sound judgment is not the sole question, if indeed it is any part of it. A universal feeling, whether well or ill founded, cannot be safely disregarded. We cannot then make them equals. It does seem to me that systems of gradual emancipation might be adopted, but for their tardiness in this I will not undertake to judge our brethren of the South.

When they remind us of their constitutional rights, I acknowledge them—not grudgingly, but fully and fairly; and I would give them any legislation for the reclaiming of their fugitives which should not in its stringency be more likely to carry a free man into slavery than our ordinary criminal laws are to hang an innocent one.

But all this, to my judgment, furnishes no more excuse for permitting slavery to go into our own free territory than it would for reviving the African slave trade by law. The law which forbids the bringing of slaves from Africa, and that which has so long forbidden the taking of them into Nebraska, can hardly be distinguished on any moral principle, and the repeal of the former could find quite as plausible excuses as that of the latter.

The arguments by which the repeal of the Missouri Compromise is sought to be justified are these: first, that the Nebraska country needed a territorial government; second, that in various ways the public had repudiated that compromise and demanded the repeal, and therefore should not now complain of it; and, lastly, that the repeal establishes a principle which is intrinsically right.

I will attempt an answer to each of them in its turn. First, then: If that country was in need of a territorial organization, could it not have had it as well without as with a repeal? Iowa and Minnesota, to both of which the Missouri restriction applied, had, without its repeal, each in succession, territorial organizations. And even the year before, a bill for Nebraska itself was within an ace of passing without the repealing clause, and this in the hands of the same men who are now the champions of repeal. Why no necessity then for repeal? But still later, when this very bill was first brought in, it contained no repeal. But, say they, because the people had demanded, or rather commanded, the repeal, the repeal was to accompany the organization whenever that should occur.

Now, I deny that the public ever demanded any such thing —ever repudiated the Missouri Compromise, ever commanded its repeal. I deny it, and call for the proof. It is not contended, I believe, that any such command has ever been given in express terms. It is only said that it was done in principle. The support of the Wilmot Proviso is the first fact mentioned to prove that the Missouri restriction was repudiated in principle, and the second is the refusal to extend the Missouri line over the country acquired from Mexico. These are near enough alike to be treated together. The one was to exclude the chances of slavery from the whole new acquisition by the lump, and the other was to reject a division of it, by which one half was to be given up to those chances. Now, whether this was a repudiation of the Missouri line in principle depends upon whether the Missouri law contained any principle requiring the line to be extended over the country acquired from Mexico. I contend it did not. I insist that it contained no general principle, but that it was, in every sense, specific. That its terms limit it to the country purchased from France is undenied and undeniable. It could have no principle beyond the intention of those who made it. They did not intend to extend the line to country which they did not own. If they intended to extend it in the event of acquiring additional territory, why did they not say so? It was just as easy to say that "in all the country west of the Mississippi which we now own, or may hereafter acquire, there shall never be slavery," as to say what they did say; and they would have said it if they had meant it. An intention to extend the law is not only not mentioned in the law, but is not mentioned in any contemporaneous history. Both the law itself, and the history of the times, are a blank as to any principle of extension; and by neither the known rules of construing statutes and contracts, nor by common sense, can any such principle be inferred.

Another fact showing the specific character of the Missouri law—showing that it intended no more than it expressed, showing that the line was not intended as a universal dividing line between free and slave territory, present and prospective, north of which slavery could never go—is the fact that by that very law Missouri came in as a slave state, north of the line. If that law contained any prospective principle, the whole law must be looked to in order to ascertain what the principle was. And by this rule the South could fairly contend that, inasmuch as they got one slave state north of the line at the inception of the law, they have the right to have another given them north of it occasionally, now and then, in the indefinite westward extension of the line. This demonstrates the absurdity of attempting to deduce a prospective principle from the Missouri Compromise line.

When we voted for the Wilmot Proviso we were voting to keep slavery out of the whole Mexican acquisition, and little did we think we were thereby voting to let it into Nebraska lying several hundred miles distant. When we voted against extending the Missouri line, little did we think we were voting to destroy the old line, then of near thirty years' standing.

To argue that we thus repudiated the Missouri Compromise is no less absurd than it would be to argue that because we have so far forborne to acquire Cuba, we have thereby, in principle, repudiated our former acquisitions and determined to throw them out of the Union. No less absurd than it would be to say that because I may have refused to build an addition to my house, I thereby have decided to destroy the existing house! And if I catch you setting fire to my house, you will turn upon me and say I instructed you to do it!

The most conclusive argument, however, that while for the Wilmot Proviso, and while voting against the extension of the Missouri line, we never thought of disturbing the original Missouri Compromise, is found in the fact that there was then, and still is, an unorganized tract of fine country, nearly as large as the state of Missouri, lying immediately west of Arkansas and south of the Missouri Compromise line, and that we never attempted to prohibit slavery as to it. I wish particular attention to this. It adjoins the original Missouri Compromise line by its northern boundary, and consequently is part of the country into which by implication slavery was permitted to go by that compromise. There it has lain open ever since, and there it still lies, and yet no effort has been made at any time to wrest it from the South. In all our struggles to prohibit slavery within our Mexican acquisitions, we never so much as lifted a finger to prohibit it as to this tract. Is not this entirely conclusive that at all times we have held the Missouri Compromise as a sacred thing, even when against ourselves as well as when for us? . . .

Again, is not Nebraska, while a territory, a part of us? Do we not own the country? And if we surrender the control of it, do we not surrender the right of self-government? It is part of ourselves. If you say we shall not control it, because it is only part, the same is true of every other part; and when all the parts are gone, what has become of the whole? What is then left of us? What use for the general government, when there is nothing left for it to govern?

But you say this question should be left to the people of Nebraska, because they are more particularly interested. If this be the rule, you must leave it to each individual to say for himself whether he will have slaves. What better moral right have thirty-one citizens of Nebraska to say that the thirty-second shall not hold slaves than the people of the thirty-one states have to say that slavery shall not go into the thirty-second state at all?

But if it is a sacred right for the people of Nebraska to take and hold slaves there, it is equally their sacred right to buy them where they can buy them cheapest; and that, undoubtedly, will be on the coast of Africa, provided you will consent not to hang them for going there to buy them. You must remove this restriction, too, from the sacred right of self-government. I am aware you say that taking slaves from the states to Nebraska does not make slaves of freemen; but the African slave-trader can say just as much. He does not catch free Negroes and bring them here. He finds them already slaves in the hands of their black captors, and he honestly buys them at the rate of a red cotton handkerchief a head. This is very cheap, and it is a great abridgment of the sacred right of self-government to hang men for engaging in this profitable trade.

Another important objection to this application of the right of self-government is that it enables the first few to deprive the succeeding many of a free exercise of the right of self-government. The first few may get slavery in, and the subsequent many cannot easily get it out. How common is the remark now in the slave states, "If we were only clear of our slaves, how much better it would be for us." They are actually deprived of the privilege of governing themselves as they would, by the action of a very few in the beginning. The same thing was true of the whole nation at the time our Constitution was formed.

Whether slavery shall go into Nebraska, or other new territories, is not a matter of exclusive concern to the people who may go there. The whole nation is interested that the best use shall be made of these territories. We want them for homes of free white people. This they cannot be, to any considerable extent, if slavery shall be planted within them. Slave states are places for poor white people to remove from, not to remove to. New free states are the places for poor people to go to, and better their condition. For this use the nation needs these territories. . . .

The Missouri Compromise ought to be restored. For the sake of the Union, it ought to be restored. We ought to elect a House of Representatives which will vote its restoration. If by any means we omit to do this, what follows? Slavery may or may not be established in Nebraska. But whether it be or not, we shall have repudiated—discarded from the councils of the nation—the spirit of compromise; for who, after this, will ever trust in a national compromise? The spirit of mutual concession —that spirit which first gave us the Constitution, and which has thrice saved the Union—we shall have strangled and cast from us forever. And what shall we have in lieu of it? The South flushed with triumph and tempted to excess; the North, betrayed as they believe, brooding on wrong and burning for revenge. One side will provoke, the other resent. The one will taunt, the other defy; one aggresses, the other retaliates. Already a few in the North defy all constitutional restraints, resist the execution of the Fugitive Slave Law, and even menace the institution of slavery in the states where it exists. Already a few in the South claim the constitutional right to take and to hold slaves in the free states, demand the revival of the slave trade, and demand a treaty with Great Britain by which fugitive slaves may be reclaimed from Canada. As yet they are but few on either side. It is a grave question for lovers of the Union whether the final destruction of the Missouri Compromise, and with it the spirit of all compromise, will or will not embolden and embitter each of these, and fatally increase the number of both.

But restore the compromise, and what then? We thereby restore the national faith, the national confidence, the national feeling of brotherhood. We thereby reinstate the spirit of concession and compromise, that spirit which has never failed us in past perils, and which may be safely trusted for all the future. The South ought to join in doing this. The peace of the nation is as dear to them as to us. In memories of the past and hopes of the future, they share as largely as we. It would be on their part a great act—great in its spirit, and great in its effect. It would be worth to the nation a hundred years' purchase of peace and prosperity. And what of sacrifice would they make? They only surrender to us what they gave us for a consideration long, long ago; what they have not now asked for, struggled or cared for; what has been thrust upon them, not less to their astonishment than to ours. . . .

I particularly object to the new position which the avowed principle of this Nebraska law gives to slavery in the body politic. I object to it because it assumes that there can be moral right in the enslaving of one man by another. I object to it as a dangerous dalliance for a free people—a sad evidence that, feeling prosperity, we forget right; that liberty, as a principle, we have ceased to revere. I object to it because the fathers of the Republic eschewed and rejected it. The argument of "necessity" was the only argument they ever admitted in favor of slavery; and so far, and so far only, as it carried them did they ever go. They found the institution existing among us, which they could not help, and they cast blame upon the British king for having permitted its introduction. Before the Constitution they prohibited its introduction into the Northwestern Territory, the only country we owned then free from it. At the framing and adoption of the Constitution, they forbore to so much as mention the word "slave" or "slavery" in the whole instrument. In the provision for the recovery of fugitives, the slave is spoken of as a "person held to service or labor." In that prohibiting the abolition of the African slave trade for twenty years, that trade is spoken of as "the migration or importation of such persons as any of the states now existing shall think proper to admit," etc. These are the only provisions alluding to slavery. Thus the thing is hid away in the Constitution, just as an afflicted man hides away a wen or cancer which he dares not cut out at once, lest he bleed to death—with the promise, nevertheless, that the cutting may begin at a certain time. Less than this our fathers could not do, and more they would not do. Necessity drove them so far, and farther they would not go. But this is not all. The earliest Congress under the Constitution took the same view of slavery. They hedged and hemmed it in to the narrowest limits of necessity.

In 1794 they prohibited an outgoing slave trade—that is, the taking of slaves from the United States to sell. In 1798 they prohibited the bringing of slaves from Africa into the Mississippi Territory, this territory then comprising what are now the states of Mississippi and Alabama. This was ten years before they had the authority to do the same thing as to the states existing at the adoption of the Constitution. In 1800 they prohibited American citizens from trading in slaves between foreign countries, as, for instance, from Africa to Brazil. In 1803 they passed a law in aid of one or two slave-state laws in restraint of the internal slave trade. In 1807, in apparent hot haste, they passed the law, nearly a year in advance—to take effect the first day of 1808, the very first day the Constitution would permit— prohibiting the African slave trade by heavy pecuniary and corporal penalties. In 1820, finding these provisions ineffectual, they declared the slave trade piracy, and annexed to it the extreme penalty of death. While all this was passing in the general government, five or six of the original slave states had adopted systems of gradual emancipation, by which the institution was rapidly becoming extinct within their limits. Thus we see that the plain, unmistakable spirit of that age toward slavery was hostility to the principle and toleration only by necessity.

But now it is to be transformed into a "sacred right." Nebraska brings it forth, places it on the highroad to extension and perpetuity, and with a pat on its back says to it, "Go, and God speed you." Henceforth it is to be the chief jewel of the nation —the very figurehead of the ship of state. Little by little, but steadily as man's march to the grave, we have been giving up the old for the new faith. Near eighty years ago we began by declaring that all men are created equal; but now from that beginning we have run down to the other declaration, that for some men to enslave others is a "sacred right of self-government." These principles cannot stand together. They are as opposite as God and Mammon; and whoever holds to the one must despise the other. When Pettit, in connection with his support of the Nebraska bill, called the Declaration of Independence "a self-evident lie," he only did what consistency and candor require all other Nebraska men to do. Of the forty-odd Nebraska senators who sat present and heard him, no one rebuked him. Nor am I apprised that any Nebraska newspaper, or any Nebraska orator, in the whole nation has ever yet rebuked him. If this had been said among Marion's men, Southerners though they were, what would have become of the man who said it? If this had been said to the men who captured André, the man who said it would probably have been hung sooner than André was. If it had been said in old Independence Hall seventy-eight years ago, the very doorkeeper would have throttled the man and thrust him into the street. Let no one be deceived. The spirit of '76 and the spirit of Nebraska are utter antagonisms; and the former is being rapidly displaced by the latter.

Fellow countrymen, Americans, South as well as North, shall we make no effort to arrest this? Already the liberal party throughout the world express the apprehension that "the one retrograde institution in America is undermining the principles of progress, and fatally violating the noblest political system the world ever saw." This is not the taunt of enemies, but the warning of friends. Is it quite safe to disregard it—to despise it? Is there no danger to liberty itself in discarding the earliest practice and first precept of our ancient faith? In our greedy chase to make profit of the Negro, let us beware lest we "cancel and tear in pieces" even the white man's charter of freedom.

Our republican robe is soiled and trailed in the dust. Let us repurify it. Let us turn and wash it white in the spirit, if not the blood, of the Revolution. Let us turn slavery from its claims of "moral right" back upon its existing legal rights and its arguments of "necessity." Let us return it to the position our fathers gave it, and there let it rest in peace. Let us readopt the Declaration of Independence, and with it the practices and policy which harmonize with it. Let North and South—let all Americans—let all lovers of liberty everywhere join in the great and good work. If we do this, we shall not only have saved the Union, but we shall have so saved it as to make and to keep it forever worthy of the saving. We shall have so saved it that the succeeding millions of free happy people the world over shall rise up and call us blessed to the latest generations.

LETTER TO
JOSHUA F. SPEED

Springfield, August 24, 1855

Dear Speed:

You know what a poor correspondent I am. Ever since I received your very agreeable letter of the 22d of May I have been intending to write you an answer to it. You suggest that in political action, now, you and I would differ. I suppose we would; not quite as much, however, as you may think. You know I dislike slavery, and you fully admit the abstract wrong of it. So far there is no cause of difference. But you say that sooner than yield your legal right to the slave, especially at the bidding of those who are not themselves interested, you would see the Union dissolved. I am not aware that anyone is bidding you yield that right; very certainly I am not. I leave that matter entirely to yourself. I also acknowledge your rights and my obligations under the Constitution in regard to your slaves. I confess I hate to see the poor creatures hunted down and caught and carried back to their stripes and unrequited toil; but I bite my lips and keep quiet.

In 1841 you and I had together a tedious low-water trip on a steamboat from Louisville to St. Louis. You may remember, as I well do, that from Louisville to the mouth of the Ohio there were on board ten or a dozen slaves shackled together with irons. That sight was a continued torment to me, and I see something like it every time I touch the Ohio or any other slave border. It is not fair for you to assume that I have no interest in a thing which has, and continually exercises, the power of making me miserable. You ought rather to appreciate how much the great body of the Northern people do crucify their feelings, in order to maintain their loyalty to the Constitution and the

Union. I do oppose the extension of slavery because my judgment and feeling so prompt me, and I am under no obligations to the contrary. If for this you and I must differ, differ we must.

You say, if you were president, you would send an army and hang the leaders of the Missouri outrages upon the Kansas elections; still, if Kansas fairly votes herself a slave state she must be admitted or the Union must be dissolved. But how if she votes herself a slave state unfairly, that is, by the very means for which you say you would hang men? Must she still be admitted, or the Union dissolved? That will be the phase of the question when it first becomes a practical one. In your assumption that there may be a fair decision of the slavery question in Kansas, I plainly see you and I would differ about the Nebraska law. I look upon that enactment not as a law, but as a violence from the beginning. It was conceived in violence, is maintained in violence, and is being executed in violence. I say it was conceived in violence, because the destruction of the Missouri Compromise, under the circumstances, was nothing less than violence. It was passed in violence because it could not have passed at all but for the votes of many members in violence of the known will of their constituents. It is maintained in violence, because the elections since clearly demand its repeal; and the demand is openly disregarded.

You say men ought to be hung for the way they are executing the law; I say the way it is being executed is quite as good as any of its antecedents. It is being executed in the precise way which was intended from the first, else why does no Nebraska man express astonishment or condemnation? Poor Reeder is the only public man who has been silly enough to believe that anything like fairness was ever intended, and he has been bravely undeceived.

That Kansas will form a slave constitution, and with it will ask to be admitted into the Union, I take to be already a settled question, and so settled by the very means you so pointedly condemn. By every principle of law ever held by any court

North or South, every Negro taken to Kansas is free; yet, in utter disregard of this—in the spirit of violence merely—that beautiful legislature gravely passes a law to hang any man who shall venture to inform a Negro of his legal rights. This is the subject and real object of the law. If, like Haman, they should hang upon the gallows of their own building, I shall not be among the mourners for their fate. In my humble sphere, I shall advocate the restoration of the Missouri Compromise so long as Kansas remains a territory, and when, by all these foul means, it seeks to come into the Union as a slave state, I shall oppose it. I am very loath in any case to withhold my assent to the enjoyment of property acquired or located in good faith; but I do not admit that good faith in taking a Negro to Kansas to be held in slavery is a probability with any man. Any man who has sense enough to be the controller of his own property has too much sense to misunderstand the outrageous character of the whole Nebraska business.

But I digress. In my opposition to the admission of Kansas I shall have some company, but we may be beaten. If we are, I shall not on that account attempt to dissolve the Union. I think it probable, however, we shall be beaten. Standing as a unit among yourselves, you can, directly and indirectly, bribe enough of our men to carry the day, as you could on the open proposition to establish a monarchy. Get hold of some man in the North whose position and ability is such that he can make the support of your measure, whatever it may be, a Democratic party necessity, and the thing is done. Apropos of this, let me tell you an anecdote. Douglas introduced the Nebraska bill in January. In February afterward there was a called session of the Illinois legislature. Of the one hundred members composing the two branches of that body, about seventy were Democrats. These latter held a caucus in which the Nebraska bill was talked of, if not formally discussed. It was thereby discovered that just three, and no more, were in favor of the measure. In a day or two Douglas's orders came on to have resolutions passed approving the bill; and they were passed by large majorities! The truth of this is vouched for by a bolting Democratic member. The masses, too, Democratic as well as Whig, were even nearer unanimous against it; but, as soon as the party necessity of supporting it became apparent, the way the Democrats began to see the wisdom and justice of it was perfectly astonishing.

You say that if Kansas fairly votes herself a free state, as a Christian you will rejoice at it. All decent slaveholders talk that way, and I do not doubt their candor. But they never vote that way. Although in a private letter or conversation you will express your preference that Kansas shall be free, you would vote for no man for Congress who would say the same thing publicly. No such man could be elected from any district in a slave state. You think Stringfellow and company ought to be hung; and yet at the next presidential election you will vote for the exact type and representative of Stringfellow. The slave-breeders and slave-traders are a small, odious, and detested class among you; and yet in politics they dictate the course of all of you, and are as completely your masters as you are the master of your own Negroes. You inquire where I now stand. That is a disputed point. I think I am a Whig; but others say there are no Whigs, and that I am an abolitionist. When I was at Washington, I voted for the Wilmot Proviso as good as forty times; and I never heard of anyone attempting to un-Whig me for that. I now do no more than oppose the extension of slavery. I am not a Know-Nothing; that is certain. How could I be? How can anyone who abhors the oppression of Negroes be in favor of degrading classes of white people? Our progress in degeneracy appears to me to be pretty rapid. As a nation we began by declaring that "all men are created equal." We now practically read it "all men are created equal, except Negroes." When the Know-Nothings get control, it will read "all men are created equal, except Negroes and foreigners and Catholics." When it comes to this, I shall prefer emigrating to some country where they make no pretense of loving liberty—to Russia, for instance, where despotism can be taken pure, and without the base alloy of hypocrisy.

Mary will probably pass a day or two in Louisville in October. My kindest regards to Mrs. Speed. On the leading subject of this letter I have more of her sympathy than I have of yours; and yet let me say I am,

Your friend forever,
A. LINCOLN

Speech Before the First Republican State Convention of Illinois

Bloomington, May 29, 1856

Mr. Chairman and Gentlemen: I was over at [Cries: "Platform!" "Take the platform!"]—I say, that while I was at Danville Court, some of our friends of anti-Nebraska got together in Springfield and elected me as one delegate to represent old Sangamon with them in this convention, and I am here certainly as a sympathizer in this movement and by virtue of that meeting and selection. But we can hardly be called delegates strictly, inasmuch as, properly speaking, we represent nobody but ourselves. I think it altogether fair to say that we have no anti-Nebraska party in Sangamon, although there is a good deal of anti-Nebraska feeling there; but I say for myself, and I think I may speak also for my colleagues, that we who are here fully approve of the platform and of all that has been done [A voice: "Yes!"], and even if we are not regularly delegates, it will be right for me to answer your call to speak. I suppose we truly stand for the public sentiment of Sangamon on the great question of the repeal, although we do not yet represent many numbers who have taken a distinct position on the question.

We are in a trying time—it ranges above mere party—and this movement to call a halt and turn our steps backward needs all the help and good counsels it can get; for unless popular opinion makes itself very strongly felt, and a change is made in our present course, *blood will flow on account of Nebraska, and brother's hands will be raised against brother!*

I have listened with great interest to the earnest appeal made to Illinois men by the gentleman from Lawrence [James S. Emery] who has just addressed us so eloquently and forcibly. I was deeply moved by his statement of the wrongs done to free-state men out there. I think it just to say that all true men North should sympathize with them, and ought to be willing to do any possible and needful thing to right their wrongs. But we must not promise what we ought not, lest we be called on to perform what we cannot; we must be calm and moderate, and consider the whole difficulty, and determine what is possible and just. We must not be led by excitement and passion to do that which our sober judgments would not approve in our cooler moments. We have higher aims; we will have more serious business than to dally with temporary measures.

We are here to stand firmly for a principle—to stand firmly for a right. We know that great political and moral wrongs are done, and outrages committed, and we denounce those wrongs and outrages, although we cannot, at present, do much more. But we desire to reach out beyond those personal outrages and establish a rule that will apply to all, and so prevent any future outrages.

We have seen today that every shade of popular opinion is represented here, with *freedom,* or rather *free soil,* as the basis. We have come together as in some sort representatives of popular opinion against the extension of slavery into territory now free in fact as well as by law, and the pledged word of the statesmen of the nation who are now no more. We come—we are here assembled together—to protest as well as we can against a great wrong, and to take measures, as well as we now can, to make that wrong right; to place the nation, as far as it may be possible now, as it was before the repeal of the Missouri Compromise; and the plain way to do this is to restore the Compromise, and to demand and determine that *Kansas shall be free!*

While we affirm, and reaffirm, if necessary, our devotion to the principles of the Declaration of Independence, let our practical work here be limited to the above. We know that there is not a perfect agreement of sentiment here on the public questions which might be rightfully considered in this convention, and that the indignation which we all must feel cannot be helped; but all of us must give up something for the good of the cause. There is one desire which is uppermost in the mind, one wish common to us all, to which no dissent will be made; and I counsel you earnestly to bury all resentment, to sink all personal feeling, make all things work to a common purpose in which we are united and agreed about, and which all present will agree is absolutely necessary—which *must* be done by any rightful mode if there be such: *Slavery must be kept out of Kansas!* The test—the pinch—is right there. If we lose Kansas to freedom, an example will be set which will prove fatal to freedom in the end. We, therefore, in the language of the Bible, must "lay the axe to the root of the tree." Temporizing will not do longer; now is the time for decision—for firm, persistent, resolute action.

The Nebraska bill, or rather Nebraska law, is not one of wholesome legislation, but was and is an act of legislative usurpation, whose result, if not indeed intention, is to make slavery national; and unless headed off in some effective way, we are in a fair way to see this land of boasted freedom converted into a land of slavery in fact. Just open your two eyes, and see if this be not so. I need do no more than state, to command universal approval, that almost the entire North, as well as a large following in the border states, is radically opposed to the planting of slavery in free territory. Probably in a popular vote throughout the nation nine tenths of the voters in the free states, and at least one half in the border states, if they could express their sentiments freely, would vote *no* on such an issue; and it is safe to say that two thirds of the votes of the entire nation would be opposed to it. And yet, in spite of this overbalancing of sentiment in this free country, we are in a fair way to see Kansas present itself for admission as a slave state. Indeed, it is a felony, by the local law of Kansas, to deny that slavery exists there even now. By every principle of law, a Negro in Kansas is free; yet the *bogus* legislature makes it an infamous crime to tell him that he is free!

The party lash and the fear of ridicule will overawe justice and liberty; for it is a singular fact, but nonetheless a fact, and well known by the most common experience, that men will do things under the terror of the party lash that they would not on any account or for any consideration do otherwise; while men who will march up to the mouth of a loaded cannon without shrinking will run from the terrible name of "abolitionist," even when pronounced by a worthless creature whom they, with good reason, despise. For instance—to press this point a little —Judge Douglas introduced his Nebraska bill in January; and we had an extra session of our legislature in the succeeding February, in which were seventy-five Democrats; and at a party caucus, fully attended, there were just three votes, out of the whole seventy-five, for the measure. But in a few days orders came on from Washington, commanding them to approve the measure; the party lash was applied, and it was brought up again in caucus, and passed by a large majority. The masses were against it, but party necessity carried it; and it was passed through the lower house of Congress against the will of the people, for the same reason. Here is where the greatest danger lies—that, while we profess to be a government of law and reason, law will give way to violence on demand of this awful and crushing power. Like the great juggernaut—I think that is the name—the great idol, it crushes everything that comes in its way, and makes a slave—as I read once, in a blackletter law book—"a human being who is legally not a *person* but a *thing.*" And if the safeguards to liberty are broken down, as is now attempted, when they have made *things* of all the free Negroes, how long, think you, before they will begin to make *things* of poor white men? Be not deceived. Revolutions do not go backward. The founder of the Democratic party declared that *all* men were created equal. His successor in the leadership has written the word "white" before men, making it read "all *white* men are created equal." Pray, will or may not the Know-Nothings, if they should get in power, add the word "Protestant," making it read *"all Protestant white men"*?

Meanwhile the hapless Negro is the fruitful subject of reprisals in other quarters. John Pettit, whom Tom Benton paid his respects to, you will recollect, calls the immortal Declaration "a self-evident lie"; while at the birthplace of freedom—in the shadow of Bunker Hill and of the "cradle of liberty," at the home of the Adamses and Warren and Otis—Choate, from our side of the house, dares to fritter away the birthday promise of liberty by proclaiming the Declaration to be "a string of glittering generalities"; and the Southern Whigs, working hand in hand with proslavery Democrats, are making Choate's theories practical. Thomas Jefferson, a slaveholder, mindful of the moral element in slavery, solemnly declared that he trembled for his country when he remembered that God is just; while Judge Douglas, with an insignificant wave of the hand, "don't care whether slavery is voted up or voted down." Now, if slavery is right, or even negative, he has a right to treat it in this trifling manner. But if it is a moral and political wrong, as all Christendom considers it to be, how can he answer to God for this attempt to spread and fortify it?

But no man, and Judge Douglas no more than any other, can maintain a negative, or merely neutral, position on this question; and, accordingly, he avows that the Union was made *by* white men and *for* white men and their descendants. As a matter of fact, the first branch of the proposition is historically true; the government was made by white men, and they were and are the superior race. This I admit. But the cornerstone of the government, so to speak, was the declaration that *"all* men are created equal," and all entitled to "life, liberty, and the pursuit of happiness."

And not only so, but the framers of the Constitution were particular to keep out of that instrument the word "slave," the reason being that slavery would ultimately come to an end, and they did not wish to have any reminder that in this free country human beings were ever prostituted to slavery. Nor is it any argument that we are superior and the Negro inferior—that he has but one talent while we have ten. Let the Negro possess the little he has in independence; if he has but one talent, he should be permitted to keep the little he has. But slavery will endure no test of reason or logic; and yet its advocates, like Douglas, use a sort of bastard logic, or noisy assumption it might better be termed, like the above, in order to prepare the mind for the gradual, but none the less certain, encroachments of the Moloch of slavery upon the fair domain of freedom. But however much you may argue upon it, or smother it in soft phrase, slavery can only be maintained by force—by violence. The repeal of the Missouri Compromise was by violence. It was a violation of both law and the sacred obligations of honor, to overthrow and trample under foot a solemn compromise, obtained by the fearful loss to freedom of one of the fairest of our western domains. Congress violated the will and confidence of its constituents in voting for the bill; and while public sentiment, as shown by the elections of 1854, demanded the restoration of this Compromise, Congress violated its trust by refusing simply because it had the force of numbers to hold onto it. And murderous violence is being used now, in order to force slavery on to Kansas; for it cannot be done in any other way.

The necessary result was to establish the rule of violence—force, instead of the rule of law and reason—to perpetuate and spread slavery, and in time to make it general. We see it at both ends of the line. In Washington, on the very spot where the outrage was started, the fearless Sumner is beaten to insensibility, and is now slowly dying—while senators who claim to be gentlemen and Christians stood by, countenancing the act, and even applauding it afterward in their places in the Senate. Even Douglas, our man, saw it all and was within helping distance, yet let the murderous blows fall unopposed. Then, at the other end of the line, at the very time Sumner was being murdered,

Lawrence was being destroyed for the crime of freedom. It was the most prominent stronghold of liberty in Kansas, and must give way to the all-dominating power of slavery. Only two days ago, Judge Trumbull found it necessary to propose a bill in the Senate to prevent a general civil war and to restore peace in Kansas.

We live in the midst of alarms; anxiety beclouds the future; we expect some new disaster with each newspaper we read. Are we in a healthful political state? Are not the tendencies plain? Do not the signs of the times point plainly the way in which we are going?

In the early days of the Constitution slavery was recognized, by South and North alike, as an evil, and the division of sentiment about it was not controlled by geographical lines or considerations of climate, but by moral and philanthropic views. Petitions for the abolition of slavery were presented to the very first Congress by Virginia and Massachusetts alike. To show the harmony which prevailed, I will state that a Fugitive Slave Law was passed in 1793, with no dissenting voice in the Senate, and but seven dissenting votes in the House. It was, however, a wise law, moderate, and, under the Constitution, a just one. Twenty-five years later, a more stringent law was proposed and defeated; and thirty-five years after that, the present law, drafted by Mason of Virginia, was passed by Northern votes. I am not, just now, complaining of this law, but I am trying to show how the current sets; for the proposed law of 1817 was far less offensive than the present one. In 1774 the Continental Congress pledged itself, without a dissenting vote, to wholly discontinue the slave trade, and to neither purchase nor import any slave; and less than three months before the passage of the Declaration of Independence, the same Congress which adopted that declaration unanimously resolved that *"no slave be imported into any of the thirteen United Colonies."*

On the second day of July 1776, the draft of a Declaration of Independence was reported to Congress by the committee, and in it the slave trade was characterized as "an execrable commerce," as "a piratical warfare," as the "opprobrium of infidel powers," and as "a cruel war against human nature." All agreed on this except South Carolina and Georgia, and in order to preserve harmony, and from the necessity of the case, these expressions were omitted. Indeed, abolition societies existed as far south as Virginia; and it is a well-known fact that Washington, Jefferson, Madison, Lee, Henry, Mason, and Pendleton were qualified abolitionists, and much more radical on that subject than we of the Whig and Democratic parties claim to be today. On March 1, 1784, Virginia ceded to the confederation all its lands lying northwest of the Ohio River. Jefferson, Chase of Maryland, and Howell of Rhode Island, as a committee on that and territory thereafter *to be ceded,* reported that no slavery should exist after the year 1800. Had this report been adopted, not only the Northwest, but Kentucky, Tennessee, Alabama, and Mississippi also would have been free; but it required the assent of nine states to ratify it. North Carolina was divided, and thus its vote was lost; and Delaware, Georgia, and New Jersey refused to vote. In point of fact, as it was, it was assented to by six states. Three years later on a square vote to exclude slavery from the Northwest, only one vote, and that from New York, was against it. And yet, thirty-seven years later, five thousand citizens of Illinois, out of a voting mass of less than twelve thousand, deliberately, after a long and heated contest, voted to introduce slavery in Illinois; and, today, a large party in the free state of Illinois are willing to vote to fasten the shackles of slavery on the fair domain of Kansas, notwithstanding it received the dowry of freedom long before its birth as a political community.

I repeat, therefore, the question: Is it not plain in what direction we are tending? In the colonial time, Mason, Pendleton, and Jefferson were as hostile to slavery in Virginia as Otis, Ames, and the Adamses were in Massachusetts; and Virginia made as earnest an effort to get rid of it as old Massachusetts did. But circumstances were against them and they failed; but not that the good will of its leading men was lacking. Yet within less than fifty years Virginia changed its tune, and made Negro-breeding for the cotton and sugar states one of its leading industries.

In the Constitutional Convention, George Mason of Virginia made a more violent abolition speech than my friends Lovejoy or Codding would desire to make here today—a speech which could not be safely repeated anywhere on Southern soil in this enlightened year. But, while there were some differences of opinion on this subject even then, discussion was allowed; but as you see by the Kansas slave code, which, as you know, is the Missouri slave code, merely ferried across the river, it is a felony to even express an opinion hostile to that foul blot in the land of Washington and the Declaration of Independence.

In Kentucky—my state—in 1849, on a test vote, the mighty influence of Henry Clay and many other good men there could not get a symptom of expression in favor of gradual emancipation on a plain issue of marching toward the light of civilization with Ohio and Illinois; but the state of Boone and Hardin and Henry Clay, with a "nigger" under each arm, took the black trail toward the deadly swamps of barbarism. Is there—can there be—any doubt about this thing? And is there any doubt that we must all lay aside our prejudices and march, shoulder to shoulder, in the great army of Freedom?

Every Fourth of July our young orators all proclaim this to be "the land of the *free* and the home of the brave!" Well, now, when you orators get that off next year, and maybe this very year, how would you like some old grizzled farmer to get up in the grove and deny it? How would you like that? But suppose Kansas comes in as a slave state, and all the "border ruffians" have barbecues about it, and free-state men come trailing back to the dishonored North, like whipped dogs with their tails between their legs, it is—ain't it?—evident that this is no more the "land of the free"; and if we let it go so, we won't dare to say "home of the brave" out loud.

Can any man doubt that, even in spite of the people's will,

slavery will triumph through violence, unless that will be made manifest and enforced? Even Governor Reeder claimed at the outset that the contest in Kansas was to be fair, but he got his eyes open at last; and I believe that, as a result of this moral and physical violence, Kansas will soon apply for admission as a slave state. And yet we can't mistake that the people don't want it so, and that it is a land which is free both by natural and political law. *No law is free law!* Such is the understanding of all Christendom. In the Somerset case, decided nearly a century ago, the great Lord Mansfield held that slavery was of such a nature that it must take its rise in *positive* (as distinguished from *natural*) law, and that in no country or age could it be traced back to any other source. Will someone please tell me where is the *positive* law that establishes slavery in Kansas? [A voice: "The *bogus* laws."] Aye, the *bogus* laws! And, on the same principle, a gang of Missouri horse-thieves could come into Illinois and declare horse-stealing to be legal, and it would be just as legal as slavery is in Kansas. But by express statute, in the land of Washington and Jefferson, we may soon be brought face to face with the discreditable fact of showing to the world by our acts that we prefer slavery to freedom—darkness to light!

It is, I believe, a principle in law that when one party to a contract violates it so grossly as to chiefly destroy the object for which it is made, the other party may rescind it. I will ask Browning if that ain't good law. [Voices: "Yes!"] Well, now if that be right, I go for rescinding the whole, entire Missouri Compromise and thus turning Missouri into a free state; and I should like to know the difference—should like for anyone to point out the difference—between *our* making a free state of Missouri and *their* making a slave state of Kansas. There ain't one bit of difference, except that our way would be a great mercy to humanity. But I have never said, and the Whig party has never said, and those who oppose the Nebraska bill do not as a body say, that they have any intention of interfering with slavery in the slave states. Our platform says just the contrary.

We allow slavery to exist in the slave states, not because slavery is right or good, but from the necessities of our Union. We grant a fugitive slave law because it is so "nominated in the bond"; because our fathers so stipulated—had to—and we are bound to carry out this agreement. But they did not agree to introduce slavery in regions where it did not previously exist. On the contrary, they said by their example and teachings that they did not deem it expedient—did not consider it right—to do so; and it is wise and right to do just as they did about it. [Voices: "Good!"] And that is what we propose—not to interfere with slavery where it exists (we have never tried to do it), and to give them a reasonable and efficient fugitive slave law. [A voice: "No!"] I say *yes!* It was part of the bargain, and I'm for living up to it; but I go no further; I'm not bound to do more, and I won't agree any further.

We, here in Illinois, should feel especially proud of the provision of the Missouri Compromise excluding slavery from what is now Kansas; for an Illinois man, Jesse B. Thomas, was its father. Henry Clay, who is credited with the authorship of the Compromise in general terms, did not even vote for that provision, but only advocated the ultimate admission by a second compromise; and Thomas was, beyond all controversy, the real author of the "slavery restriction" branch of the Compromise. To show the generosity of the Northern members toward the Southern side: on a test vote to exclude slavery from Missouri, ninety voted not to exclude, and eighty-seven to exclude, every vote from the slave states being ranged with the former and fourteen votes from the free states, of whom seven were from New England alone; while on a vote to exclude slavery from what is now Kansas, the vote was 134 *for* to 42 *against*. The scheme, as a whole, was, of course, a Southern triumph. It is idle to contend otherwise, as is now being done by the Nebraskites; it was so shown by the votes and quite as emphatically by the expressions of representative men. Mr. Lowndes of South Carolina was never known to commit a political mistake; his was the great judgment of that section; and he declared that this measure "would restore tranquillity to the country—a result demanded by every consideration of discretion, of moderation, of wisdom, and of virtue." When the measure came before President Monroe for his approval, he put to each member of his cabinet this question: "Has Congress the constitutional power to prohibit slavery in a territory?" And John C. Calhoun and William H. Crawford from the South, equally with John Quincy Adams, Benjamin Rush, and Smith Thompson from the North, alike answered *yes!* without qualification or equivocation; and this measure, of so great consequence to the South, was passed; and Missouri was, by means of it, finally enabled to knock at the door of the Republic for an open passage to its brood of slaves. And, in spite of this, Freedom's share is about to be taken by violence—by the force of misrepresentative votes, not called for by the popular will. What name can I, in common decency, give to this wicked transaction?

But even then the contest was not over; for when the Missouri constitution came before Congress for its approval, it forbade any free Negro or mulatto from entering the state. In short, our Illinois "black laws" were hidden away in their constitution, and the controversy was thus revived. Then it was that Mr. Clay's talents shone out conspicuously, and the controversy that shook the Union to its foundation was finally settled to the satisfaction of the conservative parties on both sides of the line, though not to the extremists on either, and Missouri was admitted by the small majority of six in the lower house. How great a majority, do you think, would have been given had Kansas also been secured for slavery? [A voice: "A majority the other way."] "A majority the other way" is answered. Do you think it would have been safe for a Northern man to have confronted his constituents after having voted to consign both Missouri and Kansas to hopeless slavery? And yet this man Douglas, who misrepresents his constituents and who has exerted his highest talents in that direction, will be carried in triumph through the state and hailed with honor while applauding that act. [Three groans of "Dug!"] And this shows whither we are tending. This thing of slavery is more powerful than its supporters—even than the high priests that minister at its altar. It debauches even our greatest men. It gathers strength, like a rolling snowball, by its own infamy. Monstrous crimes are committed in its name by persons collectively which they would not dare to commit as individuals. Its aggressions and encroachments almost surpass belief. In a despotism, one might not wonder to see slavery advance steadily and remorselessly into new dominions; but is it not wonderful, is it not even alarming, to see its steady advance in a land dedicated to the proposition that "all men are created equal"?

It yields nothing itself; it keeps all it has, and gets all it can besides. It really came dangerously near securing Illinois in 1824; it did get Missouri in 1821. The first proposition was to admit what is now Arkansas *and* Missouri as one slave state. But the territory was divided and Arkansas came in, without serious question, as a slave state; and afterwards Missouri, not, as a sort of equality, *free,* but also as a slave state. Then we had Florida and Texas; and now Kansas is about to be forced into the dismal procession. And so it is wherever you look. We have not forgotten—it is but six years since—how dangerously near California came to being a slave state. Texas is a slave state, and four other slave states may be carved from its vast domain. And yet, in the year 1829, slavery was abolished throughout that vast region by a royal decree of the then sovereign of Mexico. Will you please tell me by what *right* slavery exists in Texas today? By the same right as, and no higher or greater than, slavery is seeking dominion in Kansas: by political force—peaceful, if that will suffice; by the torch (as in Kansas) and the bludgeon (as in the Senate chamber), if required. And so history repeats itself; and even as slavery has kept its course by craft, intimidation, and violence in the past, so it will persist, in my judgment, until met and dominated by the will of a people bent on its restriction.

We have, this very afternoon, heard bitter denunciations of Brooks in Washington, and Titus, Stringfellow, Atchison, Jones, and Shannon in Kansas—the battleground of slavery. I certainly am not going to advocate or shield them; but they and their acts are but the necessary outcome of the Nebraska law. We should reserve our highest censure for the authors of the mischief, and not for the catspaws which they use. I believe it was Shakespeare who said, "Where the offense lies, there let the axe fall"; and, in my opinion, this man Douglas and the Northern men in Congress who advocate "Nebraska" are more guilty than a thousand Joneses and Stringfellows, with all their murderous practices, can be.

We have made a good beginning here today. As our Methodist friends would say, "I feel it is good to be here." While extremists may find some fault with the moderation of our platform, they should recollect that "the battle is not always to the strong, nor the race to the swift." In grave emergencies, moderation is generally safer than radicalism; and as this struggle is likely to be long and earnest, we must not, by our action, repel any who are in sympathy with us in the main, but rather win all that we can to our standard. We must not belittle nor overlook the facts of our condition—that we are new and comparatively weak, while our enemies are entrenched and relatively strong. They have the administration and the political power; and, right or wrong, at present they have the numbers. Our friends who urge an appeal to arms with so much force and eloquence should recollect that the government is arrayed against us, and that the numbers are now arrayed against us as well; or, to state it nearer to the truth, they are not yet expressly and affirmatively for us; and we should repel friends rather than gain them by anything savoring of revolutionary methods. As it now stands, we must appeal to the sober sense and patriotism of the people. We will make converts day by day; we will grow strong by calmness and moderation; we will grow strong by the violence and injustice of our adversaries. And, unless truth be a mockery and justice a hollow lie, we will be in the majority after a while, and then the revolution which we will accomplish will be none the less radical from being the result of pacific measures. The battle of freedom is to be fought out on principle. Slavery is a violation of the eternal right. We have temporized with it from the necessities of our condition; but as sure as God reigns and schoolchildren read, *that black, foul lie can never be consecrated into God's hallowed truth!*

One of our greatest difficulties is that men who *know* that slavery is a detestable crime and ruinous to the nation are compelled, by our peculiar condition and other circumstances, to advocate it concretely, though damning it in the raw. Henry Clay was a brilliant example of this tendency; others of our purest statesmen are compelled to do so; and thus slavery secures actual support from those who detest it at heart. Yet Henry Clay perfected and forced through the compromise which secured to slavery a great state as well as a political advantage. Not that he hated slavery less, but that he loved the whole Union more. As long as slavery profited by his great compromise, the hosts of proslavery could not sufficiently cover him with praise; but now that this compromise stands in their way

> they never mention him,
> His name is never heard:
> Their lips are now forbid to speak
> That once familiar word.

They have slaughtered one of his most cherished measures, and his ghost would arise to rebuke them.

Now, let us harmonize, my friends, and appeal to the moderation and patriotism of the people—to the sober second thought, to the awakened public conscience. The repeal of the sacred Missouri Compromise has installed the weapons of violence: the bludgeon, the incendiary torch, the death-dealing rifle, the bristling cannon—the weapons of kingcraft, of the inquisition, of ignorance, of barbarism, of oppression. We see its fruits in the dying bed of the heroic Sumner; in the ruins of the "Free

State" hotel; in the smoking embers of the *Herald of Freedom;* in the free-state governor of Kansas chained to a stake on freedom's soil like a horse-thief, for the crime of freedom. We see it in Christian statesmen, and Christian newspapers, and Christian pulpits applauding *the cowardly act of a low bully, who crawled upon his victim behind his back and dealt the deadly blow.* We note our political demoralization in the catchwords that are coming into such common use; on the one hand, "freedom-shriekers," and sometimes "freedom-screechers," and, on the other hand, "border ruffians," and that fully deserved. And the significance of catchwords cannot pass unheeded, for they constitute a sign of the times. Everything in this world "jibes" in with everything else, and all the fruits of this Nebraska bill are like the poisoned source from which they come. I will not say that we may not sooner or later be compelled to meet force by force; but the time has not yet come, and, if we are true to ourselves, may never come. Do not mistake that the ballot is stronger than the bullet. Therefore let the legions of slavery use bullets; but let us wait patiently till November and fire ballots at them in return; and by that peaceful policy I believe we shall ultimately win.

It was by that policy that here in Illinois the early fathers fought the good fight and gained the victory. In 1824 the free men of our state, led by Governor Coles—who was a native of Maryland and President Madison's private secretary—determined that those beautiful groves should never reecho the dirge of one who has no title to himself. By their resolute determination, the winds that sweep across our broad prairies shall never cool the parched brow, nor shall the unfettered streams that bring joy and gladness to our free soil water the tired feet, of a *slave;* but so long as those heavenly breezes and sparkling streams bless the land, or the groves and their fragrance or memory remain, the humanity to which they minister *shall be forever free!* Palmer, Yates, Williams, Browning, and some more in this convention came from Kentucky to Illinois (instead of going to Missouri), not only to better their conditions, but also to get away from slavery. They have said so to me, and it is understood among us Kentuckians that we don't like it one bit. Now, can we, mindful of the blessings of liberty which the early men of Illinois left to us, refuse a like privilege to the free men who seek to plant Freedom's banner on our western outposts? [Cries: "No!" "No!"] Should we not stand by our neighbors who seek to better their conditions in Kansas and Nebraska? [Cries: "Yes!" "Yes!"] Can we as Christian men, and strong and free ourselves, wield the sledge or hold the iron which is to manacle anew an already oppressed race? [Cries: "No!" "No!"] "Woe unto them," it is written, "that decree unrighteous decrees and that write grievousness which they have prescribed." Can we afford to sin any more deeply against human liberty? [Cries: "No!" "No!"]

One great trouble in the matter is that slavery is an insidious and crafty power, and gains equally by open violence of the brutal as well as by sly management of the peaceful. Even after the Ordinance of 1787, the settlers in Indiana and Illinois (it was all one government then) tried to get Congress to allow slavery temporarily, and petitions to that end were sent from Kaskaskia, and General Harrison, the governor, urged it from Vincennes, the capital. If that had succeeded, good-bye to liberty here. But John Randolph of Virginia made a vigorous report against it; and although they persevered so well as to get three favorable reports for it, yet the United States Senate, with the aid of some slave states, finally squelched it for good. And that is why this hall is today a temple for free men instead of a Negro livery stable. Once let slavery get planted in a locality, by ever so weak or doubtful a title, and in ever so small numbers, and it is like the Canada thistle or Bermuda grass—you can't root it out. You yourself may detest slavery; but your neighbor has five or six slaves, and he is an excellent neighbor, or your son has married his daughter, and they beg you to help save their property, and you vote against your interests and principle to accommodate a neighbor, hoping that your vote will be on the losing side. And others do the same; and in those ways slavery gets a sure foothold. And when that is done the whole mighty Union—the force of the nation—is committed to its support. And that very process is working in Kansas today. And you must recollect that the slave property is worth a billion of dollars; while free-state men must work for sentiment alone. Then there are "blue lodges"—as they call them—everywhere doing their secret and deadly work.

It is a very strange thing, and not solvable by any moral law that I know of, that if a man loses his horse, the whole country will turn out to help hang the thief; but if a man but a shade or two darker than I am is himself stolen, the same crowd will hang one who aids in restoring him to liberty. Such are the inconsistencies of slavery, where a horse is more sacred than a man; and the essence of squatter or popular sovereignty—I don't care how you call it—is that if one man chooses to make a slave of another, no third man shall be allowed to object. And if you can do this in free Kansas, and it is allowed to stand, the next thing you will see is shiploads of Negroes from Africa at the wharf at Charleston, for one thing is as truly lawful as the other; and these are the bastard notions we have got to stamp out, else they will stamp us out.

Two years ago, at Springfield, Judge Douglas avowed that Illinois came into the Union as a slave state, and that slavery was weeded out by the operation of his great, patent, everlasting principle of "popular sovereignty." Well, now, that argument must be answered, for it has a little grain of truth at the bottom. I do not mean that it is true in essence, as he would have us believe. It could not be essentially true if the Ordinance of 1787 was valid. But, in point of fact, there were some degraded beings called slaves in Kaskaskia and the other French settlements when our first state constitution was adopted; that is a fact, and I don't deny it. Slaves were brought here as early as 1720, and were kept here in spite of the Ordinance of 1787 against it. But slavery did not thrive here. On the contrary, under the influence of the ordinance the number *decreased* 51 from 1810 to 1820; while under the influence of *squatter* sovereignty, right across the river in Missouri, they *increased* 7,211 in the same time; and slavery finally faded out in Illinois, under the influence of the law of freedom, while it grew stronger and stronger in Missouri, under the law or practice of "popular sovereignty." In point of fact there were but 117 slaves in Illinois one year after its admission, or 1 to every 470 of its population; or, to state it in another way, if Illinois was a slave state in 1820, so were New York and New Jersey much greater slave states from having had greater numbers, slavery having been established there in very early times. But there is this vital difference between all these states and the judge's Kansas experiment: that they sought to disestablish slavery which had been already established, while the judge seeks, so far as he can, to disestablish freedom, which had been established there by the Missouri Compromise.

The Union is undergoing a fearful strain; but it is a stout old ship, and has weathered many a hard blow, and "the stars in their courses," aye, an invisible Power, greater than the puny efforts of men, will fight for us. But we ourselves must not decline the burden of responsibility, nor take counsel of unworthy passions. Whatever duty urges us to do or to omit must be done or omitted; and the recklessness with which our adversaries break the laws, or counsel their violation, should afford no example for us. Therefore, let us revere the Declaration of Independence; let us continue to obey the Constitution and the laws; let us keep step to the music of the Union. Let us draw a cordon, so to speak, around the slave states, and the hateful institution, like a reptile poisoning itself, will perish by its own infamy.

But we cannot be free men if this is, by our national choice, to be a land of slavery. Those who deny freedom to others deserve it not for themselves; and, under the rule of a just God, cannot long retain it.

Did you ever, my friends, seriously reflect upon the speed with which we are tending downwards? Within the memory of men now present the leading statesman of Virginia could make genuine, red-hot abolitionist speeches in old Virginia! And, as I have said, now even in "free Kansas" it is a crime to declare that it is "free Kansas." The very sentiments that I and others have just uttered would entitle us, and each of us, to the ignominy and seclusion of a dungeon; and yet I suppose that, like Paul, we were "free born." But if this thing is allowed to continue, it will be but one step further to impress the same rule in Illinois.

The conclusion of all is, that we must restore the Missouri Compromise. We must highly resolve that *Kansas must be free!* We must reinstate the birthday promise of the Republic; we must reaffirm the Declaration of Independence; we must make good in essence as well as in form Madison's avowal that "the word *slave* ought not to appear in the Constitution"; and we must even go further, and decree that only local law, and not that time-honored instrument, shall shelter a slaveholder. We must make this a land of liberty in fact, as it is in name. But in seeking to attain these results—so indispensable if the liberty which is our pride and boast shall endure—we will be loyal to the Constitution and to the "flag of our Union," and no matter what our grievance—even though Kansas shall come in as a slave state; and no matter what theirs—even if we shall restore the Compromise—we will say to the Southern disunionists, "We won't go out of the Union, and you *shan't!*"

But let us, meanwhile, appeal to the sense and patriotism of the people, and not to their prejudices; let us spread the floods of enthusiasm here aroused all over these vast prairies, so suggestive of freedom. Let us commence by electing the gallant soldier Governor [Colonel] Bissell who stood for the honor of our state alike on the plains and amidst the chaparral of Mexico and on the floor of Congress, while he defied the Southern Hotspur; and that will have a greater moral effect than all the border ruffians can accomplish in all their raids on Kansas. There is both a power and a magic in popular opinion. To that let us now appeal; and while, in all probability, no resort to force will be needed, our moderation and forbearance will stand us in good stead when, if ever, *we must make an appeal to battle and to the God of hosts!*

Speech Before the 1858 Republican State Convention of Illinois

A House Divided

Springfield, June 17, 1858

Mr. President and Gentlemen of the Convention: If we could first know where we are, and whither we are tending, we could better judge what to do, and how to do it. We are now far into the fifth year since a policy was initiated with the avowed object and confident promise of putting an end to slavery agitation. Under the operation of that policy, that agitation has not only not ceased, but has constantly augmented. In my opinion, it will not cease until a crisis shall have been reached and passed. *"A house divided against itself cannot stand."* I believe this government cannot endure permanently half slave and half free. I do not expect the Union to be dissolved; I do not expect the house to fall; but I do expect it will cease to be divided. It will become all one thing, or all the other. Either the opponents of slavery will arrest the further spread of it, and place it where the public mind shall rest in the belief that it is in the course of ultimate extinction, or its advocates will push it forward till it shall become alike lawful in all the states, old as well as new, North as well as South.

Have we no tendency to the latter condition?

Let anyone who doubts, carefully contemplate that now almost complete legal combination—piece of machinery, so to speak—compounded of the Nebraska doctrine and the *Dred*

Scott decision. Let him consider, not only what work the machinery is adapted to do, and how well adapted, but also let him study the history of its construction, and trace, if he can, or rather fail, if he can, to trace the evidences of design, and concert of action, among its chief architects, from the beginning.

The new year of 1854 found slavery excluded from more than half the states by state constitutions, and from most of the national territory by congressional prohibition. Four days later, commenced the struggle which ended in repealing that congressional prohibition. This opened all the national territory to slavery, and was the first point gained.

But, so far, Congress only had acted, and an endorsement by the people, real or apparent, was indispensable to save the point already gained, and give chance for more.

This necessity had not been overlooked, but had been provided for, as well as might be, in the notable argument of "squatter sovereignty," otherwise called "sacred right of self-government," which latter phrase, though expressive of the only rightful basis of any government, was so perverted in this attempted use of it as to amount to just this: That if any *one* man choose to enslave *another,* no *third* man shall be allowed to object. That argument was incorporated into the Nebraska bill itself, in the language which follows: "It being the true intent and meaning of this act not to legislate slavery into any territory or state, nor to exclude it therefrom, but to leave the people thereof perfectly free to form and regulate their domestic institutions in their own way, subject only to the Constitution of the United States." Then opened the roar of loose declamation in favor of "squatter sovereignty," and "sacred right of self-government." "But," said opposition members, "let us amend the bill so as to expressly declare that the people of the territory may exclude slavery." "Not we," said the friends of the measure, and down they voted the amendment.

While the Nebraska bill was passing through Congress, a *law case,* involving the question of a Negro's freedom, by reason of his owner having voluntarily taken him first into a free state, and then into a territory covered by the Congressional prohibition, and held him as a slave for a long time in each, was passing through the United States Circuit Court for the District of Missouri; and both Nebraska bill and lawsuit were brought to a decision in the same month of May 1854. The Negro's name was Dred Scott, which name now designates the decision finally made in the case. Before the then next presidential election, the law case came to, and was argued in, the Supreme Court of the United States; but the decision of it was deferred until after the election. Still, before the election, Senator Trumbull, on the floor of the Senate, requested the leading advocate of the Nebraska bill to state his opinion whether the people of a territory can constitutionally exclude slavery from their limits; and the latter answers: "That is a question for the Supreme Court."

The election came. Mr. Buchanan was elected, and the endorsement, such as it was, secured. That was the second point gained. The endorsement, however, fell short of a clear popular majority by nearly four hundred thousand votes, and so, perhaps, was not overwhelmingly reliable and satisfactory. The outgoing president, in his last annual message, as impressively as possible echoed back upon the people the weight and authority of the endorsement. The Supreme Court met again, did not announce their decision, but ordered a reargument. The presidential inauguration came, and still no decision of the court; but the incoming president, in his inaugural address, fervently exhorted the people to abide by the forthcoming decision, whatever it might be. Then, in a few days, came the decision.

The reputed author of the Nebraska bill finds an early occasion to make a speech at this capital endorsing the *Dred Scott* decision, and vehemently denouncing all opposition to it. The new president, too, seizes the early occasion of the Silliman letter to endorse and strongly construe that decision, and to express his astonishment that any different view had ever been entertained!

At length a squabble springs up between the president and the author of the Nebraska bill, on the mere question of fact, whether the Lecompton Constitution was or was not in any just sense made by the people of Kansas; and in that quarrel the latter declares that all he wants is a fair vote for the people, and that he cares not whether slavery be voted down or voted up. I do not understand his declaration, that he cares not whether slavery be voted down or voted up, to be intended by him other than as an apt definition of the policy he would impress upon the public mind—the principle for which he declares he has suffered so much, and is ready to suffer to the end. And well may he cling to that principle! If he has any parental feeling, well may he cling to it. That principle is the only shred left of his original Nebraska doctrine. Under the *Dred Scott* decision "squatter sovereignty" squatted out of existence, tumbled down like temporary scaffolding; like the mould at the foundry, served through one blast, and fell back into loose sand; helped to carry an election, and then was kicked to the winds. His late joint struggle with the Republicans, against the Lecompton Constitution, involves nothing of the original Nebraska doctrine. That struggle was made on a point—the right of a people to make their own constitution—upon which he and the Republicans have never differed.

The several points of the *Dred Scott* decision, in connection with Senator Douglas's "care not" policy, constitute the piece of machinery, in its present state of advancement. This was the third point gained. The working points of that machinery are:

First, That no Negro slave, imported as such from Africa, and no descendant of such slave, can ever be a citizen of any state, in the sense of that term as used in the Constitution of the United States. This point is made in order to deprive the Negro, in every possible event, of the benefit of that provision of the United States Constitution which declares that "the citizens of each state shall be entitled to all privileges and immunities of citizens in the several states."

Second, That, "subject to the Constitution of the United States," neither Congress nor a territorial legislature can exclude slavery from any United States territory. This point is made in order that individual men may fill up the territories with slaves, without danger of losing them as property, and thus to enhance the chances of permanency to the institution through all the future.

Third, That whether the holding a Negro in actual slavery in a free state makes him free, as against the holder, the United States courts will not decide, but will leave to be decided by the courts of any slave state the Negro may be forced into by the master. This point is made, not to be pressed immediately; but, if acquiesced in for a while, and apparently endorsed by the people at an election, then to sustain the logical conclusion that what Dred Scott's master might lawfully do with Dred Scott, in the free state of Illinois, every other master may lawfully do with any other one, or one thousand slaves, in Illinois, or in any other free state.

Auxiliary to all this, and working hand in hand with it, the Nebraska doctrine, or what is left of it, is to educate and mould public opinion, at least Northern public opinion, not to care whether slavery is voted down or voted up. This shows exactly where we now are; and partially, also, whither we are tending.

It will throw additional light on the latter, to go back and run the mind over the string of historical facts already stated. Several things will now appear less dark and mysterious than they did when they were transpiring. The people were to be left "perfectly free," "subject only to the Constitution." What the Constitution had to do with it, outsiders could not then see. Plainly enough now—it was an exactly fitted niche, for the *Dred Scott* decision to afterwards come in, and declare the perfect freedom of the people to be just no freedom at all. Why was the amendment, expressly declaring the right of the people, voted down? Plainly enough now—the adoption of it would have spoiled the niche for the *Dred Scott* decision. Why was the court decision held up? Why even a senator's individual opinion withheld, till after the presidential election? Plainly enough now—the speaking out then would have damaged the "perfectly free" argument upon which the election was to be carried. Why the outgoing president's felicitation on the endorsement? Why the delay of a reargument? Why the incoming president's advance exhortation in favor of the decision? These things look like the cautious patting and petting of a spirited horse preparatory to mounting him, when it is dreaded that he may give the rider a fall. And why the hasty afterendorsement of the decision by the president and others?

We cannot absolutely know that all these exact adaptations are the result of preconcert. But when we see a lot of framed timbers, different portions of which we know have been gotten out at different times and places and by different workmen— Stephen, Franklin, Roger, and James, for instance—and when we see these timbers joined together, and see they exactly make the frame of a house or a mill, all the tenons and mortises exactly fitting, and all the lengths and proportions of the different pieces exactly adapted to their respective places, and not a piece too many or too few—not omitting even scaffolding—or, if a single piece be lacking, we see the place in the frame exactly fitted and prepared yet to bring such piece in—in such a case, we find it impossible not to believe that Stephen and Franklin and Roger and James all understood one another from the beginning, and all worked upon a common plan or draft drawn up before the first blow was struck.

It should not be overlooked that by the Nebraska bill the people of a *state* as well as territory were to be left "perfectly free," "subject only to the Constitution." Why mention a state? They were legislating for territories, and not for or about states. Certainly the people of a state are and ought to be subject to the Constitution of the United States; but why is mention of this lugged into this merely territorial law? Why are the people of a territory and the people of a state therein lumped together, and their relation to the Constitution therein treated as being precisely the same? While the opinion of the court, by Chief Justice Taney, in the *Dred Scott* case, and the separate opinions of all the concurring judges, expressly declare that the Constitution of the United States neither permits Congress nor a territorial legislature to exclude slavery from any United States territory, they all omit to declare whether or not the same Constitution permits a state, or the people of a state, to exclude it. Possibly, this is a mere omission; but who can be quite sure, if McLean or Curtis had sought to get into the opinion a declaration of unlimited power in the people of a state to exclude slavery from their limits, just as Chase and Mace sought to get such declaration, in behalf of the people of a territory, into the Nebraska bill —I ask, who can be quite sure that it would not have been voted down in the one case as it had been in the other? The nearest approach to the point of declaring the power of a state over slavery is made by Judge Nelson. He approaches it more than once, using the precise idea, and almost the language, too, of the Nebraska act. On one occasion, his exact language is "Except in cases where the power is restrained by the Constitution of the United States, the law of the state is supreme over the subject of slavery within its jurisdiction." In what cases the power of the states is so restrained by the United States Constitution, is left an open question, precisely as the same question, as to the restraint on the power of the territories, was left open in the Nebraska act. Put this and that together, and we have another nice little niche, which we may, ere long, see filled with another Supreme Court decision, declaring that the Constitution of the United States does not permit a *state* to exclude slavery from its limits. And this may especially be expected if the doctrine of "care not whether slavery be voted down or voted up" shall gain upon the public mind sufficiently to give promise that such a decision can be maintained when made.

Such a decision is all that slavery now lacks of being alike lawful in all the states. Welcome or unwelcome, such a decision is probably coming, and will soon be upon us, unless the power of the present political dynasty shall be met and overthrown. We shall lie down pleasantly dreaming that the people of Missouri are on the verge of making their state free, and we shall awake to the reality instead that the Supreme Court has made Illinois a slave state. To meet and overthrow the power of that dynasty is the work now before all those who would prevent that consummation. That is what we have to do. How can we best do it?

There are those who denounce us openly to their own friends, and yet whisper us softly that Senator Douglas is the aptest instrument there is with which to effect that object. They wish us to infer all, from the fact that he now has a little quarrel with the present head of the dynasty, and that he has regularly voted with us on a single point, upon which he and we have never differed. They remind us that he is a great man, and that the largest of us are very small ones. Let this be granted. But "a living dog is better than a dead lion." Judge Douglas, if not a dead lion, for this work is at least a caged and toothless one. How can he oppose the advances of slavery? He don't care anything about it. His avowed mission is impressing the "public heart" to *care nothing about it*.

A leading Douglas Democratic newspaper thinks Douglas's superior talent will be needed to resist the revival of the African slave trade. Does Douglas believe an effort to revive that trade is approaching? He has not said so. Does he really think so? But if it is, how can he resist it? For years he has labored to prove it a sacred right of white men to take Negro slaves into the new territories. Can he possibly show that it is less a sacred right to buy them where they can be bought cheapest? And unquestionably they can be bought cheaper in Africa than in Virginia. He has done all in his power to reduce the whole question of slavery to one of a mere right of property; and, as such, how can he oppose the foreign slave trade—how can he refuse that trade in that "property" shall be "perfectly free"—unless he does it as a protection to the home production? And as the home producers will probably not ask the protection, he will be wholly without a ground of opposition.

Senator Douglas holds, we know, that a man may rightfully be wiser today than he was yesterday; that he may rightfully change when he finds himself wrong. But can we, for that reason, run ahead, and infer that he will make any particular change, of which he himself has given no intimation? Can we safely base our action upon any such vague inference? Now, as ever, I wish not to misrepresent Judge Douglas's position, question his motives, or do aught that can be personally offensive to him. Whenever, if ever, he and we can come together on principle so that our cause may have assistance from his great ability, I hope to have interposed no adventitious obstacles. But clearly he is not now with us; he does not pretend to be—he does not promise ever to be.

Our cause, then, must be entrusted to, and conducted by, its own undoubted friends—those whose hands are free, whose hearts are in the work, who *do care* for the result. Two years ago the Republicans of the nation mustered over thirteen hundred thousand strong. We did this under the single impulse of resistance to a common danger, with every external circumstance against us. Of strange, discordant, and even hostile elements we gathered from the four winds, and formed and fought the battle through, under the constant hot fire of a disciplined, proud, and pampered enemy. Did we brave all then to falter now—now, when that same enemy is wavering, dissevered, and belligerent? The result is not doubtful. We shall not fail; if we stand firm, *we shall not fail*. Wise counsels may accelerate, or mistakes delay it, but, sooner or later, the victory is sure to come.

Letter to Senator
Stephen A. Douglas

Springfield, July 29, 1858

Dear Sir:

Yours of the 24th in relation to an arrangement to divide time, and address the same audiences, is received; and, in apology for not sooner replying, allow me to say that when I sat by you at dinner yesterday, I was not aware that you had answered my note, nor, certainly, that my own note had been presented to you. An hour after, I saw a copy of your answer in the Chicago *Times,* and reaching home, I found the original awaiting me. Protesting that your insinuations of attempted unfairness on my part are unjust, and with the hope that you did not very considerately make them, I proceed to reply. To your statement that "It has been suggested, recently, that an arrangement had been made to bring out a third candidate for the United States Senate, who, with yourself, should canvass the state in opposition to me," etc., I can only say, that such suggestion must have been made by yourself, for certainly none such has been made by or to me, or otherwise, to my knowledge. Surely you did not *deliberately* conclude, as you insinuate, that I was expecting to draw you into an arrangement of terms, to be agreed on by yourself, by which a third candidate and myself, "in concert, might be able to take the opening and closing speech in every case."

As to your surprise that I did not sooner make the proposal to divide time with you, I can only say, I made it as soon as I resolved to make it. I did not know but that such proposal would come from you; I waited, respectfully, to see. It may have been well known to you that you went to Springfield for the purpose of agreeing on the plan of campaign; but it was not so known to me. When your appointments were announced in the papers, extending only to the 21st of August, I for the first time considered it certain that you would make no proposal to me, and then resolved that, if my friends concurred, I would make one to you. As soon thereafter as I could see and consult with friends satisfactorily, I did make the proposal. It did not occur to me that the proposed arrangement could derange your plans after the latest of your appointments already made. After that, there was, before the election, largely over two months of clear time.

For you to say that we have already spoken at Chicago and Springfield, and that on both occasions I had the concluding speech, is hardly a fair statement. The truth rather is this. At Chicago, July 9, you made a carefully prepared conclusion on my speech of June 16. Twenty-four hours after, I made a hasty conclusion on yours of the 9th. You had six days to prepare, and concluded on me again at Bloomington on the 16th. Twenty-four hours after, I concluded again on you at Springfield. In the mean time, you had made another conclusion on me at Springfield, which I did not hear, and of the contents of which I knew nothing when I spoke; so that your speech made in daylight, and mine at night, on the 17th, at Springfield, were both made in perfect independence of each other. The dates of making all these speeches will show, I think, that in the matter of time for preparation the advantage has all been on your side, and that none of the external circumstances have stood to my advantage.

I agree to an arrangement for us to speak at the seven places you have named, and at your own times, provided you name the times at once, so that I as well as you can have to myself the time not covered by the arrangement. As to the other details, I wish perfect reciprocity and no more. I wish as much time as you, and that conclusions shall alternate. That is all.

Your obedient servant,
A. LINCOLN

P.S. As matters now stand, I shall be at no more of your exclusive meetings, and for about a week from today a letter from you will reach me at Springfield.

A.L.

SPEECH AT THE FIRST LINCOLN-DOUGLAS DEBATE

Ottawa, Illinois, August 21, 1858

My Fellow Citizens: When a man hears himself somewhat misrepresented, it provokes him,—at least, I find it so with myself; but when misrepresentation becomes very gross and palpable, it is more apt to amuse him. The first thing I see fit to notice is the fact that Judge Douglas alleges, after running through the history of the old Democratic and the old Whig parties, that Judge Trumbull and myself made an arrangement in 1854, by which I was to have the place of General Shields in the United States Senate, and Judge Trumbull was to have the place of Judge Douglas. Now, all I have to say upon that subject is that I think no man—not even Judge Douglas—can prove it, *because it is not true.* I have no doubt he is "conscientious" in saying it. As to those resolutions that he took such a length of time to read, as being the platform of the Republican party in 1854, I say I never had anything to do with them, and I think Trumbull never had. Judge Douglas cannot show that either of us ever did have anything to do with them.

I believe *this* is true about those resolutions: There was a call for a convention to form a Republican party at Springfield, and I think that my friend Mr. Lovejoy, who is here upon this stand, had a hand in it. I think this is true, and I think if he will remember accurately he will be able to recollect that he tried to get me into it, and I would not go in. I believe it is also true that I went away from Springfield when the convention was in session, to attend court in Tazewell County. It is true they did place my name, though without authority, upon the committee, and afterward wrote me to attend the meeting of the committee; but I refused to do so, and I never had anything to do with that organization. This is the plain truth about all that matter of the resolutions.

Now, about this story that Judge Douglas tells of Trumbull bargaining to sell out the old Democratic party, and Lincoln agreeing to sell out the old Whig party, I have the means of *knowing* about that: Judge Douglas cannot have; and I know there is no substance to it whatever. Yet I have no doubt he is "conscientious" about it. I know that after Mr. Lovejoy got into the legislature that winter, he complained of me that I had told all the old Whigs of his district that the old Whig party was good enough for them, and some of them voted against him because I told them so. Now, I have no means of totally disproving such charges as this which the judge makes. A man cannot prove a negative; but he has a right to claim that when a man makes an affirmative charge, he must offer some proof to show the truth of what he says. I certainly cannot introduce testimony to show the negative about things, but I have a right to claim that if a man says he *knows* a thing, then he must show *how* he knows it. I always have a right to claim this, and it is not satisfactory to me that he may be "conscientious" on the subject.

Now, gentlemen, I hate to waste my time on such things; but in regard to that general abolition tilt that Judge Douglas makes, when he says that I was engaged at that time in selling out and abolitionizing the old Whig party, I hope you will permit me to read a part of a printed speech that I made then at Peoria, which will show altogether a different view of the position I took in that contest of 1854. [A voice: "Put on your specs."] Yes, sir, I am obliged to do so; I am no longer a young man. [Lincoln reads an extensive extract from the 1854 Peoria speech on the Kansas-Nebraska Act, the portion beginning and ending as follows.]

This is the *repeal* of the Missouri Compromise. The foregoing history may not be precisely accurate in every particular, but I am sure it is sufficiently so for all the uses I shall attempt to make of it, and in it we have before us the chief materials enabling us to correctly judge whether the repeal of the Missouri Compromise is right or wrong.

I think, and shall try to show, that it is wrong—wrong in its direct effect, letting slavery into Kansas and Nebraska, and wrong in its prospective principle, allowing it to spread to every other part of the wide world where men can be found inclined to take it. . . .

But all this, to my judgment, furnishes no more excuse for permitting slavery to go into our own free territory than it would for reviving the African slave trade by law. The law which forbids the bringing of slaves *from* Africa, and that which has so long forbid the taking of them *to* Nebraska, can hardly be distinguished on any moral principle; and the repeal of the former could find quite as plausible excuses as that of the latter.

I have reason to know that Judge Douglas *knows* that I said this. I think he has the answer here to one of the questions he put to me. I do not mean to allow him to catechize me unless he pays back for it in kind. I will not answer questions one after another, unless he reciprocates; but as he has made this inquiry, and I have answered it before, he has got it without my getting anything in return. He has got my answer on the Fugitive Slave Law.

Now, gentlemen, I don't want to read at any greater length; but this is the true complexion of all I have ever said in regard to the institution of slavery and the black race. This is the whole of it; and anything that argues me into his idea of perfect social and political equality with the Negro is but a specious and fantastic arrangement of words, by which a man can prove a horse-chestnut to be a chestnut horse. I will say here, while upon this subject, that I have no purpose, directly or indirectly, to interfere with the institution of slavery in the states where it exists. I believe I have no lawful right to do so, and I have no inclination to do so. I have no purpose to introduce political and social equality between the white and the black races. There is a physical difference between the two which, in my judgment, will probably forever forbid their living together upon the footing of perfect equality; and inasmuch as it becomes a necessity that there must be a difference, I, as well as Judge Douglas, am in favor of the race to which I belong having the superior position. I have never said anything to the contrary, but I hold that, notwithstanding all this, there is no reason in the world why the Negro is not entitled to all the natural rights enumerated in the Declaration of Independence—the right to life, liberty, and the pursuit of happiness. I hold that he is as much entitled to these as the white man. I agree with Judge Douglas he is not my equal in many respects—certainly not in color, perhaps not in moral or intellectual endowment. But in the right to eat the bread, without the leave of anybody else, which his own hand earns, *he is my equal, and the equal of Judge Douglas, and the equal of every living man.*

Now I pass on to consider one or two more of these little follies. The judge is woefully at fault about his early friend Lincoln being a "grocery-keeper." I don't know as it would be a great sin, if I had been; but he is mistaken. Lincoln never kept a grocery anywhere in the world. It is true that Lincoln did work the latter part of one winter in a little still-house, up at the head of a hollow. And so I think my friend the judge is equally at fault when he charges me at the time when I was in Congress of having opposed our soldiers who were fighting in the Mexican War. The judge did not make his charge very distinctly, but I can tell you what he can prove, by referring to the record. You remember I was an old Whig, and whenever the Democratic party tried to get me to vote that the war had been righteously begun by the president, I would not do it. But whenever they asked for any money, or land-warrants, or anything to pay the soldiers there, during all that time, I gave the same vote that Judge Douglas did. You can think as you please as to whether that was consistent. Such is the truth; and the judge has the right to make all he can out of it. But when he, by a general charge, conveys the idea that I withheld supplies from the soldiers who were fighting in the Mexican War, or did anything else to hinder the soldiers, he is, to say the least, grossly and altogether mistaken, as a consultation of the records will prove to him.

As I have not used up so much of my time as I had supposed, I will dwell a little longer upon one or two of these minor topics upon which the judge has spoken. He has read from my speech in Springfield, in which I say that "a house divided against itself cannot stand." Does the judge say it *can* stand? I don't know whether he does or not. The judge does not seem to be attending to me just now, but I would like to know if it is his opinion that a house divided against itself *can stand*. If he does, then there is a question of veracity, not between him and me, but between the judge and an Authority of a somewhat higher character.

Now, my friends, I ask your attention to this matter for the purpose of saying something seriously. I know that the judge may readily enough agree with me that the maxim which was put forth by the Savior is true, but he may allege that I misapply it; and the judge has a right to urge that, in my application, I do misapply it, and then I have a right to show that I do *not* misapply it. When he undertakes to say that because I think this nation, so far as the question of slavery is concerned, will all become one thing or all the other, I am in favor of bringing about a dead uniformity in the various states, in all their institutions, he argues erroneously. The great variety of the local institutions in the states, springing from differences in the soil, differences in the face of the country, and in the climate, are bonds of Union. They do not make "a house divided against itself," but they make a house united. If they produce in one section of the country what is called for by the wants of another section, and this other section can supply the wants of the first, they are not matters of discord, but bonds of union, true bonds of union. But can this question of slavery be considered as among *these* varieties in the institutions of the country?

I leave it to you to say whether, in the history of our government, this institution of slavery has not always failed to be a bond of union, and, on the contrary, been an apple of discord and an element of division in the house. I ask you to consider whether, so long as the moral constitution of men's minds shall continue to be the same, after this generation and assemblage shall sink into the grave, and another race shall arise, with the same moral and intellectual development we have—whether, if that institution is standing in the same irritating position in which it now is, it will not continue an element of division? If so, then I have a right to say that, in regard to this question, the Union is a house divided against itself; and when the judge reminds me that I have often said to him that the institution of slavery has existed for eighty years in some states, and yet it does not exist in some others, I agree to the fact, and I account for it by looking at the position in which our fathers originally placed it—restricting it from the new territories where it had not gone, and legislating to cut off its source by the abrogation of the slave trade, thus putting the seal of legislation *against its spread*. The public mind *did* rest in the belief that it was in the course of ultimate extinction. But lately, I think—and in this I charge nothing on the judge's motives—lately, I think that he, and those acting with him, have placed that institution on a new basis, which looks to the *perpetuity and nationalization of slavery*. And while it is placed upon this new basis, I say, and I have said, that I believe we shall not have peace upon the question until the opponents of slavery arrest the further spread of it, and place it where the public mind shall rest in the belief that it is in the course of ultimate extinction; or, on the other hand, that its advocates will push it forward until it shall become alike lawful in all the states, old as well as new, North as well as South. Now, I believe if we could arrest the spread, and place it where Washington and Jefferson and Madison placed it, it *would be* in the course of ultimate extinction, and the public mind *would*, as for eighty years past, believe that it was in the course of ultimate extinction. The crisis would be past, and the institution might be let alone for a hundred years, if it should live so long, in the states where it exists; yet it would be going out of existence in the way best for both the black and the white races.

[A voice: "Then do you repudiate popular sovereignty?"]

Well, then, let us talk about popular sovereignty! What is popular sovereignty? Is it the right of the people to have slavery or not have it, as they see fit, in the territories? I will state—and I have an able man to watch me—my understanding is that popular sovereignty, as now applied to the question of slavery, does allow the people of a territory to have slavery if they want to, but does not allow them *not* to have it if they *do not* want it. I do not mean that if this vast concourse of people were in a territory of the United States, any one of them would be obliged to have a slave if he did not want one; but I do say that, as I understand the *Dred Scott* decision, if any one man wants slaves, all the rest have no way of keeping that one man from holding them.

When I made my speech at Springfield, of which the judge complains, and from which he quotes, I really was not thinking of the things which he ascribes to me at all. I had no thought in the world that I was doing anything to bring about a war between the free and slave states. I had no thought in the world that I was doing anything to bring about a political and social equality of the black and white races. It never occurred to me that I was doing anything or favoring anything to reduce to a dead uniformity all the local institutions of the various states. But I must say, in all fairness to him, if he thinks I am doing something which leads to these bad results, it is none the better that I did not mean it. It is just as fatal to the country, if I have any influence in producing it, whether I intend it or not.

But can it be true that placing this institution upon the original basis—the basis upon which our fathers placed it—can have any tendency to set the Northern and the Southern states at war with one another, or that it can have any tendency to make the people of Vermont raise sugarcane, because they raise it in Louisiana, or that it can compel the people of Illinois to cut pine logs on the Grand Prairie, where they will not grow, because they cut pine logs in Maine, where they do grow? The judge says this is a new principle started in regard to this question. Does the judge claim that he is working on the plan of the founders of government? I think he says in some of his speeches —indeed, I have one here now—that he saw evidence of a policy to allow slavery to be south of a certain line, while north of it it should be excluded, and he saw an indisposition on the part of the country to stand upon that policy, and therefore he set about studying the subject upon *original principles,* and upon *original principles* he got up the Nebraska bill! I am fighting it upon these "original principles"—fighting it in the Jeffersonian, Washingtonian, and Madisonian fashion.

Now, my friends, I wish you to attend for a little while to one or two other things in that Springfield speech. My main object was to show, so far as my humble ability was capable of showing, to the people of this country what I believed was the truth—that there was a *tendency,* if not a conspiracy, among those who have engineered this slavery question for the last four or five years, to make slavery perpetual and universal in this nation. Having made that speech principally for that object, after arranging the evidences that I thought tended to prove my proposition, I concluded with this bit of comment:

> We cannot absolutely know that these exact adaptations are the result of preconcert; but when we see a lot of framed timbers, different portions of which we know have been gotten out at different times and places, and by different workmen—Stephen, Franklin, Roger, and James, for instance—and when we see these timbers joined together, and see they exactly make the frame of a house or a mill, all the tenons and mortises exactly fitting, and all the lengths and proportions of the different pieces exactly adapted to their respective places, and not a piece too many or too few—not omitting even the scaffolding—or if a single piece be lacking, we see the place in the frame exactly fitted and prepared yet to bring such piece in—in such a case we feel it impossible not to believe that Stephen and Franklin and

Roger and James all understood one another from the beginning, and all worked upon a common plan or draft drawn before the first blow was struck.

When my friend Judge Douglas came to Chicago on the ninth of July, this speech having been delivered on the sixteenth of June, he made an harangue there, in which he took hold of this speech of mine, showing that he had carefully read it; and while he paid no attention to *this* matter at all, but complimented me as being a "kind, amiable, and intelligent gentleman," notwithstanding I had said this, he goes on and eliminates, or draws out, from my speech this tendency of mine to set the states at war with one another, to make all the institutions uniform, and set the "niggers" and white people to marrying together. Then, as the judge had complimented me with these pleasant titles (I must confess to my weakness), I was a little taken, for it came from a great man. I was not very much accustomed to flattery, and it came the sweeter to me. I was rather like the Hoosier, with the gingerbread, when he said he reckoned he loved it better than any other man, and got less of it. As the judge had so flattered me, I could not make up my mind that he meant to deal unfairly with me; so I went to work to show him that he misunderstood the whole scope of my speech, and that I really never intended to set the people at war with one another.

As an illustration, the next time I met him, which was at Springfield, I used this expression, that I claimed no right under the Constitution, nor had I any inclination, to enter into the slave states and interfere with the institutions of slavery. He says upon that: Lincoln will not enter into the slave states, but will go to the banks of the Ohio, on this side, and shoot over! He runs on, step by step, in the horse-chestnut style of argument, until in the Springfield speech he says: "Unless he shall be successful in firing his batteries until he shall have extinguished slavery in all the states, the Union shall be dissolved." Now, I don't think that was exactly the way to treat "a kind, amiable, intelligent gentleman." I know if I had asked the judge to show when or where it was I had said that if I didn't succeed in firing into the slave states until slavery should be extinguished, the Union should be dissolved, he could not have shown it. I understand what he would do. He would say: I don't mean to quote from you, but this was the *result* of what you say. But I have the right to ask, and I do ask now, Did you not put it in such a form that an ordinary reader or listener would take it as an expression *from me?*

In a speech at Springfield, on the night of the seventeenth, I thought I might as well attend to my own business a little, and I recalled his attention as well as I could to this charge of conspiracy to nationalize slavery. I called his attention to the fact that he had acknowledged in my hearing twice that he had carefully read the speech, and, in the language of the lawyers, as he had twice read the speech, and still had put in no plea or answer, I took a default on him. I insisted that I had a right then to renew that charge of conspiracy. Ten days afterward I met the judge at Clinton—that is to say, I was on the ground, but not in the discussion—and heard him make a speech. Then he comes in with his plea to this charge, for the first time; and his plea when put in, as well as I can recollect it, amounted to this: that he never had any talk with Judge Taney or the president of the United States with regard to the *Dred Scott* decision before it was made.

I ought to know that the man who makes a charge without knowing it to be true falsifies as much as he who knowingly tells a falsehood; and, lastly, that he would pronounce the whole thing a falsehood; but, he would make no personal application of the charge of falsehood, not because of any regard for the "kind, amiable, intelligent gentleman," but because of his own personal self-respect! I have understood since then—but [turning to Judge Douglas] will not hold the judge to it if he is not willing—that he has broken through the "self-respect," and has got to saying the thing *out.* The judge nods to me that it is so. It is fortunate for me that I can keep as good-humored as I do, when the judge acknowledges that he has been trying to make a question of veracity with me. I know the judge is a great man, while I am only a small man, but *I feel that I have got him*. I demur to that plea. I waive all objections that it was not filed till after default was taken, and demur to it upon the merits. What if Judge Douglas never did talk with Chief Justice Taney and the president before the *Dred Scott* decision was made—does it follow that he could not have had as perfect an understanding without talking as with it? I am not disposed to stand upon my legal advantage. I am disposed to take his denial as being like an answer in chancery, that he neither had any knowledge, information, or belief in the existence of such a conspiracy. I am disposed to take his answer as being as broad as though he had put it in these words. And now, I ask, even if he had done so, have not I a right to *prove it on him,* and to offer the evidence of more than two witnesses, by whom to prove it; and if the evidence proves the existence of the conspiracy, does his broader answer denying all knowledge, information, or belief, disturb the fact? It can only show that he was *used* by conspirators, and was not a *leader* of them.

Now, in regard to his reminding me of the moral rule that persons who tell what they do not know to be true falsify as much as those who knowingly tell falsehoods. I remember the rule, and it must be borne in mind that in what I have read to you, I do not say that I *know* such a conspiracy to exist. To that I reply, *I believe it*. If the judge says that I do *not* believe it, then *he* says what *he* does not know, and falls within his own rule, that he who asserts a thing which he does not know to be true, falsifies as much as he who knowingly tells a falsehood. I want to call your attention to a little discussion on that branch of the case, and the evidence which brought my mind to the conclusion which I expressed as my *belief*. If, in arraying that evidence I had stated anything which was false or erroneous, it needed but that Judge Douglas should point it out, and I would have taken it back, with all the kindness in the world. I do not deal in that way. If I have brought forward anything not a fact, if he will point it out, it will not even ruffle me to take it back. But if he will not point out anything erroneous in the evidence, is it not rather for him to show, by a comparison of the evidence, that I have *reasoned* falsely, than to call the "kind, amiable, intelligent gentleman" a liar? If I have reasoned to a false conclusion, it is the vocation of an able debater to show by argument that I have wandered to an erroneous conclusion. I want to ask your attention to a portion of the Nebraska bill, which Judge Douglas has quoted: "It being the true intent and meaning of this act, not to legislate slavery into any territory or state, nor to exclude it therefrom, but to leave the people thereof perfectly free to form and regulate their domestic institutions in their own way, subject only to the Constitution of the United States." Thereupon Judge Douglas and others began to argue in favor of "popular sovereignty"—the right of the people to have slaves if they wanted them, and to exclude slavery if they did not want them. "But," said, in substance, a senator from Ohio—Mr. Chase, I believe—"we more than suspect that you do not mean to allow the people to exclude slavery if they wish to; and if you do mean it, accept an amendment which I propose, expressly authorizing the people to exclude slavery." I believe I have the amendment here before me, which was offered, and under which the people of the territory, through their representatives, might, if they saw fit, prohibit the existence of slavery therein. And now I state it as a *fact,* to be taken back if there is any mistake about it, that Judge Douglas and those acting with him *voted that amendment down.* I now think that those men who voted it down had a *real reason* for doing so. They know what that reason was. It looks to us, since we have seen the *Dred Scott* decision pronounced, holding that "under the Constitution" the people cannot exclude slavery—I say it looks to outsiders, poor, simple, "amiable, intelligent gentlemen," as though the niche was left as a place to put that *Dred Scott* decision in—a niche which would have been spoiled by adopting the amendment. And now, I say again, if *this* was not the reason, it will avail the judge much more to calmly and good-humoredly point out to these people what that *other* reason was for voting the amendment down, than, swelling himself up, to vociferate that he may be provoked to call somebody a liar.

Again: There is in that same quotation from the Nebraska bill this clause: "It being the true intent and meaning of this bill not to legislate slavery into any territory or state." I have always been puzzled to know what business the word "state" had in that connection. Judge Douglas knows. *He. put it there.* He knows what he put it there for. We outsiders cannot say what he put it there for. The law they were passing was not about states, and was not making provisions for states. What was it placed there for? After seeing the *Dred Scott* decision, which holds that the people cannot exclude slavery from a *territory,* if another *Dred Scott* decision shall come, holding that they cannot exclude it from a *state,* we shall discover that when the word was originally put there, it was in view of something which was to come in due time, we shall see that it was the *other half* of something. I now say again, if there is any different reason for putting it there, Judge Douglas, in a good-humored way, without calling anybody a liar, *can tell what the reason was.*

Speech at the Second Lincoln-Douglas Debate

Freeport, Illinois, August 27, 1858

Ladies and Gentlemen: On Saturday last, Judge Douglas and myself first met in public discussion. He spoke one hour, I an hour and a half, and he replied for half an hour. The order is now reversed. I am to speak an hour, he an hour and a half, and then I am to reply for half an hour. I propose to devote myself during the first hour to the scope of what was brought within the range of his half-hour speech at Ottawa. Of course there was brought within the scope in that half-hour's speech something of his own opening speech. In the course of that opening argument Judge Douglas proposed to me seven distinct interrogatories. In my speech of an hour and a half, I attended to some other parts of his speech, and incidentally, as I thought, intimated to him that I would answer the rest of his interrogatories on condition only that he should agree to answer as many for me. He made no intimation at the time of the proposition, nor did he in his reply allude at all to that suggestion of mine. I do him no injustice in saying that he occupied at least half of his reply in dealing with me as though I had *refused* to answer his interrogatories. I now propose that I will answer any of the interrogatories, upon condition that he will answer questions from me not exceeding the same number. I give him an opportunity to respond.

The judge remains silent. I now say that I will answer his interrogatories, whether he answers mine or not; and that after I have done so, I shall propound mine to him.

I have supposed myself, since the organization of the Republican party at Bloomington, in May 1856, bound as a party man by the platforms of the party, then and since. If in any interrogatories which I shall answer I go beyond the scope of what is within these platforms, it will be perceived that no one is responsible but myself.

Having said thus much, I will take up the judge's interrogatories as I find them printed in the Chicago *Times,* and answer them *seriatim.* In order that there may be no mistake about it, I have copied the interrogatories in writing, and also my answers to them. The first one of these interrogatories is in these words:

QUESTION 1. "I desire to know whether Lincoln today stands, as he did in 1854, in favor of the unconditional repeal of the Fugitive Slave Law?"

ANSWER. I do not now, nor ever did, stand in favor of the unconditional repeal of the Fugitive Slave Law.

QUESTION 2. "I desire him to answer whether he stands pledged today, as he did in 1854, against the admission of any more slave states into the Union, even if the people want them?"

ANSWER. I do not now, nor ever did, stand pledged against the admission of any more slave states into the Union.

QUESTION 3. "I want to know whether he stands pledged against the admission of a new state into the Union with such a constitution as the people of that state may see fit to make?"

ANSWER. I do not stand pledged against the admission of a new state into the Union, with such a constitution as the people of that state may see fit to make.

QUESTION 4. "I want to know whether he stands today pledged to the abolition of slavery in the District of Columbia?"

ANSWER. I do not stand today pledged to the abolition of slavery in the District of Columbia.

QUESTION 5. "I desire him to answer whether he stands pledged to the prohibition of the slave trade between the different states?"

ANSWER. I do not stand pledged to the prohibition of the slave trade between the different states.

QUESTION 6. "I desire to know whether he stands pledged to prohibit slavery in all the territories of the United States, north as well as south of the Missouri Compromise line?"

ANSWER. I am impliedly, if not expressly, pledged to a belief in the *right* and *duty* of Congress to prohibit slavery in all the United States territories.

QUESTION 7. "I desire him to answer whether he is opposed to the acquisition of any new territory unless slavery is first prohibited therein?"

ANSWER. I am not generally opposed to honest acquisition of territory; and, in any given case, I would or would not oppose such acquisition, accordingly as I might think such acquisition would or would not aggravate the slavery question among ourselves.

Now, my friends, it will be perceived, upon an examination of these questions and answers, that so far I have only answered that I was not *pledged* to this, that, or the other. The judge has not framed his interrogatories to ask me anything more than this, and I have answered in strict accordance with the interrogatories, and have answered truly, that I am not *pledged* at all upon any of the points to which I have answered. But I am not disposed to hang upon the exact form of his interrogatory. I am rather disposed to take up at least some of these questions, and state what I really think upon them.

As to the first one, in regard to the Fugitive Slave law, I have never hesitated to say, and I do not now hesitate to say, that I think, under the Constitution of the United States, the people of the Southern states are entitled to a congressional Fugitive Slave Law. Having said that, I have had nothing to say in regard to the existing Fugitive Slave Law, further than that I think it should have been framed so as to be free from some of the objections that pertain to it, without lessening its efficiency. And inasmuch as we are not now in an agitation in regard to an alteration or modification of that law, I would not be the man to introduce it as a new subject of agitation upon the general question of slavery.

In regard to the other question, of whether I am pledged to the admission of any more slave states into the Union, I state to you very frankly that I would be exceedingly sorry ever to be put in a position of having to pass upon that question. I should be exceedingly glad to know that there would never be another slave state admitted into the Union; but I must add that if slavery shall be kept out of the territories during the territorial existence of any one given territory, and then the people shall, having a fair chance and a clear field, when they come to adopt the constitution, do such an extraordinary thing as to adopt a slave constitution, uninfluenced by the actual presence of the institution among them, I see no alternative, if we own the country, but to admit them into the Union.

The third interrogatory is answered by the answer to the second, it being, as I conceive, the same as the second.

The fourth one is in regard to the abolition of slavery in the District of Columbia. In relation to that, I have my mind very distinctly made up. I should be exceedingly glad to see slavery abolished in the District of Columbia. I believe that Congress possesses the constitutional power to abolish it. Yet as a member of Congress, I should not, with my present views, be in favor of *endeavoring* to abolish slavery in the District of Columbia, unless it would be upon these conditions: first, that the abolition should be gradual; second, that it should be on a vote of the majority of qualified voters in the District; and third, that compensation should be made to unwilling owners. With these three conditions, I confess I would be exceedingly glad to see Congress abolish slavery in the District of Columbia, and, in the language of Henry Clay, "sweep from our capital that foul blot upon our nation."

In regard to the fifth interrogatory, I must say here that, as to the question of the abolition of the slave trade between the different states, I can truly answer, as I have, that I am *pledged* to nothing about it. It is a subject to which I have not given that mature consideration that would make me feel authorized to state a position so as to hold myself entirely bound by it. In other words, that question has never been prominently enough before me to induce me to investigate whether we really have the constitutional power to do it. I could investigate it if I had sufficient time to bring myself to a conclusion upon that subject; but I have not done so, and I say so frankly to you here, and to Judge Douglas. I must say, however, that if I should be of opinion that Congress does possess the constitutional power to abolish the slave trade among the different states, I should still not be in favor of the exercise of that power, unless upon some conservative principle as I conceive it, akin to what I have said in relation to the abolition of slavery in the District of Columbia.

My answer as to whether I desire that slavery should be prohibited in all the territories of the United States is full and explicit within itself, and cannot be made clearer by any comments of mine. So I suppose in regard to the question whether I am opposed to the acquisition of any more territory unless slavery is first prohibited therein, my answer is such that I could add nothing by way of illustration, or making myself better understood, than the answer which I have placed in writing.

Now in all this the judge has me, and he has me on the record. I suppose he had flattered himself that I was really entertaining one set of opinions for one place, and another set for another place; that I was afraid to say at one place what I uttered at another. What I am saying here I suppose I say to a vast audience as strongly tending to abolitionism as any audience in the state of Illinois, and I believe I am saying that which, if it would be offensive to any persons and render them enemies to myself, would be offensive to persons in this audience.

Speech at the Third Lincoln-Douglas Debate

Jonesboro, Illinois, September 15, 1858

Ladies and Gentlemen: There is very much in the principles that Judge Douglas has here enunciated that I most cordially approve, and over which I shall have no controversy with him. In so far as he has insisted that all the states have the right to do exactly as they please about all their domestic relations, including that of slavery, I agree entirely with him. He places me wrong in spite of all I can tell him, though I repeat it again and again, insisting that I have no difference with him upon this subject. I have made a great many speeches, some of which have been printed, and it will be utterly impossible for him to find anything that I have ever put in print contrary to what I now say upon this subject. I hold myself under constitutional obligations to allow the people in all the states, without interference, direct or indirect, to do exactly as they please; and I deny that I have any inclination to interfere with them, even if there were no such constitutional obligation. I can only say again that I am placed improperly—altogether improperly, in spite of all I can say—when it is insisted that I entertain any other view or purposes in regard to that matter.

While I am upon this subject, I will make some answers briefly to certain propositions that Judge Douglas has put. He says, "Why can't this Union endure permanently half slave and half free?" I have said that I supposed it could not, and I will try, before this new audience, to give briefly some of the reasons for entertaining that opinion. Another form of his question is, "Why can't we let it stand as our fathers placed it?" That is the exact difficulty between us. I say that Judge Douglas and his friends have changed it from the position in which our fathers originally placed it. I say, in the way our fathers originally left the slavery question, the institution was in the course of ultimate extinction, and the public mind rested in the belief that it *was* in the course of ultimate extinction.

I say when this government was first established it was the policy of its founders to prohibit the spread of slavery into the new territories of the United States, where it had not existed. But Judge Douglas and his friends have broken up that policy, and placed it upon a new basis, by which it is to become national and perpetual. All I have asked or desired anywhere is that it should be placed back again upon the basis that the fathers of our government originally placed it upon. I have no doubt that it *would* become extinct, for all time to come, if we but readopted the policy of the fathers, by restricting it to the limits it has already covered—restricting it from the new territories.

I do not wish to dwell at great length on this branch of the subject at this time, but allow me to repeat one thing that I have stated before. Brooks—the man who assaulted Senator Sumner on the floor of the Senate, and who was complimented with dinners, and silver pitchers, and gold-headed canes, and a good many other things for that feat—in one of his speeches declared that when this government was originally established, nobody expected that the institution of slavery would last until this day. That was but the opinion of one man, but it was such an opinion as we can never get from Judge Douglas or anybody in favor of slavery, in the North, at all. You *can* sometimes get it from a Southern man. He said at the same time that the framers of our government did not have the knowledge that experience has taught us; that experience and the invention of the cotton gin have taught us that the perpetuation of slavery is a necessity. He insisted, therefore, upon its being changed from the basis upon which the fathers of the government left it to the basis of its perpetuation and nationalization.

I insist that this is the difference between Judge Douglas and myself—that Judge Douglas is helping that change along. I insist upon this government being placed where our fathers originally placed it.

I remember Judge Douglas once said that he saw the evidences on the statute books of Congress of a policy in the origin of government to divide slavery and freedom by a geographical line; that he saw an indisposition to maintain that policy, and therefore he set about studying up a way to settle the institution on the right basis—the basis which he thought it ought to have been placed upon at first; and in that speech he confesses that he seeks to place it, not upon the basis that the fathers placed it upon, but upon one gotten up on "original principles." When he asks me why we cannot get along with it in the attitude where our fathers placed it, he had better clear up the evidences that he has himself changed it from that basis, that he has himself been chiefly instrumental in changing the policy of the fathers. Anyone who will read his speech of the twenty-second of last March will see that he there makes an open confession, showing that he set about fixing the institution upon an altogether different set of principles. I think I have fully answered him when he asks me why we cannot let it alone upon the basis where our fathers left it, by showing that he has himself changed the whole policy of the government in that regard. . . .

He tries to persuade us that there must be a variety in the different institutions of the states of the Union; that that variety necessarily proceeds from the variety of soil, climate, of the face of the country, and the difference in the natural features of the states. I agree to all that. Have these very matters ever produced any difficulty amongst us? Not at all. Have we ever had any quarrel over the fact that they have laws in Louisiana designed to regulate the commerce that springs from the production of sugar? Or because we have a different class relative to the production of flour in this state? Have they produced any differences? Not at all. They are the very cements of this Union. They don't make the house a house divided against itself. They are the props that hold up the house and sustain the Union.

But has it been so with this element of slavery? Have we not always had quarrels and difficulties over it? And when will we cease to have quarrels over it? Like causes produce like effects. It is worthwhile to observe that we have generally had comparative peace upon the slavery question, and that there has been no cause for alarm until it was excited by the effort to spread it into new territory. Whenever it has been limited to its present bounds, and there has been no effort to spread it, there has been peace. All the trouble and convulsion has proceeded from efforts to spread it over more territory. It was thus at the date of the Missouri Compromise. It was so again with the annexation of Texas; so with the territory acquired by the Mexican War; and it is so now. Whenever there has been an effort to spread it, there has been agitation and resistance. Now, I appeal to this audience—very few of whom are my political friends—as national men, whether we have reason to expect that the agitation in regard to this subject will cease while the causes that tend to reproduce agitation are actively at work? Will not the same cause that produced agitation in 1820, when the Missouri Compromise was formed, that which produced the agitation upon the annexation of Texas, and at other times, work out the same results always? Do you think that the nature of man will be changed, that the same causes that produced agitation at one time will not have the same effect at another?

This has been the result so far as my observation of the slavery question and my reading in history extends. What right have we then to hope that the trouble will cease—that the agitation will come to an end—until it shall either be placed back where it originally stood, and where the fathers originally placed it, or on the other hand, until it shall entirely master all opposition? This is the view I entertain, and this is the reason why I entertained it, as Judge Douglas has read from my Springfield speech. . . .

I wish to ask one other question. It being understood that the Constitution of the United States guarantees property in slaves in the territories, if there is any infringement of the right of that property, would not the United States courts, organized for the government of the territory, apply such remedy as might be necessary in that case? It is a maxim held by the courts that there is no wrong without its remedy; and the courts have a remedy for whatever is acknowledged and treated as a wrong.

Again: I will ask you, my friends, if you were elected members of the legislature, what would be the first thing you would have to do before entering upon your duties? *Swear to support the Constitution of the United States.* Suppose you believe, as Judge Douglas does, that the Constitution of the United States guarantees to your neighbor the right to hold slaves in that territory, that they are his property: how can you clear your oaths unless you give him such legislation as is necessary to enable him to enjoy that property? What do you understand by supporting the Constitution of a state, or of the United States? Is it not to give such constitutional helps to the rights established by that Constitution as may be practically needed? Can you, if you swear to support the Constitution, and believe that the Constitution establishes a right, clear your oath, without giving it support? Do you support the Constitution if, knowing or believing there is a right established under it which needs specific legislation, you withhold that legislation? Do you not violate and disregard your oath? I can conceive of nothing plainer in the world. There can be nothing in the words "support the Constitution," if you may run counter to it by refusing support to any right established under the Constitution. And what I say here will hold with still more force against the judge's doctrine of "unfriendly legislation." How could you, having sworn to support the Constitution, and believing it guaranteed the right to hold slaves in the territories, assist in legislation *intended to defeat that right?* That would be violating your own view of the Constitution. Not only so, but if you were to do so, how long would it take the courts to hold your votes unconstitutional and void? Not a moment.

Lastly, I would ask: Is not Congress itself under obligation to give legislative support to any right that is established under the United States Constitution? I repeat the question: Is not Congress itself bound to give legislative support to any right that is established in the United States Constitution? A member of Congress swears to support the Constitution of the United States: and if he sees a right established by that Constitution which needs specific legislative protection, can he clear his oath without giving that protection? Let me ask you why many of us who are opposed to slavery upon principle give our acquiescence to a Fugitive Slave Law? Why do we hold ourselves under obligations to pass such a law, and abide by it when it is passed? Because the Constitution makes provision that the owners of slaves shall have the right to reclaim them. It gives the right to reclaim slaves; and that right is, as Judge Douglas says, a barren right, unless there is legislation that will enforce it.

The mere declaration "No person held to service or labor in one state under the laws thereof, escaping into another, shall in consequence of any law or regulation therein be discharged from such service or labor, but shall be delivered up on claim of the party to whom such service or labor may be due" is powerless without specific legislation to enforce it. Now, on what ground would a member of Congress, who is opposed to slavery in the abstract, vote for a fugitive law, as I would deem it my duty to do? Because there is a constitutional right which needs legislation to enforce it. And although it is distasteful to me, I have sworn to support the Constitution; and having so sworn, I cannot conceive that I do support it if I withhold from that right any necessary legislation to make it practical. And if that is true in regard to a Fugitive Slave Law, is the right to have fugitive slaves reclaimed any better fixed in the Constitution than the right to hold slaves in the territories? For this decision is a just exposition of the Constitution, as Judge Douglas thinks. Is the one right any better than the other? Is there any man who, while a member of Congress, would give support to the one any more than the other? If I wished to refuse to give legislative support to slave property in the territories, if a member of

Congress, I could not do it, holding the view that the Constitution establishes that right. If I did it at all, it would be because I deny that this decision properly construes the Constitution. But if I acknowledge, with Judge Douglas, that this decision properly construes the Constitution, I cannot conceive that I would be less than a perjured man if I should refuse in Congress to give such protection to that property as in its nature it needed.

Now, my fellow citizens, I will detain you only a little while longer; my time is nearly out. I find a report of a speech made by Judge Douglas at Joliet, since we last met at Freeport—published, I believe, in the *Missouri Republican*—on the ninth of this month, in which Judge Douglas says:

> You know at Ottawa I read this platform, and asked him if he concurred in each and all of the principles set forth in it. He would not answer these questions. At last I said frankly, I wish you to answer them, because when I get them up here where the color of your principles are a little darker than in Egypt, I intend to trot you down to Jonesboro. The very notice that I was going to take him down to Egypt made him tremble in his knees so that he had to be carried from the platform. He laid up seven days, and in the meantime held a consultation with his political physicians; they had Lovejoy and Farnsworth and all the leaders of the abolition party, they consulted it all over, and at last Lincoln came to the conclusion that he would answer, so he came up to Freeport last Friday.

Now, that statement altogether furnishes a subject for philosophical contemplation. I have been treating it in that way, and I have really come to the conclusion that I can explain it in no other way than by believing the judge is crazy. If he was in his right mind I cannot conceive how he would have risked disgusting the four or five thousand of his own friends who stood there and knew, as to my having been carried from the platform, that there was not a word of truth in it.

[Judge Douglas: "Didn't they carry you off?"]

There! that question illustrates the character of this man

Douglas exactly. He smiles now, and says, "Didn't they carry you off?" but he said then: *"He had to be carried off"*; and he said it to convince the country that he had so completely broken me down by his speech that I had to be carried away. Now he seeks to dodge it, and asks, "Didn't they carry you off?" Yes, they did. *But, Judge Douglas, why didn't you tell the truth?* I would like to know why you didn't tell the truth about it. And then again: "He laid up seven days." He put this in print for the people of the country to read as a serious document. I think if he had been in his sober senses he would not have risked that barefacedness in the presence of thousands of his own friends who knew that I made speeches within six of the seven days at Henry, Marshall County, Augusta, Hancock County, and Macomb, McDonough County, including all the necessary travel to meet him again at Freeport at the end of the six days.

Now I say there is no charitable way to look at that statement, except to conclude that he is actually crazy. There is another thing in that statement that alarmed me very greatly as he states it, that he was going to "trot me down to Egypt." Thereby he would have you infer that I would not come to Egypt unless he forced me—that I could not be got here unless he, giantlike, had hauled me down here. That statement he makes, too, in the teeth of the knowledge that I had made the stipulation to come down here and that he himself had been very reluctant to enter into the stipulation. More than all this: Judge Douglas, when he made that statement, must have been crazy and wholly out of his sober senses, or else he would have known that when he got me down here, that promise—that windy promise—of his powers to annihilate me, wouldn't amount to anything.

Now, how little do I look like being carried away trembling? Let the judge go on; and after he is done with his half hour, I want you all, if I can't go home myself, to let me stay and rot here; and if anything happens to the judge, if I cannot carry him to the hotel and put him to bed, let me stay here and rot. I say, then, here is something *extraordinary* in this statement. I ask you if you know any other living man who would make such a statement? I will ask my friend Casey, over there, if he would do such a thing? Would he send that out and have his men take it as the truth? Did the judge talk of trotting me down to Egypt to scare me to death? Why, I know this people better than he does. I was raised just a little east of here. I am a part of this people. But the judge was raised farther north, and perhaps he has some horrid idea of what this people might be induced to do.

But really I have talked about this matter perhaps longer than I ought, for it is no great thing; and yet the smallest are often the most difficult things to deal with. The judge has set about seriously trying to make the impression that when we meet at different places I am literally in his clutches—that I am a poor, helpless, decrepit mouse, and that I can do nothing at all. This is one of the ways he has taken to create that impression. I don't know any other way to meet it except this. I don't want to quarrel with him—to call him a liar; but when I come square up to him I don't know what else to call him if I must tell the truth out. I want to be at peace, and reserve all my fighting powers for necessary occasions. My time now is very nearly out, and I give up the trifle that is left to the judge, to let him set my knees trembling again, if he can.

Speech at the Fourth Lincoln-Douglas Debate

Charleston, Illinois, September 18, 1858

Ladies and Gentlemen: It will be very difficult for an audience so large as this to hear distinctly what a speaker says, and consequently it is important that as profound silence be preserved as possible.

When I was at the hotel today, an elderly gentleman called upon me to know whether I was really in favor of producing a perfect equality between the Negroes and white people. While I had not proposed to myself on this occasion to say much on that subject, yet as the question was asked me I thought I would occupy perhaps five minutes in saying something in regard to it. I will say, then, that I am not, nor ever have been, in favor of bringing about in any way the social and political equality of the white and black races; that I am not, nor ever have been, in favor of making voters or jurors of Negroes, nor of qualifying them to hold office, nor to intermarry with white people; and I will say, in addition to this, that there is a physical difference between the white and black races which I believe will forever forbid the two races living together on terms of social and political equality. And inasmuch as they cannot so live, while they do remain together there must be the position of superior and inferior, and I as much as any other man am in favor of having the superior position assigned to the white race. I say upon this occasion I do not perceive that because the white man is to have the superior position the Negro should be denied everything. I do not understand that because I do not want a Negro woman for a slave I must necessarily want her for a wife.

My understanding is that I can just let her alone. I am now in my fiftieth year, and I certainly never have had a black woman for either a slave or a wife. So it seems to me quite possible for us to get along without making either slaves or wives of Negroes.

I will add to this that I have never seen, to my knowledge, a man, woman, or child who was in favor of producing a perfect equality, social and political, between Negroes and white men. I recollect of but one distinguished instance that I ever heard of so frequently as to be entirely satisfied of its correctness, and that is the case of Judge Douglas's old friend Colonel Richard M. Johnson. I will also add to the remarks I have made . . . that I have never had the least apprehension that I or my friends would marry Negroes if there was no law to keep them from it; but as Judge Douglas and his friends seem to be in great apprehension that they might, if there were no law to keep them from it, I give him the most solemn pledge that I will to the very last stand by the law of this state which forbids the marrying of white people with Negroes. I will add one further word, which is this: that I do not understand that there is any place where an alteration of the social and political relations of the Negro and the white man can be made, except in the state legislature—not in the Congress of the United States; and as I do not really apprehend the approach of any such thing myself, and as Judge Douglas seems to be in constant horror that some such danger is rapidly approaching, I propose as the best means to prevent it that the judge be kept at home, and placed in the state legislature to fight the measure. I do not propose dwelling longer at this time on this subject.

SPEECH AT THE FIFTH LINCOLN-DOUGLAS DEBATE

Galesburg, Illinois, October 7, 1858

My Fellow Citizens: A very large portion of the speech which Judge Douglas has addressed to you has previously been delivered and put in print. I do not mean that for a hit upon the judge at all. If I had not been interrupted, I was going to say that such an answer as I was able to make to a very large portion of it had already been more than once made and published. There has been an opportunity afforded to the public to see our respective views upon the topics discussed in a large portion of the speech which he has just delivered. I make these remarks for the purpose of excusing myself for not passing over the entire ground that the judge has traversed. I however desire to take up some of the points that he has attended to, and ask your attention to them, and I shall follow him backwards upon some notes which I have taken, reversing the order, by beginning where he concluded.

The judge has alluded to the Declaration of Independence, and insisted that Negroes are not included in that Declaration; and that it is a slander upon the framers of that instrument to suppose that Negroes were meant therein. And he asks you: Is it possible to believe that Mr. Jefferson, who penned the immortal paper, could have supposed himself applying the language of that instrument to the Negro race, and yet held a portion of that race in slavery? Would he not at once have freed them? I only have to remark upon this part of the judge's speech (and that, too, very briefly, for I shall not detain myself, or you, upon that point for any great length of time), that I believe the entire

155

records of the world, from the date of the Declaration of Independence up to within three years ago, may be searched in vain for one single affirmation, from one single man, that the Negro was not included in the Declaration of Independence; I think I may defy Judge Douglas to show that he ever said so, that Washington ever said so, that any president ever said so, that any member of Congress ever said so, or that any living man upon the whole earth ever said so, until the necessities of the present policy of the Democratic party, in regard to slavery, had to invent that affirmation. And I will remind Judge Douglas and this audience that while Mr. Jefferson was the owner of slaves, as undoubtedly he was, in speaking upon this very subject he used the strong language that "he trembled for his country when he remembered that God was just"; and I will offer the highest premium in my power to Judge Douglas if he will show that he, in all his life, ever uttered a sentiment at all akin to that of Jefferson. . . .

The judge has also detained us awhile in regard to the distinction between his party and our party. His he assumes to be a national party—ours a sectional one. He does this in asking the question whether this country has any interest in the maintenance of the Republican party. He assumes that our party is altogether sectional, that the party to which he adheres is national; and the argument is that no party can be a rightful party—can be based upon rightful principles—unless it can announce its principles everywhere.

I presume that Judge Douglas could not go into Russia and announce the doctrine of our national democracy; he could not denounce the doctrine of kings and emperors and monarchies in Russia; and it may be true of this country that in some places we may not be able to proclaim a doctrine as clearly true as the truth of democracy, because there is a section so directly opposed to it that they will not tolerate us in doing so. Is it the true test of the soundness of a doctrine that in some places people won't let you proclaim it? Is that the way to test the truth of any doctrine? Why, I understood that at one time the people of

Chicago would not let Judge Douglas preach a certain favorite doctrine of his. I commend to his consideration the question whether he takes that as a test of the unsoundness of what he wanted to preach.

There is another thing to which I wish to ask attention for a little while on this occasion. What has always been the evidence brought forward to prove that the Republican party is a sectional party? The main one was that in the Southern portion of the Union the people did not let the Republicans proclaim their doctrines amongst them. That has been the main evidence brought forward—that they had no supporters, or substantially none, in the slave states. The South have not taken hold of our principles as we announce them; nor does Judge Douglas now grapple with those principles. We have a Republican State Platform, laid down in Springfield in June last, stating our position all the way through the questions before the country. We are now far advanced in this canvass. Judge Douglas and I have made perhaps forty speeches apiece, and we have now for the fifth time met face to face in debate, and up to this day I have not found either Judge Douglas or any friend of his taking hold of the Republican platform, or laying his finger upon anything in it that is wrong. I ask you all to recollect that. Judge Douglas turns away from the platform of principles to the fact that he can find people somewhere who will not allow us to announce those principles. If he had great confidence that our principles were wrong, he would take hold of them and demonstrate them to be wrong. But he does not do so. The only evidence he has of their being wrong is in the fact that there are people who won't allow us to preach them. I ask again, is that the way to test the soundness of a doctrine?

I ask his attention also to the fact that by the rule of nationality he is himself fast becoming sectional. I ask his attention to the fact that his speeches would not go as current now south of the Ohio River as they have formerly gone there. I ask his attention to the fact that he felicitates himself today that all the Democrats of the free states are agreeing with him, while he omits to tell us that the Democrats of any slave state agree with him. If he has not thought of this, I commend to his consideration the evidence in his own declaration, on this day, of his becoming sectional too. I see it rapidly approaching. Whatever may be the result of this ephemeral contest between Judge Douglas and myself, I see the day rapidly approaching when his pill of sectionalism, which he has been thrusting down the throats of Republicans for years past, will be crowded down his own throat.

Now, in regard to what Judge Douglas said (in the beginning of his speech) about the Compromise of 1850 containing the principles of the Nebraska bill, although I have often presented my views upon that subject, yet as I have not done so in this canvass, I will, if you please, detain you a little with them. I have always maintained, so far as I was able, that there was nothing of the principle of the Nebraska bill in the Compromise of 1850 at all—nothing whatever. Where can you find the principle of the Nebraska bill in that Compromise? If anywhere, in the two pieces of the Compromise organizing the territories of New Mexico and Utah. It was expressly provided in these two acts that when they came to be admitted into the Union they should be admitted with or without slavery, as they should choose, by their own constitutions. Nothing was said in either of those acts as to what was to be done in relation to slavery during the territorial existence of those territories, while Henry Clay constantly made the declaration (Judge Douglas recognizing him as a leader) that, in his opinion, the old Mexican laws would control that question during the territorial existence, and that these old Mexican laws excluded slavery. How can that be used as a principle for declaring that during the territorial existence as well as at the time of framing the constitution the people, if you please, might have slaves if they wanted them? . . .

The judge tells, in proceeding, that he is opposed to making any odious distinctions between free and slave states. I am altogether unaware that the Republicans are in favor of making any odious distinctions between the free and slave states. But there is still a difference, I think, between Judge Douglas and the Republicans in this. I suppose that the real difference between Judge Douglas and his friends, and the Republicans on the contrary, is, that the judge is not in favor of making any difference between slavery and liberty; that he is in favor of eradicating, of pressing out of view, the questions of preference in this country for free or slave institutions; and consequently every sentiment he utters discards the idea that there is any wrong in slavery. Everything that emanates from him or his coadjutors in their course of policy carefully excludes the thought that there is anything wrong in slavery. All their arguments if you will consider them, will be seen to exclude the thought that there is anything whatever wrong in slavery. If you will take the judge's speeches, and select the short and pointed sentences expressed by him—as his declaration that he "don't care whether slavery is voted up or down"—you will see at once that this is perfectly logical, if you do not admit that slavery is wrong. If you do admit that it is wrong, Judge Douglas cannot logically say he don't care whether a wrong is voted up or voted down.

Judge Douglas declares that if any community wants slavery they have a right to have it. He can say that logically, if he says that there is no wrong in slavery; but if you admit that there is a wrong in it, he cannot logically say that anybody has a right to do wrong. He insists that upon the score of equality the owners of slaves and owners of property—of horses and every other sort of property—should be alike, and hold them alike in a new territory. That is perfectly logical if the two species of property are alike and are equally founded in right. But if you admit that one of them is wrong, you cannot institute any equality between right and wrong. And from this difference of sentiment—the belief on the part of one that the institution is wrong, and a policy springing from that belief which looks to the arrest of the enlargement of that wrong, and this other sentiment, that it is not wrong, and a policy sprung from that sentiment, which will tolerate no idea of preventing the wrong from growing larger, and looks to there never being an end to it through all the existence of things—arises the real difference between Judge Douglas and his friends on the one hand and the Republicans on the other.

Now, I confess myself as belonging to that class in the country who contemplate slavery as a moral, social, and political evil, having due regard for its actual existence amongst us and the difficulties of getting rid of it in any satisfactory way, and to all the constitutional obligations which have been thrown about it—but, nevertheless, desire a policy that looks to the prevention of it as a wrong, and looks hopefully to the time when as a wrong it may come to an end.

SPEECH AT THE SIXTH LINCOLN-DOUGLAS DEBATE

Quincy, Illinois, October 13, 1858

Ladies and Gentlemen: I have had no immediate conference with Judge Douglas, but I will venture to say that he and I will perfectly agree that your entire silence both when I speak and when he speaks, will be most agreeable to us.

In the month of May 1856, the elements in the state of Illinois which have since been consolidated into the Republican party assembled together in a state convention at Bloomington. They adopted at that time what, in political language, is called a platform. In June of the same year the elements of the Republican party in the nation assembled together in a national convention at Philadelphia. They adopted what is called the National Platform. In June 1858—the present year—the Republicans of Illinois reassembled at Springfield, in state convention, and adopted again their platform, as I suppose not differing in any essential particular from either of the former ones, but perhaps adding something in relation to the new developments of political progress in the country.

The convention that assembled in June last did me the honor, if it be one, and I esteem it such, to nominate me as their candidate for the United States Senate. I have supposed that, in entering upon this canvass, I stood generally upon these platforms. We are now met together on the thirteenth of October of the same year, only four months from the adoption of the last platform, and I am unaware that in this canvass, from the beginning until today, any one of our adversaries has taken hold of our platforms, or laid his finger upon anything that he calls wrong in them. . . .

We have in this nation this element of domestic slavery. It is a matter of absolute certainty that it is a disturbing element. It is the opinion of all the great men who have expressed an opinion upon it, that it is a dangerous element. We keep up a controversy in regard to it. That controversy necessarily springs from difference of opinion; and if we can learn exactly—can reduce to the lowest elements—what that difference of opinion is, we perhaps shall be better prepared for discussing the different systems of policy that we would propose in regard to that disturbing element.

I suggest that the difference of opinion, reduced to its lowest of terms, is no other than the difference between the men who think slavery a wrong and those who do not think it wrong. The Republican party think it wrong; we think it is a moral, a social, and a political wrong. We think it as a wrong not confining itself merely to the persons or the states where it exists, but that it is a wrong in its tendency, to say the least, that extends itself to the existence of the whole nation. Because we think it wrong, we propose a course of policy that shall deal with it as a wrong. We deal with it as with any other wrong, in so far as we can prevent its growing any larger, and so deal with it that in the run of time there may be some promise of an end to it. We have a due regard to the actual presence of it amongst us, and the difficulties of getting rid of it in any satisfactory way, and all the constitutional obligations thrown about it.

I suppose that in reference both to its actual existence in the nation, and to our constitutional obligations, we have no right at all to disturb it in the states where it exists, and we profess that we have no more inclination to disturb it than we have the right to do it. We go further than that: we don't propose to disturb it where, in one instance, we think the Constitution would permit us. We think the Constitution would permit us to disturb it in the District of Columbia. Still, we do not propose to do that, unless it should be in terms which I don't suppose the nation is very likely soon to agree to—the terms of making the emancipation gradual, and compensating the unwilling owners.

Where we suppose we have the constitutional right, we restrain ourselves in reference to the actual existence of the institution and the difficulties thrown about it. We also oppose it as an evil so far as it seeks to spread itself. We insist on the policy that shall restrict it to its present limits. We don't suppose that in doing this we violate anything due to the actual presence of the institution, or anything due to the constitutional guaranties thrown around it.

We oppose the *Dred Scott* decision in a certain way, upon which I ought perhaps to address you a few words. We do not propose that when Dred Scott has been decided to be a slave by the court, we, as a mob, will decide him to be free. We do not propose that, when any other one, or one thousand, shall be decided by that court to be slaves, we will in any violent way disturb the rights of property thus settled; but we nevertheless do oppose that decision as a political rule which shall be binding on the voter to vote for nobody who thinks it wrong, which shall be binding on the members of Congress or the president to favor no measure that does not actually concur with the principles of that decision. We do not propose to be bound by it as a political rule in that way, because we think it lays the foundation, not merely of enlarging and spreading out what we consider an evil, but it lays the foundation for spreading that evil into the states themselves. We propose so resisting it as to have it reversed if we can, and a new judicial rule established upon this subject.

I will add this: that if there be any man who does not believe that slavery is wrong in the three aspects which I have mentioned, or in any one of them, that man is misplaced, and ought to leave us; while on the other hand, if there be any man in the Republican party who is impatient over the necessity springing from its actual presence, and is impatient of the constitutional guaranties thrown around it, and would act in disregard of these, he too is misplaced, standing with us. He will find his place somewhere else; for we have a due regard, so far as we are capable of understanding them, for all these things. This, gentlemen, as well as I can give it, is a plain statement of our principles in all their enormity.

I will say now that there is a sentiment in the country contrary to me—a sentiment which holds that slavery is not wrong, and therefore it goes for the policy that does not propose dealing with it as a wrong. That policy is the Democratic policy, and that sentiment is the Democratic sentiment. If there be a doubt in the mind of anyone in this vast audience that this is really the central idea of the Democratic party in relation to this subject, I ask him to bear with me while I state a few things tending, as I think, to prove that proposition.

In the first place, the leading man—I think I may do my friend Judge Douglas the honor of calling him such—advocating the present Democratic policy never himself says it is wrong. He has the high distinction, so far as I know, of never having said slavery is either right or wrong. Almost everybody else says one or the other, but the judge never does. If there be a man in the Democratic party who thinks it is wrong, and yet clings to that party, I suggest to him, in the first place, that his leader don't talk as he does, for he never says that it is wrong.

In the second place, I suggest to him that if he will examine the policy proposed to be carried forward, he will find that he carefully excludes the idea that there is anything wrong in it. If you will examine the arguments that are made on it, you will find that everyone carefully excludes the idea that there is anything wrong in slavery. Perhaps that Democrat who says he is as much opposed to slavery as I am will tell me that I am wrong about this. I wish him to examine his own course in regard to this matter a moment, and then see if his opinion will not be changed a little. You say it is wrong; but don't you constantly object to anybody else saying so? Do you not constantly argue that this is not the right place to oppose it? You say it must not be opposed in the free states, because slavery is not here; it must not be opposed in the slave states, because it is there; it must not be opposed in politics, because that will make a fuss; it must not be opposed in the pulpit, because it is not religion. Then where is the place to oppose it? There is no suitable place to oppose it. There is no place in the country to oppose this evil overspreading the continent, which you say yourself is coming. . . .

So I say, again, that in regard to the arguments that are made, when Judge Douglas says he "don't care whether slavery is voted up or voted down," whether he means that as an individual expression of sentiment, or only as a sort of statement of his views on national policy, it is alike true to say that he can thus argue logically if he don't see anything wrong in it; but he cannot say so logically if he admits that slavery is wrong. He cannot say that he would as soon see a wrong voted up as voted down.

When Judge Douglas says that whoever or whatever community wants slaves, they have a right to have them, he is perfectly logical, if there is nothing wrong in the institution; but if you admit that it is wrong, he cannot logically say that anybody has a right to do wrong. When he says that slave property and horse and hog property are alike to be allowed to go into the territories, upon the principles of equality, he is reasoning truly, if there is no difference between them as property; but if the one is property held rightfully, and the other is wrong, then there is no equality between the right and wrong; so that, turn it in any way you can, in all the arguments sustaining the Democratic policy, and in that policy itself, there is a careful, studied exclusion of the idea that there is anything wrong in slavery.

Let us understand this. I am not, just here, trying to prove that we are right, and they are wrong. I have been stating where we and they stand, and trying to show what is the real difference between us; and I now say that whenever we can get the question distinctly stated, can get all these men who believe that slavery is in some of these respects wrong to stand and act with us in treating it as a wrong—then, and not till then, I think we will in some way come to an end of this slavery agitation.

Speech at the Seventh Lincoln-Douglas Debate

Alton, Illinois, October 15, 1858

Ladies and Gentlemen: I have been somewhat, in my own mind, complimented by a large portion of Judge Douglas's speech— I mean that portion which he devotes to the controversy between himself and the present administration. This is the seventh time Judge Douglas and myself have met in these joint discussions, and he has been gradually improving in regard to his war with the administration. At Quincy, day before yesterday, he was a little more severe upon the administration than I had heard him upon any occasion, and I took pains to compliment him for it. I then told him to give it to them with all the power he had; and as some of them were present, I told them I would be very much obliged if they would *give it to him* in about the same way. I take it he has now vastly improved upon the attack he made then upon the administration. I flatter myself he has really taken my advice on this subject. All I can say now is to recommend to him and to them what I then commended— to prosecute the war against one another in the most vigorous manner. I say to them again: "Go it, husband! Go it, bear!"

There is one other thing I will mention before I leave this branch of the discussion—although I do not consider it much of my business, anyway. I refer to that part of the judge's remarks where he undertakes to involve Mr. Buchanan in an inconsistency. He reads something from Mr. Buchanan, from which he undertakes to involve him in an inconsistency; and he gets something of a cheer for having done so. I would only remind the judge that while he is very valiantly fighting for the Nebraska bill and the repeal of the Missouri Compromise, it has been but a little while since he was the *valiant advocate* of the Missouri Compromise. I want to know if Buchanan has not as much right to be inconsistent as Douglas has? Has Douglas the *exclusive right,* in this country, of being *on all sides of all questions?* Is nobody allowed that high privilege but himself? Is he to have an entire *monopoly* on that subject?

So far as Judge Douglas addressed his speech to me, or so far as it was about me, it is my business to pay some attention to it. I have heard the judge state two or three times what he has stated today—that in a speech which I made at Springfield, Illinois, I had in a very especial manner complained that the Supreme Court in the *Dred Scott* case had decided that a Negro could never be a citizen of the United States. I have omitted by some accident heretofore to analyze this statement, and it is required of me to notice it now. In point of fact it is *untrue.* I never have complained *especially* of the *Dred Scott* decision because it held that a Negro could not be a citizen, and the judge is always wrong when he says I ever did so complain of it. I have the speech here, and I will thank him or any of his friends to show where I said that a Negro should be a citizen, and complained especially of the *Dred Scott* decision because it declared he could not be one. I have done no such thing; and Judge Douglas, so persistently insisting that I have done so, has strongly impressed me with the belief of a predomination on his part to misrepresent me. He could not get his foundation for insisting that I was in favor of this Negro equality anywhere else as well as he could by assuming that untrue proposition.

Let me tell this audience what is true in regard to that matter; and the means by which they may correct me if I do not tell them truly is by a recurrence to the speech itself. I spoke of the *Dred Scott* decision in my Springfield speech, and I was then endeavoring to prove that the *Dred Scott* decision was a portion of a system or scheme to make slavery national in this country. I pointed out what things had been decided by the court. I mentioned as a fact that they had decided that a Negro could not be a citizen; that they had done so, as I supposed, to deprive the Negro, under all circumstances, of the remotest possibility of ever becoming a citizen and claiming the rights of a citizen of the United States under a certain clause of the Constitution. I stated that, without making any complaint of it at all. I then went on and stated the other points decided in the case; namely, that the bringing of a Negro into the state of Illinois and holding him in slavery for two years here was a matter in regard to which they would not decide whether it would make him free or not; that they decided the further point that taking him into a United States territory where slavery was prohibited by act of Congress did not make him free, because that act of Congress, as they held, was unconstitutional.

I mentioned these three things as making up the points decided in that case. I mentioned them in a lump, taken in connection with the introduction of the Nebraska bill, and the amendment of Chase, offered at the time, declaratory of the right of the people of the territories to *exclude slavery,* which was voted down by the friends of the bill. I mentioned all these things together, as evidence tending to prove a combination and conspiracy to make the institution of slavery national. In that connection and in that way I mentioned the decision on the point that a Negro could not be a citizen, and in no other connection.

Out of this Judge Douglas builds up his beautiful fabrication of my purpose to introduce a perfect social and political equality between the white and black races. His assertion that I made an "especial objection"—that is his exact language—to the decision on this account is untrue in point of fact. . . .

I have stated upon former occasions, and I may as well state again, what I understand to be the real issue in this controversy between Judge Douglas and myself. On the point of my wanting to make war between the free and the slave states, there has been no issue between us. So, too, when he assumes that I am in favor of introducing a perfect social and political equality between the white and black races. These are false issues, upon which Judge

Douglas has tried to force the controversy. There is no foundation in truth for the charge that I maintain either of these propositions.

The real issue in this controversy—the one pressing upon every mind—is the sentiment on the part of one class that looks upon the institution of slavery *as a wrong,* and of another class that *does not* look upon it as a wrong. The sentiment that contemplates the institution of slavery in this country as a wrong is the sentiment of the Republican party. It is the sentiment around which all their actions, all their arguments, circle, from which all their propositions radiate. They look upon it as being a moral, social, and political wrong; and while they contemplate it as such, they nevertheless have due regard for its actual existence among us, and the difficulties of getting rid of it in any satisfactory way, and to all the constitutional obligations thrown about it. Yet, having a due regard for these, they desire a policy in regard to it that looks to its not creating any more danger. They insist that it should, as far as may be, *be treated* as a wrong; and one of the methods of treating it as a wrong is to *make provision that it shall grow no larger.* They also desire a policy that looks to a peaceful end of slavery at some time as being wrong.

These are the views they entertain in regard to it as I understand them; and all their sentiments, all their arguments and propositions, are brought within this range. I have said, and I repeat it here, that if there be a man amongst us who does not think that the institution of slavery is wrong in any one of the aspects of which I have spoken, he is misplaced, and ought not to be with us. And if there be a man amongst us who is so impatient of it as a wrong as to disregard its actual presence among us and the difficulty of getting rid of it suddenly in a satisfactory way, and to disregard the constitutional obligations thrown about it, that man is misplaced if he is on our platform. We disclaim sympathy with him in practical action. He is not placed properly with us.

On this subject of treating it as a wrong, and limiting its

spread, let me say a word. Has anything ever threatened the existence of this Union save and except this very institution of slavery? What is it that we hold most dear amongst us? Our own liberty and prosperity. What has ever threatened our liberty and prosperity, save and except this institution of slavery? If this is true, how do you propose to improve the condition of things by enlarging slavery—by spreading it out and making it bigger? You may have a wen or cancer upon your person, and not be able to cut it out, lest you bleed to death; but surely it is no way to cure it, to engraft it and spread it over your whole body. That is no proper way of treating what you regard a wrong. You see this peaceful way of dealing with it as a wrong—restricting the spread of it, and not allowing it to go into new countries where it has not already existed. That is the peaceful way, the old-fashioned way, the way in which the fathers themselves set us the example.

On the other hand, I have said there is a sentiment which treats it as *not* being wrong. That is the Democratic sentiment of this day. I do not mean to say that every man who stands within that range positively asserts that it is right. That class will include all who positively assert that it is right, and all who, like Judge Douglas, treat it as indifferent and do not say it is either right or wrong. These two classes of men fall within the general class of those who do not look upon it as a wrong. And if there be among you anybody who supposes that he, as a Democrat, can consider himself "as much opposed to slavery as anybody," I would like to reason with him. You never treat it as a wrong. What other thing that you consider as a wrong do you deal with as you deal with that? Perhaps you *say* it is wrong, *but your leader never does, and you quarrel with anybody who says it is wrong.*

Although you pretend to say so yourself, you can find no fit place to deal with it as a wrong. You must not say anything about it in the free states, *because it is not here.* You must not say anything about it in the slave states, *because it is there.* You must not say anything about it in the pulpit, because that is religion, and has nothing to do with it. You must not say anything about it in politics, because that will disturb the security of "my place." There is no place to talk about it as being a wrong, although you say yourself it is a wrong.

But, finally, you will screw yourself up to the belief that if the people of the slave states should adopt a system of gradual emancipation on the slavery question, you would be in favor of it. You would be in favor of it. You say that is getting it in the right place, and you would be glad to see it succeed. But you are deceiving yourself. You all know that Frank Blair and Gratz Brown, down there in St. Louis, undertook to introduce that system in Missouri. They fought as valiantly as they could for the system of gradual emancipation which you pretend you would be glad to see succeed. Now, I will bring you to the test. After a hard fight they were beaten, and when the news came over here, you threw up your hats and *hurrahed for democracy.*

More than that, take all the argument made in favor of the system you have proposed, and it carefully excludes the idea that there is anything wrong in the institution of slavery. The arguments to sustain that policy carefully exclude it. Even here today you heard Judge Douglas quarrel with me because I uttered a wish that it might sometime come to an end. Although Henry Clay could say he wished every slave in the United States was in the country of his ancestors, I am denounced by those pretending to respect Henry Clay for uttering a wish that it might sometime, in some peaceful way, come to an end.

The Democratic policy in regard to that institution will not tolerate the merest breath, the slightest hint, of the least degree of wrong about it. Try it by some of Judge Douglas's arguments. He says he "don't care whether it is voted up or voted down" in the territories. I do not care myself, in dealing with that expression, whether it is intended to be expressive of his individual sentiments on the subject, or only of the national policy he desires to have established. It is alike valuable for my purpose.

Any man can say that who does not see anything wrong in

slavery; but no man can logically say it who does see a wrong in it, because no man can logically say he don't care whether a wrong is voted up or voted down. He may say he don't care whether an indifferent thing is voted up or down, but he must logically have a choice between a right thing and a wrong thing. He contends that whatever community wants slaves has a right to have them. So they have, if it is not a wrong. But if it is a wrong, he cannot say people have a right to do wrong. He says that upon the score of equality slaves should be allowed to go in a new territory, like other property. This is strictly logical if there is no difference between it and other property. If it and other property are equal, this argument is entirely logical. But if you insist that one is wrong and the other right, there is no use to institute a comparison between right and wrong. You may turn over everything in the Democratic policy from beginning to end, whether in the shape it takes on the statute book, in the shape it takes in the *Dred Scott* decision, in the shape it takes in conversation, or the shape it takes in short maximlike arguments—it everywhere carefully excludes the idea that there is anything wrong in it.

That is the real issue. That is the issue that will continue in this country when these poor tongues of Judge Douglas and myself shall be silent. It is the eternal struggle between these two principles—right and wrong—throughout the world. They are the two principles that have stood face to face from the beginning of time, and will ever continue to struggle. The one is the common right of humanity, and the other the divine right of kings. It is the same principle in whatever shape it develops itself. It is the same spirit that says, "You work and toil and earn bread, and I'll eat it." No matter in what shape it comes, whether from the mouth of a king who seeks to bestride the people of his own nation and live by the fruit of their labor, or from one race of men as an apology for enslaving another race, it is the same tyrannical principle.

I was glad to express my gratitude at Quincy, and I reexpress it here, to Judge Douglas—*that he looks to no end of the institution of slavery*. That will help the people to see where the struggle really is. It will hereafter place with us all men who really do wish the wrong may have an end. And whenever we can get rid of the fog which obscures the real question, when we can get Judge Douglas and his friends to avow a policy looking to its perpetuation—we can get out from among that class of men and bring them to the side of those who treat it as a wrong. Then there will soon be an end of it, and that end will be its "ultimate extinction."

Whenever the issue can be distinctly made, and all extraneous matter thrown out so that men can fairly see the real difference between the parties, this controversy will soon be settled, and it will be done peaceably too. There will be no war, no violence. It will be placed again where the wisest and best men of the world placed it. Brooks of South Carolina once declared that when this Constitution was framed its framers did not look to the institution existing until this day. When he said this, I think he stated a fact that is fully borne out by the history of the times. But he also said they were better and wiser men than the men of these days, yet the men of these days had experience which they had not, and by the invention of the cotton gin it became a necessity in this country that slavery should be perpetual. I now say that, willingly or unwillingly, purposely or without purpose, Judge Douglas has been the most prominent instrument in changing the position of the institution of slavery—which the fathers of the government expected to come to an end ere this—and putting it upon Brooks's cotton gin basis—placing it where he openly confesses he has no desire there shall ever be an end of it.

I understand I have ten minutes yet. I will employ it in saying something about this argument Judge Douglas uses, while he sustains the *Dred Scott* decision, that the people of the territories can still somehow exclude slavery. The first thing I ask attention to is the fact that Judge Douglas constantly said, before the decision, that whether they could or not, was a question for the Supreme Court. But after the court had made the decision he virtually says it is *not* a question for the Supreme Court, but for the people. And how is it he tells us they can exclude it? He says it needs "police regulations," and that admits of "unfriendly legislation." Although it is a right established by the Constitution of the United States to take a slave into a territory of the United States and hold him as property, yet unless the territorial legislature will give friendly legislation, and more especially if they adopt unfriendly legislation, they can practically exclude him.

Now, without meeting this proposition as a matter of fact, I pass to consider the real constitutional obligation. Let me take the gentleman who looks me in the face before me, and let us suppose that he is a member of the territorial legislature. The first thing he will do will be to swear that he will support the Constitution of the United States. His neighbor by his side in the territory has slaves and needs territorial legislation to enable him to enjoy that constitutional right. Can he withhold the legislation which his neighbor needs for the enjoyment of a right which is fixed in his favor in the Constitution of the United States which he has sworn to support? Can he withhold it without violating his oath? And, more especially, can he pass unfriendly legislation to violate his oath? Why, this is a *monstrous* sort of talk about the Constitution of the United States! *There has never been as outlandish or lawless a doctrine from the mouth of any respectable man on earth.* I do not believe it is a constitutional right to hold slaves in a territory of the United States. I believe the decision was improperly made and I go for reversing it. Judge Douglas is furious against those who go for reversing a decision. But he is for legislating it out of all force while the law itself stands. I repeat that there has never been so monstrous a doctrine uttered from the mouth of a respectable man.

I suppose most of us—I know it of myself—believe that the people of the Southern states are entitled to a congressional Fugitive Slave Law—that is a right fixed in the Constitution. But it cannot be made available to them without Congressional legislation. In the judge's language, it is a "barren right," which needs legislation before it can become efficient and valuable to the persons to whom it is guaranteed. And as the right is constitutional, I agree that the legislation shall be granted to it—and that not that we like the institution of slavery. We profess to have no taste for running and catching "niggers"—at least, I profess no taste for that job at all. Why then do I yield support to a Fugitive Slave Law? Because I do not understand that the Constitution, which guarantees that right, can be supported without it. And if I believed that the right to hold a slave in a territory was equally fixed in the Constitution with the right to reclaim fugitives, I should be bound to give it the legislation necessary to support it. I say that no man can deny his obligation to give the necessary legislation to support slavery in a territory, who believes it is a constitutional right to have it there. No man can, who does not give the abolitionists an argument to deny the obligation enjoined by the Constitution to enact a Fugitive Slave Law. Try it now. It is the strongest abolition argument ever made.

I say if that *Dred Scott* decision is correct, then the right to hold slaves in a territory is equally a constitutional right with the right of a slaveholder to have his runaway returned. No one can show the distinction between them. The one is express, so that we cannot deny it. The other is construed to be in the Constitution, so that he who believes the decision to be correct believes in the right. And the man who argues that by unfriendly legislation, in spite of that constitutional right, slavery may be driven from the territories, cannot avoid furnishing an argument by which abolitionists may deny the obligation to return fugitives, and claim the power to pass laws unfriendly to the right of the slaveholder to reclaim his fugitive.

I do not know how such an argument may strike a popular assembly like this, but I defy anybody to go before a body of men whose minds are educated to estimating evidence and reasoning, and show that there is an iota of difference between the constitutional right to reclaim a fugitive and the constitutional right to hold a slave, in a territory, provided this *Dred Scott* decision is correct, I defy any man to make an argument that will justify unfriendly legislation to deprive a slaveholder of his right to hold his slave in a territory, that will not equally, in all its length, breadth, and thickness, furnish an argument for nullifying the Fugitive Slave Law. *Why, there is not such an abolitionist in the nation as Douglas, after all!*

LETTER TO
HENRY L. PIERCE
AND OTHERS

Springfield, Illinois, April 6, 1859

Gentlemen:

Your kind note inviting me to attend a festival in Boston, on the 28th instant, in honor of the birthday of Thomas Jefferson, was duly received. My engagements are such that I cannot attend.

Bearing in mind that about seventy years ago two great political parties were first formed in this country, that Thomas Jefferson was the head of one of them and Boston the headquarters of the other, it is both curious and interesting that those supposed to descend politically from the party opposed to Jefferson should now be celebrating his birthday in their own original seat of empire, while those claiming political descent from him have nearly ceased to breathe his name everywhere.

Remembering, too, that the Jefferson party was formed upon its supposed superior devotion to the personal rights of men, holding the rights of property to be secondary only, and greatly inferior, and assuming that the so-called Democracy of today are the Jefferson, and their opponents the anti-Jefferson, party, it will be equally interesting to note how completely the two have changed hands as to the principle upon which they were originally supposed to be divided. The Democracy of today hold the liberty of one man to be absolutely nothing, when in conflict with another man's right of property; Republicans, on the contrary, are for both the man and the dollar, but in case of conflict the man before the dollar.

I remember being once much amused at seeing two partially

intoxicated men engaged in a fight with their greatcoats on, which fight, after a long and rather harmless contest, ended in each having fought himself out of his own coat and into that of the other. If the two leading parties of this day are really identical with the two in the days of Jefferson and Adams, they have performed the same feat as the two drunken men.

But soberly, it is now no child's play to save the principles of Jefferson from total overthrow in this nation. One would state with great confidence that he could convince any sane child that the simpler propositions of Euclid are true; but nevertheless he would fail, utterly, with one who should deny the definitions and axioms. The principles of Jefferson are the definitions and axioms of free society. And yet they are denied and evaded, with no small show of success. One dashingly calls them "glittering generalities." Another bluntly calls them "self-evident lies." And others insidiously argue that they apply to "superior races." These expressions, differing in form, are identical in object and effect—the supplanting the principles of free government, and restoring those of classification, caste, and legitimacy. They would delight a convocation of crowned heads plotting against the people. They are the vanguard, the miners and sappers, of returning despotism. We must repulse them, or they will subjugate us. This is a world of compensation; and he who would be no slave must consent to have no slave. Those who deny freedom to others deserve it not for themselves, and, under a just God, cannot long retain it. All honor to Jefferson—to the man who, in the concrete pressure of a struggle for national independence by a single people, had the coolness, forecast, and capacity to introduce into a mere revolutionary document an abstract truth, applicable to all men and all times, and so to embalm it there that today and in all coming days it shall be a rebuke and a stumbling block to the very harbingers of reappearing tyranny and oppression.

> Your obedient servant,
> A. LINCOLN

LETTER TO
SAMUEL GALLOWAY

Springfield, Illinois, July 28, 1859

My dear Sir:

Your very complimentary, not to say flattering, letter of the 23d instant is received. Dr. Reynolds had induced me to expect you here; and I was disappointed not a little by your failure to come. And yet I fear you have formed an estimate of me which can scarcely be sustained on a personal acquaintance.

Two things done by the Ohio Republican convention—the repudiation of Judge Swan, and the "plank" for a repeal of the Fugitive Slave Law—I very much regretted. These two things are of a piece; and they are viewed by many good men, sincerely opposed to slavery, as a struggle against, and in disregard of, the Constitution itself. And it is the very thing that will greatly endanger our cause, if it be not kept out of our national convention. There is another thing our friends are doing which gives me some uneasiness. It is their leaning toward "popular sovereignty."

There are three substantial objections to this: First, no party can command respect which sustains this year what it opposed last. Second, Douglas (who is the most dangerous enemy of liberty, because the most insidious one) would have little support in the North, and by consequence, no capital to trade on in the South, if it were not for his friends thus magnifying him and his humbug. But lastly, and chiefly, Douglas's popular sovereignty, accepted by the public mind as a just principle, nationalizes slavery, and revives the African slave trade inevitably. Taking slaves into new territories, and buying slaves in Africa, are identical things, identical rights or identical wrongs, and the argument which establishes one will establish the other. Try a thousand years for a sound reason why Congress shall not hinder the people of Kansas from having slaves, and, when you have found it, it will be an equally good one why Congress should not hinder the people of Georgia from importing slaves from Africa.

As to Governor Chase, I have a kind side for him. He was one of the few distinguished men of the nation who gave us, in Illinois, their sympathy last year. I never saw him, but suppose him to be able and right-minded; but still he may not be the most suitable as a candidate for the presidency.

I must say I do not think myself fit for the presidency. As you propose a correspondence with me, I shall look for your letters anxiously.

I have not met Dr. Reynolds since receiving your letter; but when I shall, I will present your respects as requested.

Yours very truly,
A. LINCOLN

LETTER TO
JESSE W. FELL

INCLUDING AN AUTOBIOGRAPHY

Springfield, December 20, 1859

My dear Sir:

Herewith is a little sketch, as you requested. There is not much of it, for the reason, I suppose, that there is not much of me. If anything be made out of it, I wish it to be modest, and not to go beyond the material. If it were thought necessary to incorporate anything from any of my speeches I suppose there would be no objection. Of course it must not appear to have been written by myself.

Yours very truly,
A. LINCOLN

I was born February 12, 1809, in Hardin County, Kentucky. My parents were both born in Virginia, of undistinguished families —second families, perhaps I should say. My mother, who died in my tenth year, was of a family of the name of Hanks, some of whom now reside in Adams, and others in Macon County, Illinois. My paternal grandfather, Abraham Lincoln, emigrated from Rockingham County, Virginia, to Kentucky about 1781 or 1782, where a year or two later he was killed by the Indians, not in battle, but by stealth, when he was laboring to open a farm in the forest. His ancestors, who were Quakers, went to Virginia from Berks County, Pennsylvania. An effort to identify them with the New England family of the same name ended in nothing more definite than a similarity of Christian names in both families, such as Enoch, Levi, Mordecai, Solomon, Abraham, and the like.

My father, at the death of his father, was but six years of age, and he grew up literally without education. He removed from Kentucky to what is now Spencer County, Indiana, in my eighth year. We reached our new home about the time that state came into the Union. It was a wild region, with many bears and other wild animals still in the woods. There I grew up. There were some schools, so called, but no qualification was ever required of a teacher beyond "readin', writin', and cipherin' " to the Rule of Three. If a straggler supposed to understand Latin happened to sojourn in the neighborhood he was looked upon as a wizard. There was absolutely nothing to excite ambition for education. Of course, when I came of age I did not know much. Still, somehow, I could read, write, and cipher to the Rule of Three, but that was all. I have not been to school since. The little advance I now have upon this store of education I have picked up from time to time under the pressure of necessity.

I was raised to farm work, which I continued till I was twenty-two. At twenty-one I came to Illinois, Macon County. Then I got to New Salem, at that time in Sangamon, now in Menard County, where I remained a year as a sort of clerk in a store. Then came the Black Hawk War; and I was elected a captain of volunteers, a success which gave me more pleasure than any I have had since. I went the campaign, was elated, ran for the legislature the same year (1832), and was beaten—the only time I ever have been beaten by the people. The next and three succeeding biennial elections I was elected to the legislature. I was not a candidate afterwards. During this legislative period I had studied law, and removed to Springfield to practice it. In 1846 I was once elected to the lower House of Congress. Was not a candidate for reelection. From 1849 to 1854, both inclusive, practiced law more assiduously than ever before. Always a Whig in politics; and generally on the Whig electoral tickets, making active canvasses. I was losing interest in politics when the repeal of the Missouri Compromise aroused me again. What I have done since then is pretty well known.

If any personal description of me is thought desirable, it may be said I am, in height, six feet four inches, nearly; lean in flesh, weighing on an average one hundred and eighty pounds; dark complexion, with coarse black hair and gray eyes. No other marks or brands recollected.

SPEECH AT NEW HAVEN, CONNECTICUT

March 6, 1860

Mr. President, and Fellow Citizens of New Haven: If the Republican party of this nation shall ever have the national house entrusted to its keeping, it will be the duty of that party to attend to all the affairs of national housekeeping. Whatever matters of importance may come up, whatever difficulties may arise in its way of administration of the government, that party will then have to attend to. It will then be compelled to attend to other questions, besides this question which now assumes an overwhelming importance—the question of slavery.

It is true that in the organization of the Republican party this question of slavery was more important than any other: indeed, so much more important has it become that no more national question can even get a hearing just at present. The old question of tariff—a matter that will remain one of the chief affairs of national housekeeping to all time; the question of the management of financial affairs; the question of the disposition of the public domain—how shall it be managed for the purpose of getting it well settled, and of making there the homes of a free and happy people?—these will remain open and require attention for a great while yet, and these questions will have to be attended to by whatever party has the control of the government. Yet, just now, they cannot even obtain a hearing, and I do not propose to detain you upon these topics or what sort of hearing they should have when opportunity shall come.

For, whether we will or not, the question of slavery is the question, the all-absorbing topic of the day. It is true that all of us—and by that I mean, not the Republican party alone, but the whole American people, here and elsewhere—all of us wish this question settled, wish it out of the way. It stands in the way, and prevents the adjustment, and the giving of necessary attention to other questions of national housekeeping. The people of the whole nation agree that this question ought to be settled, and yet it is not settled. And the reason is that they are not yet agreed *how* it shall be settled. All wish it done, but some wish one way and some another, and some a third, or fourth, or fifth; different bodies are pulling in different directions, and none of them, having a decided majority, are able to accomplish the common object.

In the beginning of the year 1854, a new policy was inaugurated with the avowed object and confident promise that it would entirely and forever put an end to the slavery agitation. It was again and again declared that under this policy, when once successfully established, the country would be forever rid of this whole question. Yet under the operation of that policy this agitation has not only not ceased, but it has been constantly augmented. And this too, although, from the day of its introduction, its friends, who promised that it would wholly end all agitation, constantly insisted, down to the time that the Lecompton bill was introduced, that it was working admirably, and that its inevitable tendency was to remove the question forever from the politics of the country. Can you call to mind any Democratic speech, made after the repeal of the Missouri Compromise, down to the time of the Lecompton bill, in which it was not predicted that the slavery agitation was just at an end, that "the abolition excitement was played out," "the Kansas question was dead," "they have made the most they can out of this question and it is now forever settled"? But since the Lecompton bill no Democrat, within my experience, has ever pretended that he could see the end. That cry has been dropped. They themselves do not pretend, now, that the agitation of this subject has come to an end yet.

The truth is that this question is one of national importance, and we cannot help dealing with it; we must do something about it, whether we will or not. We cannot avoid it; the subject is one we cannot avoid considering; we can no more avoid it than a man can live without eating. It is upon us; it attaches to the body politic as much and closely as the natural wants attach to our natural bodies. Now I think it important that this matter should be taken up in earnest, and really settled. And one way to bring about a true settlement of the question is to understand its true magnitude.

There have been many efforts made to settle it. Again and again it has been fondly hoped that it was settled, but every time it breaks out afresh, and more violently than ever. It was settled, our fathers hoped, by the Missouri Compromise, but it did not stay settled. Then the compromises of 1850 were declared to be a full and final settlement of the question. The two great parties, each in national convention, adopted resolutions declaring that the settlement made by the Compromise of 1850 was a finality —that it would last forever. Yet how long before it was unsettled again? It broke out again in 1854, and blazed higher and raged more furiously than ever before, and the agitation has not rested since.

These repeated settlements must have some faults about them. There must be some inadequacy in their very nature to the purpose to which they were designed. We can only speculate as to where that fault, that inadequacy, is, but we may perhaps profit by past experiences.

I think that one of the causes of these repeated failures is that our best and greatest men have greatly underestimated the size of this question. They have constantly brought forward small cures for great sores—plasters too small to cover the wound. That is one reason that all settlements have proved temporary—so evanescent.

Look at the magnitude of this subject. One sixth of our population, in round numbers—not quite one sixth, and yet more than a seventh—about one sixth of the whole population of the United States are slaves. The owners of these slaves consider them property. The effect upon the minds of the owners is that of property, and nothing else—it induces them to insist upon all that will favorably affect its value as property, to demand laws and institutions and a public policy that shall increase and secure its value, and make it durable, lasting, and universal. The effect on the minds of the owners is to persuade them that there is no wrong in it. The slaveholder does not like to be considered a mean fellow for holding that species of property, and hence he has to struggle within himself and sets about arguing himself into the belief that slavery is right. The property influences his mind.

The dissenting minister who argued some theological point with one of the established church was always met with the reply, "I can't see it so." He opened a Bible and pointed him a passage, but the orthodox minister replied, "I can't see it so." Then he showed him a single word—"Can you see that?" "Yes, I see it," was the reply. The dissenter laid a guinea over the word and asked, "Do you see it now?" So here. Whether the owners of this species of property do really see it as it is, it is not for me to say, but if they do, they see it as it is through two thousand millions of dollars, and that is a pretty thick coating. Certain it is that they do not see it as we see it. Certain it is that this two thousand millions of dollars, invested in this species of property, all so concentrated that the mind can grasp it at once—this immense pecuniary interest—has its influence upon their minds.

But here in Connecticut and at the North slavery does not exist, and we see it through no such medium. To us it appears natural to think that slaves are human beings—*men,* not property—that some of the things, at least, stated about men in the Declaration of Independence apply to them as well as to us. I say we think, most of us, that this charter of freedom applies to the slaves as well as to ourselves, that the class of arguments put forward to batter down that idea are also calculated to break down the very idea of a free government, even for white men, and to undermine the very foundations of free society. We think slavery a great moral wrong, and, while we do not claim the right to touch it where it exists, we wish to treat it as a wrong in the territories, where our votes will reach it. We think that a respect for ourselves, a regard for future generations and for the God that made us, require that we put down this wrong where our votes will properly reach it. We think that species of labor an injury to free white men—in short, we think slavery a great moral, social, and political evil, tolerable only because, and so far as its actual existence makes it necessary to tolerate it, and that beyond that it ought to be treated as a wrong.

Now these two ideas, the property idea that slavery is right, and the idea that it is wrong, come into collision, and do actually produce that irrepressible conflict which Mr. Seward has been so roundly abused for mentioning. The two ideas conflict, and must conflict.

Again, in its political aspect, does anything in any way endanger the perpetuity of this Union but that single thing, slavery? Many of our adversaries are anxious to claim that they are specially devoted to the Union, and take pains to charge upon us hostility to the Union. Now we claim that we are the only true Union men, and we put to them this one proposition: Whatever endangers this Union, save and except slavery? Did any other thing ever cause a moment's fear? All men must agree that this thing alone has ever endangered the perpetuity of the Union. But if it was threatened by any other influence, would not all men say that the best thing that could be done, if we could not or ought not to destroy it, would be at least to keep it from growing any larger? Can any man believe that the way to save the Union is to extend and increase the only thing that threatens the Union, and to suffer it to grow bigger and bigger?

Whenever this question shall be settled, it must be settled on some philosophical basis. No policy that does not rest upon some philosophical opinion can be permanently maintained. And hence there are but two policies in regard to slavery that can be at all maintained. The first, based on the property view that slavery is right, conforms to that idea throughout, and demands that we shall do everything for it that we ought to do if it were right. We must sweep away all opposition, for opposition to the right is wrong; we must agree that slavery is right, and we must adopt the idea that property has persuaded the owner to believe—that slavery is morally right and socially elevating. This gives a philosophical basis for a permanent policy of encouragement.

The other policy is one that squares with the idea that slavery is wrong, and it consists in doing everything that we ought to do if it is wrong. Now, I don't wish to be misunderstood, nor to leave a gap down to be misrepresented, even. I don't mean that we ought to attack it where it exists. To me it seems that if we were to form a government anew, in view of the actual presence of slavery we should find it necessary to frame just such a government as our fathers did—giving to the slaveholder the entire control where the system was established, while we possessed the power to restrain it from going outside those limits. From the necessities of the case we should be compelled to form just such a government as our blessed fathers gave us; and, surely, if they have so made it, that adds another reason why we should let slavery alone where it exists.

If I saw a venomous snake crawling in the road, any man would say I might seize the nearest stick and kill it; but if I found that snake in bed with my children, that would be another question. I might hurt the children more than the snake, and it might bite them. Much more if I found it in bed with my neighbor's children, and I had bound myself by a solemn compact not to meddle with his children under any circumstances, it would become me to let that particular mode of getting rid of the gentleman alone. But if there was a bed newly made up, to which the children were to be taken, and it was proposed to take a batch of young snakes and put them there with them, I take it no man would say there was any question how I ought to decide!

That is just the case. The new territories are the newly made bed to which our children are to go, and it lies with the nation to say whether they shall have snakes mixed up with them or not. It does not seem as if there could be much hesitation what our policy should be!

Now I have spoken of a policy based on the idea that slavery is wrong, and a policy based on the idea that it is right. But an effort has been made for a policy that shall treat it as neither right nor wrong. It is based upon utter indifference. Its leading advocate has said, "I don't care whether it be voted up or down." "It is merely a matter of dollars and cents." "The Almighty has drawn a line across this continent, on one side of which all soil must forever be cultivated by slave labor, and on the other by free." "When the struggle is between the white man and the Negro, I am for the white man; when it is between the Negro and the crocodile, I am for the Negro." Its central idea is indifference. It holds that it makes no more difference to us whether the territories become free or slave states than whether my neighbor stocks his farm with horned cattle or puts in tobacco. All recognize this policy, the plausible sugar-coated name of which is "popular sovereignty."

This policy chiefly stands in the way of a permanent settlement of the question. I believe there is no danger of its becoming the permanent policy of the country, for it is based on a public indifference. There is nobody that "don't care." *All the people do care* one way or the other! I do not charge that its author, when he says he "don't care," states his individual opinion; he only expresses his policy for the government. I understand that he has never said as an individual whether he thought slavery right or wrong—and he is the only man in the nation that has not! Now such a policy may have a temporary run; it may spring up as necessary to the political prospects of some gentleman; but it is utterly baseless: the people are not indifferent, and it can therefore have no durability or permanence.

But suppose it could: Then it could be maintained only by a public opinion that shall say, "We don't care." There must be a change in public opinion; the public mind must be so far debauched as to square with this policy of caring not at all. The people must come to consider this as "merely a question of dollars and cents," and to believe that in some places the Almighty has made slavery necessarily eternal. This policy can be brought to prevail if the people can be brought round to say honestly, "We don't care"; if not, it can never be maintained. It is for you to say whether that can be done.

You are ready to say it cannot, but be not too fast! Remember what a long stride has been taken since the repeal of the Missouri Compromise! Do you know of any Democrat, of either branch of the party—do you know one who declares that he believes that the Declaration of Independence has any application to the Negro? Judge Taney declares that it has not, and Judge Douglas even vilifies me personally and scolds me roundly for saying that the Declaration applies to all men, and that Negroes are men. Is there a Democrat here who does not deny that the Declaration applies to the Negro? Do any of you know of one? Well, I have tried before perhaps fifty audiences, some larger and some smaller than this, to find one such Democrat, and never yet have I found one who said I did not place him right in that.

I must assume that Democrats hold that, and now, *not one of these Democrats can show that he said that five years ago!* I venture to defy the whole party to produce one man that ever uttered the belief that the Declaration did not apply to Negroes, before the repeal of the Missouri Compromise! Four or five years ago we all thought Negroes were men, and that when "all men" were named, Negroes were included. *But the whole Democratic party has deliberately taken Negroes from the class of men and put them in the class of brutes.* Turn it as you will it is simply the truth! Don't be too hasty, then, in saying that the people cannot be brought to this new doctrine, but note that long stride. One more as long completes the journey from where Negroes are estimated as men to where they are estimated as mere brutes—as rightful property!

That saying "In the struggle between white men and the Negro," etc., which I know came from the same source as this policy—that saying marks another step. There is a falsehood wrapped up in that statement. "In the struggle between the white man and the Negro" assumes that there is a struggle, in which either the white man must enslave the Negro or the Negro must enslave the white. There is no such struggle! It is merely the ingenious falsehood to degrade and brutalize the Negro. Let each let the other alone, and there is no struggle about it. If it was like two wrecked seamen on a narrow plank, when each must push the other off or drown himself, I would push the Negro off or a white man either, but it is not; the plank is large enough for both. This good earth is plenty broad enough for white man and Negro both, and there is no need of either pushing the other off.

So that saying, "In the struggle between the Negro and the crocodile," etc., is made up from the idea that down where the crocodile inhabits, a white man can't labor; it must be nothing else but crocodile or Negro; if the Negro does not, the crocodile must possess the earth; in that case he declares for the Negro. The meaning of the whole is just this: As a white man is to a Negro, so is a Negro to a crocodile; and as the Negro may rightfully treat the crocodile, so may the white man rightfully treat the Negro. This very dear phrase coined by its author, and so dear that he deliberately repeats it in many speeches, has a tendency to still further brutalize the Negro, and to bring public opinion to the point of utter indifference whether men so brutalized are enslaved or not. When that time shall come, if ever, I think that policy to which I refer may prevail. But I hope the good freemen of this country will never allow it to come, and until then the policy can never be maintained. . . .

I am glad to see that a system of labor prevails in New England under which laborers can strike when they want to, where they are not obliged to work under all circumstances, and are not tied down and obliged to labor whether you pay them or not! I *like* the system which lets a man quit when he wants to, and wish it might prevail everywhere. One of the reasons why I am opposed to slavery is just here. What is the true condition of the laborer? I take it that it is best for all to leave each man free to acquire property as fast as he can. Some will get wealthy. I don't believe in a law to prevent a man from getting rich; it would do more harm than good. So, while we do not propose any war upon capital, we do wish to allow the humblest man an equal chance to get rich with everybody else. When one starts poor, as most do in the race of life, free society is such that he knows he can better his condition; he knows that there is no fixed condition of labor for his whole life. I am not ashamed to confess that twenty-five years ago I was a hired laborer, mauling rails, at work on a flatboat—just what might happen to any poor man's son! I want every man to have a chance—and I believe a black man is entitled to it—in which he *can* better his condition; when he may look forward and hope to be a hired laborer this year and the next, work for himself afterward, and finally to hire men to work for him! That is the true system. Up here in New England, you have a soil that scarcely sprouts black-eyed beans, and yet where will you find wealthy men so wealthy, and poverty so rarely in extremity? There is not another such place on earth! I desire that if you get too thick here, and find it hard to better your condition on this soil, you may have a chance to strike and go somewhere else, where you may not be degraded, nor have your families corrupted, by forced rivalry with Negro slaves. I want you to have a clean bed and no snakes in it! Then you can better your condition, and so it may go on and on in one ceaseless round so long as man exists on the face of the earth! . . .

It is exceedingly desirable that all parts of this great confederacy shall be at peace, and in harmony one with another. Let us Republicans do our part to have it so. Even though much provoked, let us do nothing through passion and ill-temper. Even though the Southern people will not so much as listen to us, let us calmly consider their demands, and yield to them if, in our deliberate view of our duty, we possibly can. Judging by all they say and do, and by the subject and nature of their controversy with us, let us determine, if we can, what will satisfy them.

Will they be satisfied if the territories be unconditionally surrendered to them? We know they will not. In all their present complaints against us, the territories are scarcely mentioned.

Invasions and insurrections are the rage now. Will it satisfy them, in the future, if we have nothing to do with invasions and insurrections? We know it will not. We so know because we know we never had anything to do with invasions and insurrections; and yet this total abstaining does not exempt us from the charge and the denunciation.

The question recurs, What will satisfy them? Simply this: we must not only let them alone, but we must, somehow, convince them that we do let them alone. This, we know by experience, is no easy task. We have been so trying to convince them, from the very beginning of our organization, but with no success. In all our platforms and speeches, we have constantly protested our purpose to let them alone; but this had no tendency to convince them. Alike unavailing to convince them is the fact that they have never detected a man of us in any attempt to disturb them.

These natural and apparently adequate means all failing, what will convince them? This, and this only: cease to call slavery *wrong,* and join them in calling it *right.* And this must be done thoroughly—done in *acts* as well as in *words.* Silence will not be tolerated—we must place ourselves avowedly with them. Douglas's new sedition law must be enacted and enforced, suppressing all declarations that slavery is wrong, whether made in politics, in presses, in pulpits, or in private. We must arrest and return their fugitive slaves with greedy pleasure. We must pull down our free-state constitutions. The whole atmosphere must be disinfected of all taint of opposition to slavery, before they will cease to believe that all their troubles proceed from us. So long as we call slavery wrong, whenever a slave runs away they will overlook the obvious fact that he ran away because he was oppressed, and declare he was stolen off. Whenever a master cuts his slaves with a lash, and they cry out under it, he will overlook the obvious fact that the Negroes cry out because they are hurt, and insist that they were *put up to it by some rascally abolitionist.*

I am quite aware that they do not state their case precisely in this way. Most of them would probably say to us, "Let us alone, do nothing to us, and say what you please about slavery." But we do let them alone—have never disturbed them—so that, after all, it is what we say which dissatisfies them. They will continue to accuse us of doing, until we cease saying.

I am also aware that they have not as yet in terms demanded the overthrow of our free-state constitutions. Yet those constitutions declare the wrong of slavery with more solemn emphasis than do all other sayings against it; and when all these other sayings shall have been silenced, the overthrow of these constitutions will be demanded. It is nothing to the contrary that they do not demand the whole of this just now. Demanding what they do, and for the reason they do, they can voluntarily stop nowhere short of this consummation. Holding as they do that slavery is morally right, and socially elevating, they cannot cease to demand a full national recognition of it, as a legal right, and a social blessing.

Nor can we justifiably withold this on any ground save our conviction that slavery is wrong. If slavery is right, all words, acts, laws, and constitutions against it are themselves wrong and should be silenced and swept away. If it is right, we cannot justly object to its nationality—its universality: if it is wrong, they cannot justly insist upon its extension—its enlargement. All they ask, we could readily grant, if we thought slavery right; all we ask, they could as readily grant, if they thought it wrong. Their thinking it right and our thinking it wrong is the precise fact on which depends the whole controversy. Thinking it right as they do, they are not to blame for desiring its full recognition, as being right; but, thinking it wrong, as we do, can we yield to them? Can we cast our votes with their view, and against our own? In view of our moral, social, and political responsibilities, can we do this?

Wrong as we think slavery is, we can yet afford to let it alone where it is because that much is due to the necessity arising from its actual presence in the nation; but can we, while our votes will prevent it, allow it to spread into the national territories, and to overrun us here in these free states?

If our sense of duty forbids this, then let us stand by our duty, fearlessly and effectively. Let us be diverted by none of those sophistical contrivances wherewith we are so industriously plied and belabored—contrivances such as groping for some middle ground between the right and the wrong, vain as the search for a man who should be neither a living man nor a dead man—such as a policy of "don't care" on a question about which all true men do care—such as Union appeals beseeching true Union men to yield to disunionists, reversing the divine rule, and calling, not the sinners, but the righteous to repentance —such as invocations of Washington, imploring men to unsay what Washington did.

Neither let us be slandered from our duty by false accusations against us, nor frightened from it by menaces of destruction to the government, nor of dungeons to ourselves. Let us have faith that right makes might; and in that faith, let us, to the end, dare to do our duty as we understand it.

Reply to the Committee of the Republican National Convention

Informing Lincoln of His Nomination

May 19, 1860

Mr. Chairman and Gentlemen of the Committee: I tender to you, and through you to the Republican National Convention, and all the people represented in it, my profounds thanks for the high honor done me, which you now formally announce. Deeply and even painfully sensible of the great responsibility which is inseparable from this high honor—a responsibility which I could almost wish had fallen upon some one of the far more eminent men and experienced statesmen whose distinguished names were before the convention—I shall, by your leave, consider more fully the resolutions of the convention, denominated the platform, and without any unnecessary or unreasonable delay respond to you, Mr. Chairman, in writing, not doubting that the platform will be found satisfactory, and the nomination gratefully accepted.

And now I will not longer defer the pleasure of taking you, and each of you, by the hand.

LETTER TO
GEORGE ASHMUN
AND OTHERS

Springfield, Illinois, May 23, 1860

Sir:

I accept the nomination tendered me by the convention over which you presided, and of which I am formally apprised in the letter of yourself and others, acting as a committee of the convention for that purpose.

The declaration of principles and sentiments which accompanies your letter meets my approval; and it shall be my care not to violate or disregard it in any part.

Imploring the assistance of Divine Providence, and with due regard to the views and feelings of all who were represented in the convention, to the rights of all the states and territories and people of the nation, to the inviolability of the Constitution, and the perpetual union, harmony, and prosperity of all—I am most happy to cooperate for the practical success of the principles declared by the convention.

Your obliged friend and fellow citizen,
A. LINCOLN

Remarks at a Meeting in Springfield

Celebrating Lincoln's Election as President

November 20, 1860

Friends and Fellow Citizens: Please excuse me on this occasion from making a speech. I thank you in common with all those who have thought fit by their votes to endorse the Republican cause. I rejoice with you in the success which has thus far attended that cause. Yet in all our rejoicings let us neither express nor cherish any hard feelings toward any citizen who by his vote has differed with us. Let us at all times remember that all American citizens are brothers of a common country, and should dwell together in the bonds of fraternal feeling. Let me again beg you to accept my thanks, and to excuse me from further speaking at this time.

LETTER TO
THURLOW WEED

Springfield, Illinois, December 17, 1860

My dear Sir:

Yours of the 11th was received two days ago. Should the convocation of governors of which you speak seem desirous to know my views on the present aspect of things, tell them you judge from my speeches that I will be inflexible on the territorial question; but I probably think either the Missouri line extended, or Douglas's and Eli Thayer's popular sovereignty would lose us everything we gain by the election; that filibustering for all south of us and making slave states of it would follow in spite of us, in either case; also that I probably think all opposition, real and apparent, to the fugitive slave clause of the Constitution ought to be withdrawn.

I believe you can pretend to find but little, if anything, in my speeches, about secession. But my opinion is that no state can in any way lawfully get out of the Union without the consent of the others; and that it is the duty of the president and other government functionaries to run the machine as it is.

Truly yours,
A. LINCOLN

LETTER TO
ALEXANDER H. STEPHENS

Springfield, Illinois, December 22, 1860

My dear Sir:

Your obliging answer to my short note is just received, and for which please accept my thanks. I fully appreciate the present peril the country is in, and the weight of responsibility on me. Do the people of the South really entertain fears that a Republican administration would, directly or indirectly, interfere with the slaves, or with them about the slaves? If they do, I wish to assure you, as once a friend, and still, I hope, not an enemy, that there is no cause for such fears. The South would be in no more danger in this respect than it was in the days of Washington. I suppose, however, this does not meet the case. You think slavery is right and ought to be extended, while we think it is wrong and ought to be restricted. That, I suppose, is the rub. It certainly is the only substantial difference between us.

Yours very truly,
A. LINCOLN

Memorandum for a Resolution on Fugitive Slave Laws

December [22?], 1860

Resolved, That the fugitive slave clause of the Constitution ought to be enforced by a law of Congress, with efficient provisions for that object, not obliging private persons to assist in its execution, but punishing all who resist it, and with the usual safeguards to liberty, securing free men against being surrendered as slaves.

That all state laws, if there be such, really or apparently in conflict with such law of Congress, ought to be repealed; and no opposition to the execution of such law of Congress ought to be made.

That the federal Union must be preserved.

FAREWELL ADDRESS
AT SPRINGFIELD

February 11, 1861

My Friends: One who has never been placed in a like position cannot understand my feelings at this hour, nor the oppressive sadness I feel at this parting. For more than twenty-five years I have lived among you, and during all that time I have received nothing but kindness at your hands. Here the most cherished ties of earth were assumed. Here my children were born, and here one of them lies buried. To you, my friends, I owe all that I have—all that I am. All the strange checkered past seems to crowd upon my mind.

Today I leave you. I go to assume a task more difficult than that which devolved upon General Washington. Unless the great God who assisted him shall be with and aid me I cannot prevail; but if the same Almighty Arm that directed and protected him shall guide and support me I shall not fail; I shall succeed. Let us pray that the God of our fathers may not forsake us now. To Him I commend you all. Permit me to ask that with equal sincerity and faith you will all invoke His wisdom and goodness for me.

With these words I must leave you; for how long I know not. Friends, one and all, I must now wish you an affectionate farewell.

SPEECH BEFORE THE INDIANA STATE LEGISLATURE

Indianapolis, February 12, 1861

Fellow Citizens of the State of Indiana: I am here to thank you much for this magnificent welcome, and still more for the generous support given by your state to that political cause which I think is the true and just cause of the whole country and the whole world.

Solomon says there is "a time to keep silence," and when men wrangle by the mouth with no certainty that they *mean* the same *thing* while using the same *word*, it perhaps were as well if they would keep silence.

The words "coercion" and "invasion" are much used in these days, and often with some temper and hot blood. Let us make sure, if we can, the meaning of those who use them. Let us get the exact definitions of these words, not from dictionaries, but from the men themselves, who certainly deprecate the things they would represent by the use of the words.

What, then, is coercion? What is invasion? Would the marching of an army into South Carolina, without the consent of her people, and with hostile intent toward them, be invasion? I certainly think it would, and it would be coercion also, if the South Carolinians were forced to submit. But if the United States should merely hold and retake its own forts and other property, and collect the duties on foreign importations, or even withhold the mails from places where they were habitually violated, would any or all of these things be invasion or coercion? Do our professed lovers of the Union, who spitefully resolve that they will resist coercion and invasion, understand that such things as these, on the part of the United States, would be coercion or invasion of a state? If so, their idea of means to preserve the object of their great affection would seem to be exceedingly thin and airy. If sick, the little pills of the homeopathist would be much too large for it to swallow. In their view, the Union, as a family relation, would seem to be no regular marriage, but rather a sort of "free-love" arrangement, to be maintained on passional attraction.

By the way, in what consists the special sacredness of a state? I speak not of the position assigned to a state in the Union by the Constitution, for that is a bond we all recognize. That position, however, a state cannot carry out of the Union with it. I speak of that assumed primary right of a state to rule all which is less than itself, and to ruin all which is larger than itself. If a state and a country, in a given case, should be equal in number of inhabitants, in what, as a matter of principle, is the state better than the country? Would an exchange of name be an exchange of rights? Upon what principle, upon what rightful principle, may a state, being no more than one-fiftieth part of the nation in soil and population, break up the nation, and then coerce a proportionably large subdivision of itself in the most arbitrary way? What mysterious right to play tyrant is conferred on a district of country, with its people, by merely calling it a state? F 'low citizens, I am not asserting anything. I am merely asking questions for you to consider. And now allow me to bid you farewell.

Speech at Cleveland, Ohio

February 15, 1861

Mr. Chairman and Fellow Citizens of Cleveland: We have been marching about two miles through snow, rain, and deep mud. The large numbers that have turned out under these circumstances testify that you are in earnest about something or other. But do I think so meanly of you as to suppose that that earnestness is about me personally? I would be doing you an injustice to suppose you did. You have assembled to testify your respect for the Union, the Constitution, and the laws; and here let me say that it is with you, the people, to advance the great cause of the Union and the Constitution, and not with any one man. It rests with you alone.

This fact is strongly impressed upon my mind at present. In a community like this, whose appearance testifies to their intelligence, I am convinced that the cause of liberty and the Union can never be in danger. Frequent allusion is made to the excitement at present existing in our national politics, and it is as well that I should also allude to it here. I think that there is no occasion for any excitement. The crisis, as it is called, is altogether an artificial crisis. In all parts of the nation there are differences of opinion on politics. There are differences of opinion even here. You did not all vote for the person who now addresses you. What is happening now will not hurt those who are farther away from here. Have they not all their rights now as they ever have had? Do they not have their fugitive slaves returned now as ever? Have they not the same Constitution that they have lived under for seventy-odd years? Have they not a position as citizens of this common country, and have we any power to change that position? What, then, is the matter with them? Why all this excitement? Why all these complaints?

As I said before, this crisis is all artificial! It has no foundation in facts. It is not argued up, as the saying is, and cannot, therefore, be argued down. Let it alone and it will go down of itself.

This is as it should be. If Judge Douglas had been elected and had been here on his way to Washington, as I am tonight, the Republicans should have joined his supporters in welcoming him, just as his friends have joined with mine tonight. If all do not join now to save the good old ship of the Union this voyage, nobody will have a chance to pilot her on another voyage.

SPEECH AT
NEW YORK CITY

February 19, 1861

Mr. Chairman and Gentlemen: I am rather an old man to avail myself of such an excuse as I am now about to do. Yet the truth is so distinct, and presses itself so distinctly upon me, that I cannot well avoid it—and that is, that I did not understand when I was brought into this room that I was to be brought here to make a speech. It was not intimated to me that I was brought into the room where Daniel Webster and Henry Clay had made speeches, and where one in my position might be expected to do something like those men or say something worthy of myself or my audience. I therefore beg you to make allowance for the circumstances in which I have been by surprise brought before you. Now I have been in the habit of thinking and sometimes speaking upon political questions that have for some years past agitated the country; and, if I were disposed to do so, and we could take up some one of the issues, as the lawyers call them, and I were called upon to make an argument about it to the best of my ability, I could do so without much preparation. But that is not what you desire to have done here tonight.

I have been occupying a position, since the presidential election, of silence—of avoiding public speaking, of avoiding public writing. I have been doing so because I thought, upon full consideration, that was the proper course for me to take. I am brought before you now, and required to make a speech, when you all approve more than anything else of the fact that I have been keeping silence. And now it seems to me that the response you give to that remark ought to justify me in closing just here. I have not kept silence since the presidential election from any party wantonness, or from any indifference to the anxiety that pervades the minds of men about the aspect of the political affairs of this country. I have kept silence for the reason that I supposed it was peculiarly proper that I should do so until the time came when, according to the custom of the country, I could speak officially.

I still suppose that, while the political drama being enacted in this country at this time is rapidly shifting its scenes—forbidding an anticipation with any degree of certainty today of what we shall see tomorrow—it is peculiarly fitting that I should see it all, up to the last minute, before I should take ground that I might be disposed, by the shifting of the scenes afterward, also to shift. I have said several times upon this journey, and I now repeat it to you, that when the time does come, I shall then take the ground that I think is right—right for the North, for the South, for the East, for the West, for the whole country. And in doing so I hope to feel no necessity pressing upon me to say anything in conflict with the Constitution, in conflict with the continued union of these states, in conflict with the perpetuation of the liberties of this people, or anything in conflict with anything whatever that I have ever given you reason to expect from me.

And now, my friends, have I said enough? [Loud cries: "No, no!" and "Three cheers for Lincoln!"] Now, my friends, there appears to be a difference of opinion between you and me, and I really feel called upon to decide the question myself.

SPEECH AT
INDEPENDENCE HALL

Philadelphia, Pennsylvania, February 22, 1861

Mr. Cuyler: I am filled with deep emotion at finding myself standing here, in this place, where were collected together the wisdom, the devotion to principle, from which sprang the institutions under which we live. You have kindly suggested to me that in my hands is the task of restoring peace to the present distracted condition of the country. I can say in return, sir, that all the political sentiments I entertain have been drawn, so far as I have been able to draw them, from the sentiments which originated and were given to the world from this hall. I have never had a feeling politically that did not spring from the sentiments embodied in the Declaration of Independence. I have often pondered over the dangers which were incurred by the men who assembled here and framed and adopted the Declaration of Independence. I have pondered over the toils that were endured by the officers and soldiers of the army who achieved that independence. I have often inquired of myself what great principle or idea it was that kept the confederacy so long together. It was not the mere matter of separation of the colonies from the motherland, but that sentiment in the Declaration of Independence which gave liberty, not alone to the people of this country, but, I hope, to the world for all future time. It was that which gave promise that in due time the weight would be lifted from the shoulders of all men. This is the sentiment embodied in the Declaration of Independence.

Now, my friends, can the country be saved upon that basis? If it can, I will consider myself one of the happiest men in the world if I can help to save it. If it cannot be saved upon that principle, it will be truly awful. But if this country cannot be saved without giving up that principle, I was about to say I would rather be assassinated on this spot than surrender it. Now, in my view of the present aspect of affairs, there need be no bloodshed or war. There is no necessity for it. I am not in favor of such a course, and I may say, in advance, that there will be no bloodshed unless it is forced upon the government, and then it will be compelled to act in self-defense.

My friends, this is wholly an unexpected speech, and I did not expect to be called upon to say a word when I came here. I supposed it was merely to do something toward raising the flag. I may, therefore, have said something indiscreet. I have said nothing but what I am willing to live by and, if it be the pleasure of Almighty God, die by.

FIRST INAUGURAL
ADDRESS

March 4, 1861

Fellow Citizens of the United States: In compliance with a custom as old as the government itself, I appear before you to address you briefly, and to take in your presence the oath prescribed by the Constitution of the United States to be taken by the president "before he enters on the execution of his office."

I do not consider it necessary at present for me to discuss those matters of administration about which there is no special anxiety or excitement.

Apprehension seems to exist among the people of the Southern states that by the accession of a Republican administration their property and their peace and personal security are to be endangered. There has never been any reasonable cause for such apprehension. Indeed, the most ample evidence to the contrary has all the while existed and been open to their inspection. It is found in nearly all the published speeches of him who now addresses you. I do but quote from one of those speeches when I declare that "I have no purpose, directly or indirectly, to interfere with the institution of slavery in the states where it exists. I believe I have no lawful right to do so, and I have no inclination to do so." Those who nominated and elected me did so with full knowledge that I had made this and many similar declarations, and have never recanted them. And, more than this, they placed in the platform for my acceptance, and as a law to themselves and to me, the clear and emphatic resolution which I now read:

> *Resolved*, That the maintenance inviolate of the rights of the states, and especially the right of each state to order and control its own domestic institutions according to its own judgment

exclusively, is essential to that balance of power on which the perfection and endurance of our political fabric depend, and we denounce the lawless invasion by armed force of the soil of any state or territory, no matter under what pretext, as amongst the gravest of crimes.

I now reiterate these sentiments; and, in doing so, I only press upon the public attention the most conclusive evidence of which the case is susceptible, that the property, peace, and security of no section are to be in any wise endangered by the now incoming administration. I add, too, that all the protection which, consistently with the Constitution and the laws, can be given, will be cheerfully given to all the states when lawfully demanded, for whatever cause—as cheerfully to one section as to another.

There is much controversy about the delivering up of fugitives from service or labor. The clause I now read is as plainly written in the Constitution as any other of its provisions:

> No person held to service or labor in one state, under the laws thereof, escaping into another, shall in consequence of any law or regulation therein be discharged from such service or labor, but shall be delivered up on claim of the party to whom such service or labor may be due.

It is scarcely questioned that this provision was intended by those who made it for the reclaiming of what we call fugitive slaves; and the intention of the lawgiver is the law. All members of Congress swear their support to the whole Constitution—to this provision as much as to any other. To the proposition, then, that slaves whose cases come within the terms of this clause "shall be delivered up," their oaths are unanimous. Now, if they would make the effort in good temper, could they not with nearly equal unanimity frame and pass a law by means of which to keep good that unanimous oath?

There is some difference of opinion whether this clause should be enforced by national or by state authority; but surely that difference is not a very material one. If the slave is to be surrendered, it can be of but little consequence to him or to others by which authority it is done. And should anyone in any case be content that his oath shall go unkept on a merely unsubstantial controversy as to how it shall be kept?

Again, in any law upon this subject, ought not all the safeguards of liberty known in civilized and humane jurisprudence to be introduced, so that a free man be not, in any case, surrendered as a slave? And might it not be well at the same time to provide by law for the enforcement of that clause in the Constitution which guarantees that "the citizens of each state shall be entitled to all privileges and immunities of citizens in the several states"?

I take the official oath today with no mental reservations, and with no purpose to construe the Constitution or laws by any hypercritical rules. And, while I do not choose now to specify particular acts of Congress as proper to be enforced, I do suggest that it will be much safer for all, both in official and private stations, to conform to and abide by all those acts which stand unrepealed, than to violate any of them, trusting to find impunity in having them held to be unconstitutional.

It is seventy-two years since the first inauguration of a president under our national Constitution. During that period fifteen different and greatly distinguished citizens have, in succession, administered the executive branch of the government. They have conducted it through many perils, and generally with great success. Yet, with all this scope of precedent, I now enter upon the same task for the brief constitutional term of four years under great and peculiar difficulty. A disruption of the Federal Union, heretofore only menaced, is now formidably attempted.

I hold that, in contemplation of universal law and of the Constitution, the union of these states is perpetual. Perpetuity is implied, if not expressed, in the fundamental law of all national governments. It is safe to assert that no government proper ever had a provision in its organic law for its own termination. Continue to execute all the express provisions of our national

Constitution, and the Union will endure forever—it being impossible to destroy it except by some action not provided for in the instrument itself.

Again, if the United States be not a government proper, but an association of states in the nature of contract merely, can it as a contract be peaceably unmade by less than all the parties who made it? One party to a contract may violate it—break it, so to speak; but does it not require all to lawfully rescind it?

Descending from these general principles, we find the proposition that in legal contemplation the Union is perpetual confirmed by the history of the Union itself. The Union is much older than the Constitution. It was formed, in fact, by the Articles of Association in 1774. It was matured and continued by the Declaration of Independence in 1776. It was further matured, and the faith of all the then thirteen states expressly plighted and engaged that it should be perpetual, by the Articles of Confederation in 1778. And, finally, in 1787 one of the declared objects for ordaining and establishing the Constitution was "to form a more perfect Union."

But if the destruction of the Union by one or by a part only of the states be lawfully possible, the Union is less perfect than before the Constitution, having lost the vital element of perpetuity.

It follows from these views that no state upon its own mere motion can lawfully get out of the Union; that resolves and ordinances to that effect are legally void; and that acts of violence, within any state or states, against the authority of the United States, are insurrectionary or revolutionary, according to circumstances.

I therefore consider that, in view of the Constitution and the laws, the Union is unbroken; and to the extent of my ability I shall take care, as the Constitution itself expressly enjoins upon me, that the laws of the Union be faithfully executed in all the states. Doing this I deem to be only a simple duty on my part; and I shall perform it so far as practicable, unless my rightful masters, the American people, shall withhold the requisite means, or in some authoritative manner direct the contrary. I trust this will not be regarded as a menace, but only as the declared purpose of the Union that it will constitutionally defend and maintain itself.

In doing this there needs to be no bloodshed or violence; and there shall be none, unless it be forced upon the national authority. The power confided to me will be used to hold, occupy, and possess the property and places belonging to the government, and to collect the duties and imposts; but beyond what may be necessary for these objects, there will be no invasion, no using of force against or among the people anywhere. Where hostility to the United States, in any interior locality, shall be so great and universal as to prevent competent resident citizens from holding the federal offices, there will be no attempt to force obnoxious strangers among the people for that object. While the strict legal right may exist in the government to enforce the exercise of these offices, the attempt to do so would be so irritating, and so nearly impracticable withal, that I deem it better to forego for the time the uses of such offices.

The mails, unless repelled, will continue to be furnished in all parts of the Union. So far as possible, the people everywhere shall have that sense of perfect security which is most favorable to calm thought and reflection. The course here indicated will be followed unless current events and experience shall show a modification or change to be proper, and in every case and exigency my best discretion will be exercised according to circumstances actually existing, and with a view and a hope of a peaceful solution of the national troubles and the restoration of fraternal sympathies and affections.

That there are persons in one section or another who seek to destroy the Union at all events, and are glad of any pretext to do it, I will neither affirm nor deny; but if there be such, I need address no word to them. To those, however, who really love the Union may I not speak?

Before entering upon so grave a matter as the destruction of our national fabric, with all its benefits, its memories, and its hopes, would it not be wise to ascertain precisely why we do it? Will you hazard so desperate a step while there is any possibility that any portion of the ills you fly from have no real existence? Will you, while the certain ills you fly to are greater than all the real ones you fly from—will you risk the commission of so fearful a mistake?

All profess to be content in the Union if all constitutional rights can be maintained. Is it true, then, that any right, plainly written in the Constitution, has been denied? I think not. Happily the human mind is so constituted that no party can reach to the audacity of doing this. Think, if you can, of a single instance in which a plainly written provision of the Constitution has ever been denied. If by the mere force of numbers a majority should deprive a minority of any clearly written constitutional right, it might, in a moral point of view, justify revolution—certainly would if such a right were a vital one.

But such is not our case. All the vital rights of minorities and of individuals are so plainly assured to them by affirmations and negations, guaranties and prohibitions, in the Constitution, that controversies never arise concerning them. But no organic law can ever be framed with a provision specifically applicable to every question which may occur in practical administration. No foresight can anticipate, nor any document of reasonable length contain, express provisions for all possible questions. Shall fugitives from labor be surrendered by national or by state authority? The Constitution does not expressly say. *May* Congress prohibit slavery in the territories? The Constitution does not expressly say. *Must* Congress protect slavery in the territories? The Constitution does not expressly say.

From questions of this class spring all our constitutional controversies, and we divide upon them into majorities and minorities. If the minority will not acquiesce, the majority must, or the government must cease. There is no other alternative; for continuing the government is acquiescence on one side or the other.

If a minority in such case will secede rather than acquiesce, they make a precedent which in turn will divide and ruin them; for a minority of their own will secede from them whenever a majority refuses to be controlled by such minority. For instance, why may not any portion of a new confederacy a year or two hence arbitrarily secede again, precisely as portions of the present Union now claim to secede from it? All who cherish disunion sentiments are now being educated to the exact temper of doing this.

Is there such perfect identity of interests among the states to compose a new Union as to produce harmony only, and prevent renewed secession?

Plainly, the central idea of secession is the essence of anarchy. A majority held in restraint by constitutional checks and limitations, and always changing easily with deliberate changes of popular opinions and sentiments, is the only true sovereign of a free people. Whoever rejects it does, of necessity, fly to anarchy or to despotism. Unanimity is impossible; the rule of a minority, as a permanent arrangement, is wholly inadmissible; so that, rejecting the majority principle, anarchy or despotism in some form is all that is left.

I do not forget the position assumed by some, that constitutional questions are to be decided by the Supreme Court; nor do I deny that such decisions must be binding, in any case, upon the parties to a suit, as to the object of that suit, while they are also entitled to very high respect and consideration in all parallel cases by all other departments of the government. And, while it is obviously possible that such decision may be erroneous in any given case, still the evil effect following it, being limited to that particular case, with the chance that it may be overruled and never become a precedent for other cases, can better be borne than could the evils of a different practice.

At the same time, the candid citizen must confess that if the policy of the government, upon vital questions affecting the whole people, is to be irrevocably fixed by decisions of the Supreme Court, the instant they are made, in ordinary litigation between parties in personal actions, the people will have ceased to be their own rulers, having to that extent practically resigned the government into the hands of that eminent tribunal. Nor is there in this view any assault upon the court or the judges. It is a duty from which they may not shrink to decide cases properly brought before them, and it is no fault of theirs if others seek to turn their decisions to political purposes.

One section of our country believes slavery is right, and ought to be extended, while the other believes it is wrong, and ought not to be extended. This is the only substantial dispute. The fugitive slave clause of the Constitution and the law for the suppression of the foreign slave trade are each as well enforced, perhaps, as any law can ever be in a community where the moral sense of the people imperfectly supports the law itself. The great body of the people abide by the dry legal obligation in both cases, and a few break over in each. This, I think, cannot be perfectly cured; and it would be worse in both cases after the separation of the sections than before. The foreign slave trade, now imperfectly suppressed, would be ultimately revived, without restriction, in one section, while fugitive slaves, now only partially surrendered, would not be surrendered at all by the other.

Physically speaking, we cannot separate. We cannot remove our respective sections from each other, nor build an impassable wall between them. A husband and wife may be divorced and go out of the presence and beyond the reach of each other; but the different parts of our country cannot do this. They cannot but remain face to face, and intercourse, either amicable or hostile, must continue between them. Is it possible then, to make that intercourse more advantageous or more satisfactory after separation than before? Can aliens make treaties easier than friends can make laws? Can treaties be more faithfully enforced between aliens than laws can among friends? Suppose you go to war, you cannot fight always; and when, after much loss on both sides, and no gain on either, you cease fighting, the identical old questions as to terms of intercourse are again upon you.

This country, with its institutions, belongs to the people who inhabit it. Whenever they shall grow weary of the existing government, they can exercise their constitutional right of amending it, or their revolutionary right to dismember or overthrow it. I cannot be ignorant of the fact that many worthy and patriotic citizens are desirous of having the national Constitution amended. While I make no recommendation of amendments, I fully recognize the rightful authority of the people over the whole subject, to be exercised in either of the modes prescribed in the instrument itself, and I should, under existing circumstances, favor rather than oppose a fair opportunity being afforded the people to act upon it.

I will venture to add that to me the convention mode seems preferable, in that it allows amendments to originate with the people themselves, instead of only permitting them to take or reject propositions originated by others not especially chosen for the purpose, and which might not be precisely such as they would wish to either accept or refuse. I understand a proposed amendment to the Constitution—which amendment, however, I have not seen—has passed Congress, to the effect that the federal government shall never interfere with the domestic institutions of the states, including that of persons held to service. To avoid misconstruction of what I have said, I depart from my purpose not to speak of particular amendments so far as to say that, holding such a provision to now be implied constitutional law, I have no objection to its being made express and irrevocable.

The chief magistrate derives all his authority from the people, and they have conferred none upon him to fix terms for the separation of the states. The people themselves can do this also if they choose; but the executive, as such, has nothing to do with it. His duty is to administer the present government, as it came to his hands, and to transmit it, unimpaired by him, to his successor.

Why should there not be a patient confidence in the ultimate justice of the people? Is there any better or equal hope in the world? In our present differences is either party without faith of being in the right? If the Almighty Ruler of Nations, with his eternal truth and justice, be on your side of the North, or on yours of the South, that truth and that justice will surely prevail by the judgment of this great tribunal of the American people.

By the frame of the government under which we live, this same people have wisely given their public servants but little power for mischief; and have, with equal wisdom, provided for the return of that little to their own hands at very short intervals. While the people retain their virtue and vigilance, no administration, by any extreme of wickedness or folly, can very seriously injure the government in the short space of four years.

My countrymen, one and all, think calmly and well upon this whole subject. Nothing valuable can be lost by taking time. If there be an object to hurry any of you in hot haste to a step which you would never take deliberately, that object will be frustrated by taking time; but no good object can be frustrated by it. Such of you as are now dissatisfied still have the old Constitution unimpaired, and, on the sensitive point, the laws of your own framing under it; while the new administration will have no immediate power, if it would, to change either. If it were admitted that you who are dissatisfied hold the right side in the dispute, there still is no single good reason for precipitate action. Intelligence, patriotism, Christianity, and a firm reliance on Him who has never yet forsaken this favored land, are still competent to adjust in the best way all our present difficulty.

In your hands, my dissatisified fellow countrymen, and not in mine, is the momentous issue of civil war. The government will not assail you. You can have no conflict without being yourselves the aggressors. You have no oath registered in heaven to destroy the government, while I shall have the most solemn one to "preserve, protect, and defend" it.

I am loath to close. We are not enemies, but friends. We must not be enemies. Though passion may have strained, it must not break, our bonds of affection. The mystic chords of memory, stretching from every battlefield and patriot grave to every living heart and hearthstone all over this broad land, will yet swell the chorus of the Union when again touched, as surely they will be, by the better angels of our nature.

REPLY TO A COMMITTEE FROM THE VIRGINIA CONVENTION

April 13, 1861

Gentlemen: As a committee of the Virginia Convention now in session, you present me a preamble and resolution in these words:

> *Whereas,* In the opinion of this convention, the uncertainty which prevails in the public mind as to the policy which the federal executive intends to pursue toward the seceded states is extremely injurious to the industrial and commercial interests of the country, tends to keep up an excitement which is unfavorable to the adjustment of pending difficulties, and threatens a disturbance of the public peace; therefore,
> *Resolved,* That a committee of three delegates be appointed by this convention to wait upon the president of the United States, present to him this preamble and resolution, and respectfully ask him to communicate to this convention the policy which the federal executive intends to pursue in regard to the Confederate States.
> Adopted by the Convention of the State of Virginia, Richmond, April 8, 1861.

In answer I have to say that, having at the beginning of my official term expressed my intended policy as plainly as I was able, it is with deep regret and some mortification I now learn that there is great and injurious uncertainty in the public mind as to what that policy is, and what course I intend to pursue. Not having as yet seen occasion to change, it is now my purpose to pursue the course marked out in the inaugural address. I commend a careful consideration of the whole document as the best expression I can give of my purposes.

As I then and therein said, I now repeat: "The power confided to me will be used to hold, occupy, and possess the property and places belonging to the government, and to collect the duties and imposts; but beyond what is necessary for these objects, there will be no invasion, no using of force against or among the people anywhere." By the words "property and places belonging to the government," I chiefly allude to the military posts and property which were in the possession of the government when it came to my hands.

But if, as now appears to be true, in pursuit of a purpose to drive the United States authority from these places, an unprovoked assault has been made upon Fort Sumter, I shall hold myself at liberty to repossess, if I can, like places which had been seized before the government was devolved upon me. And in every event I shall, to the extent of my ability, repel force by force. In case it proves true that Fort Sumter has been assaulted, as is reported, I shall perhaps cause the United States mails to be withdrawn from all the states which claim to have seceded, believing that the commencement of actual war against the government justifies and possibly demands this.

I scarcely need to say that I consider the military posts and property situated within the states which claim to have seceded as yet belonging to the government of the United States as much as they did before the supposed secession.

Whatever else I may do for the purpose, I shall not attempt to collect the duties and imposts by any armed invasion of any part of the country; not meaning by this, however, that I may not land a force deemed necessary to relieve a fort upon a border of the country.

From the fact that I have quoted a part of the inaugural address, it must not be inferred that I repudiate any other part, the whole of which I reaffirm, except so far as what I now say of the mails may be regarded as a modification.

Proclamation
Calling Out a Militia
and Convening Congress
in Special Session

April 15, 1861

Whereas, The laws of the United States have been for some time past and now are opposed, and the execution thereof obstructed, in the states of South Carolina, Georgia, Alabama, Florida, Mississippi, Louisiana, and Texas, by combinations too powerful to be suppressed by the ordinary course of judicial proceedings, or by the powers vested in the marshals by law:

Now, therefore, I, Abraham Lincoln, President of the United States, in virtue of the power in me vested by the Constitution and the laws, have thought fit to call forth, and hereby do call forth, the militia of the several states of the Union, to the aggregate number of seventy-five thousand, in order to suppress said combinations, and to cause the laws to be duly executed.

The details for this object will be immediately communicated to the state authorities through the War Department.

I appeal to all loyal citizens to favor, facilitate, and aid this effort to maintain the honor, the integrity, and the existence of our national Union, and the perpetuity of popular government; and to redress wrongs already long enough endured.

I deem it proper to say that the first service assigned to the forces hereby called forth will probably be to repossess the forts, places, and property which have been seized from the Union; and in every event the utmost care will be observed, consistently with the objects aforesaid, to avoid any devastation, any destruction of or interference with property, or any disturbance of peaceful citizens in any part of the country.

And I hereby command the persons composing the combinations aforesaid to disperse and retire peacefully to their respective abodes within twenty days from date.

Deeming that the present condition of public affairs presents an extraordinary occasion, I do hereby, in virtue of the power in me vested by the Constitution, convene both houses of Congress. Senators and representatives are therefore summoned to assemble at their respective chambers, at twelve o'clock noon, on Thursday, the fourth day of July next, then and there to consider and determine such measures as, in their wisdom, the public safety and interest may seem to demand.

In witness whereof, I have hereunto set my hand, and caused the seal of the United States to be affixed.

Done at the city of Washington, this fifteenth day of April, in the year of Our Lord one thousand eight hundred and sixty-one, and of the independence of the United States the eighty-fifth.

PROCLAMATION AUTHORIZING A BLOCKADE OF THE REBELLIOUS STATES

April 19, 1861

Whereas, An insurrection against the government of the United States has broken out in the states of South Carolina, Georgia, Alabama, Florida, Mississippi, Louisiana, and Texas, and the laws of the United States for the collection of the revenue cannot be effectually executed therein conformably to that provision of the Constitution which requires duties to be uniform throughout the United States:

And whereas, A combination of persons engaged in such insurrection have threatened to grant pretended letters of marque to authorize the bearers thereof to commit assaults on the lives, vessels, and property of good citizens of the country lawfully engaged in commerce on the high seas, and in waters of the United States:

And whereas, An executive proclamation has been already issued requiring the persons engaged in these disorderly proceedings to desist therefrom, calling out a militia force for the purpose of repressing the same, and convening Congress in extraordinary session to deliberate and determine thereon:

Now, therefore, I, Abraham Lincoln, President of the United States, with a view to the same purposes before mentioned, and to the protection of the public peace, and the lives and property of quiet and orderly citizens pursuing their lawful occupations, until Congress shall have assembled and deliberated on the said unlawful proceedings, or until the same shall have ceased, have further deemed it advisable to set on foot a blockade of the ports within the states aforesaid, in pursuance of the laws of the United States, and of the law of nations in such case provided. For this purpose a competent force will be posted so as to prevent entrance and exit of vessels from the ports aforesaid. If, therefore, with a view to violate such blockade, a vessel shall approach or shall attempt to leave either of the said ports, she will be duly warned by the commander of one of the blockading vessels, who will endorse on her register the fact and date of such warning, and if the same vessel shall again attempt to enter or leave the blockaded port, she will be captured and sent to the nearest convenient port, for such proceedings against her and her cargo, as prize, as may be deemed advisable.

And I hereby proclaim and declare that if any person, under the pretended authority of the said states, or under any other pretense, shall molest a vessel of the United States, or the persons or cargo on board of her, such person will be held amenable to the laws of the United States for the prevention and punishment of piracy.

In witness whereof, I have hereunto set my hand and caused the seal of the United States to be affixed.

Done at the city of Washington, this nineteenth day of April, in the year of Our Lord one thousand eight hundred and sixty-one, and of the independence of the United States the eighty-fifth.

Proclamation Calling Volunteers into Service

May 3, 1861

Whereas, Existing exigencies demand immediate and adequate measures for the protection of the national Constitution and the preservation of the national Union by the suppression of the insurrectionary combinations now existing in several states for opposing the laws of the Union and obstructing the execution thereof, to which end a military force in addition to that called forth by my proclamation of the fifteenth day of April in the present year appears to be indispensably necessary:

Now, therefore, I, Abraham Lincoln, President of the United States and Commander in Chief of the Army and Navy thereof, and of the militia of the several states when called into actual service, do hereby call into the service of the United States 42,034 volunteers to serve for the period of three years, unless sooner discharged, and to be mustered into service as infantry and cavalry. The proportions of each arm and the details of enrollment and organization will be made known through the Department of War.

And I also direct that the Regular Army of the United States be increased by the addition of eight regiments of infantry, one regiment of cavalry, and one regiment of artillery, making altogether a maximum aggregate increase of 22,714 officers and enlisted men, the details of which increase will also be made known through the Department of War.

And I further direct the enlistment for not less than one or more than three years of 18,000 seamen, in addition to the present force, for the naval service of the United States. The details of the enlistment and organization will be made known through the Department of the Navy.

The call for volunteers hereby made and the direction for the increase of the Regular Army and for the enlistment of seamen hereby given, together with the plan of organization adopted for the volunteer and for the regular forces hereby authorized, will be submitted to Congress as soon as assembled.

In the meantime I earnestly invoke the cooperation of all good citizens in the measures hereby adopted for the effectual suppression of unlawful violence, for the impartial enforcement of constitutional laws, and for the speediest possible restoration of peace and order, and with these of happiness and prosperity, throughout our country.

In testimony whereof I have hereunto set my hand and caused the seal of the United States to be affixed.

Done at the city of Washington, this third day of May, A.D. 1861, and of the independence of the United States the eighty-fifth.

MESSAGE TO CONGRESS
IN SPECIAL SESSION

July 4, 1861

Fellow Citizens of the Senate and House of Representatives: Having been convened on an extraordinary occasion, as authorized by the Constitution, your attention is not called to any ordinary subject of legislation.

At the beginning of the present presidential term, four months ago, the functions of the federal government were found to be generally suspended within the several states of South Carolina, Georgia, Alabama, Mississippi, Louisiana, and Florida, excepting only those of the Post Office Department.

Within these states all the forts, arsenals, dockyards, customhouses, and the like, including the movable and stationary property in and about them, had been seized, and were held in open hostility to this government, excepting only Forts Pickens, Taylor, and Jefferson, on and near the Florida coast, and Fort Sumter, in Charleston Harbor, South Carolina. The forts thus seized had been put in improved condition, new ones had been built, and armed forces had been organized and were organizing, all avowedly with the same hostile purpose.

The forts remaining in the possession of the federal government in and near these states were either besieged or menaced by warlike preparations, and especially Fort Sumter was nearly surrounded by well-protected hostile batteries, with guns equal in quality to the best of its own, and outnumbering the latter as perhaps ten to one. A disproportionate share of the federal muskets and rifles had somehow found their way into these states, and had been seized to be used against the government. Accumulations of the public revenue lying within them had been seized for the same object. The navy was scattered in distant seas, leaving but a very small part of it within the immediate reach of the government. Officers of the federal army and navy had resigned in great numbers; and of those resigning a large proportion had taken up arms against the government.

Simultaneously, and in connection with all this, the purpose to sever the federal Union was openly avowed. In accordance with this purpose, an ordinance had been adopted in each of these states, declaring the states respectively to be separated from the national Union. A formula for instituting a combined government of these states had been promulgated; and this illegal organization, in the character of confederate states, was already invoking recognition, aid, and intervention from foreign powers.

Finding this condition of things, and believing it to be an imperative duty upon the incoming executive to prevent, if possible, the consummation of such attempt to destroy the federal Union, a choice of means to that end became indispensable. This choice was made and was declared in the inaugural address. The policy chosen looked to the exhaustion of all peaceful measures before a resort to any stronger ones. It sought only to hold the public places and property not already wrested from the government, and to collect the revenue, relying for the rest on time, discussion, and the ballot box. It promised a continuance of the mails, at government expense, to the very people who were resisting the government; and it gave repeated pledges against any disturbance to any of the people, or any of their rights. Of all that which a president might constitutionally and justifiably do in such a case, everything was forborne without which it was believed possible to keep the government on foot.

On the fifth of March (the present incumbent's first full day in office), a letter of Major Anderson, commanding at Fort Sumter, written on the twenty-eighth of February and received at the War Department on the fourth of March, was by that department placed in his hands. This letter expressed the professional opinion of the writer that reinforcements could not be thrown into that fort within the time for his relief, rendered necessary by the limited supply of provisions, and with a view of holding possession of the same, with a force of less than twenty thousand good and well-disciplined men. This opinion was concurred in by all the officers of his command, and their memoranda on the subject were made enclosures of Major Anderson's letter. The whole was immediately laid before Lieutenant-General Scott, who at once concurred with Major Anderson in opinion. On reflection, however, he took full time, consulting with other officers, both of the army and the navy, and at the end of four days came reluctantly but decidedly to the same conclusion as before. He also stated at the same time that no such sufficient force was then at the control of the government, or could be raised and brought to the ground within the time when the provisions in the fort would be exhausted. In a purely military point of view, this reduced the duty of the administration in the case to the mere matter of getting the garrison safely out of the fort.

It was believed, however, that to so abandon that position, under the circumstances, would be utterly ruinous; that the necessity under which it was to be done would not be fully understood; that by many it would be construed as a part of a voluntary policy; that at home it would discourage the friends of the Union, embolden its adversaries, and go far to insure to the latter a recognition abroad; that, in fact, it would be our national destruction consummated. This could not be allowed. Starvation was not yet upon the garrison, and ere it would be reached Fort Pickens might be reinforced. This last would be a clear indication of policy, and would better enable the country to accept the evacuation of Fort Sumter as a military necessity. An order was at once directed to be sent for the landing of the troops from the steamship *Brooklyn* into Fort Pickens. This order could not go by land, but must take the longer and slower route by sea. The first return news from the order was received just one week before the fall of Fort Sumter. The news itself was that the officer commanding the *Sabine,* to which vessel the troops had been transferred from the *Brooklyn,* acting upon some quasi-armistice of the late administration (and of the existence of which the present administration, up to the time the order was dispatched, had only too vague and uncertain rumors to fix attention), had refused to land the troops. To now reinforce Fort Pickens before a crisis would be reached at Fort Sumter was impossible—rendered so by the near exhaustion of provisions in the latter-named fort.

In precaution against such a conjuncture, the government had, a few days before, commenced preparing an expedition as well adapted as might be to relieve Fort Sumter, which expedition was intended to be ultimately used, or not, according to circumstances. The strongest anticipated case for using it was now presented, and it was resolved to send it forward. As had been intended in this contingency, it was also resolved to notify the governor of South Carolina that he might expect an attempt would be made to provision the fort; and that, if the attempt should not be resisted, there would be no effort to throw in men, arms, or ammunition, without further notice, or in case of an attack upon the fort. This notice was accordingly given; whereupon the fort was attacked and bombarded to its fall, without even awaiting the arrival of the provisioning expedition.

It is thus seen that the assault upon and reduction of Fort Sumter was in no sense a matter of self-defense on the part of the assailants. They well knew that the garrison in the fort could by no possibility commit aggression upon them. They knew— they were expressly notified—that the giving of bread to the few brave and hungry men of the garrison was all which would on that occasion be attempted, unless themselves, by resisting so much, should provoke more. They knew that this government desired to keep the garrison in the fort, not to assail them, but merely to maintain visible possession, and thus to preserve the Union from actual and immediate dissolution—trusting, as hereinbefore stated, to time, discussion, and the ballot box for final adjustment; and they assailed and reduced the fort for precisely the reverse object—to drive out the visible authority of the federal Union, and thus force it to immediate dissolution.

That this was their object the executive well understood; and having said to them in the inaugural address, "You can have no conflict without being yourselves the aggressors," he took pains not only to keep this declaration good, but also to keep the case so free from the power of ingenious sophistry that the world should not be able to misunderstand it. By the affair at Fort Sumter, with its surrounding circumstances, that point was reached. Then and thereby the assailants of the government began the conflict of arms, without a gun in sight or in expectancy to return their fire, save only the few in the fort sent to that harbor years before for their own protection, and still ready to give that protection in whatever was lawful. In this act, discarding all else, they have forced upon the country the distinct issue, "immediate dissolution or blood."

And this issue embraces more than the fate of these United States. It presents to the whole family of man the question whether a constitutional republic or democracy—a government of the people by the same people—can or cannot maintain its territorial integrity against its own domestic foes. It presents the question whether discontented individuals, too few in numbers to control administration according to organic law in any case, can always, upon the pretenses made in this case, or on any other pretenses, or arbitrarily without any pretense, break up their government, and thus practically put an end to free government upon the earth. It forces us to ask: Is there in all republics this inherent and fatal weakness? Must a government, of necessity, be too strong for the liberties of its own people, or too weak to maintain its own existence?

So viewing the issue, no choice was left but to call out the war power of the government, and so to resist force employed for its destruction by force for its preservation.

The call was made, and the response of the country was most gratifying, surpassing in unanimity and spirit the most sanguine expectation. Yet none of the states commonly called slave states, except Delaware, gave a regiment through regular state organization. A few regiments have been organized within some others of those states by individual enterprise, and received into the government service. Of course the seceded states, so called (and to which Texas had been joined about the time of the inauguration), gave no troops to the cause of the Union. The border states, so called, were not uniform in their action, some of them being almost for the Union, while in others—as Virginia, North Carolina, Tennessee, and Arkansas—the Union sentiment was nearly repressed and silenced.

The course taken in Virginia was the most remarkable—perhaps the most important. A convention elected by the people of that state to consider this very question of disrupting the federal Union was in session at the capital of Virginia when Fort Sumter fell. To this body the people had chosen a large majority of professed Union men. Almost immediately after the fall of Sumter, many members of that majority went over to the original disunion minority, and with them adopted an ordinance for withdrawing the state from the Union. Whether this change was wrought by their great approval of the assault upon Sumter, or their great resentment at the government's resistance to that assault, is not definitely known. Although they submitted the ordinance for ratification to a vote of the people, to be taken on a day then somewhat more than a month distant, the convention and the legislature (which was also in session at the same time and place), with leading men of the state not members of either, immediately commenced acting as if the state were already out of the Union. They pushed military preparations vigorously forward all over the state. They seized the United States armory at Harper's Ferry, and the navy yard at Gosport, near Norfolk. They received—perhaps invited—into their state large bodies of troops, with their warlike appointments, from the so-called seceded states. They formally entered into a treaty of temporary alliance and cooperation with the so-called Confederate States, and sent members to their congress at Montgomery. And finally, they permitted the insurrectionary government to be transferred to their capital at Richmond.

The people of Virginia have thus allowed this giant insurrection to make its nest within her borders; and this government has no choice left but to deal with it where it finds it. And it has the less regret as the loyal citizens have, in due form, claimed its protection. Those loyal citizens this government is bound to recognize and protect as being Virginia.

In the border states, so called—in fact, the middle states—there are those who favor a policy which they call "armed neutrality"; that is, an arming of those states to prevent the Union forces passing one way, or the disunion the other, over their soil. This would be disunion completed. Figuratively speaking, it would be the building of an impassable wall along the line of separation—and yet not quite an impassable one, for under the guise of neutrality it would tie the hands of Union men and freely pass supplies from among them to the insurrectionists, which it could not do as an open enemy. At a stroke it would take all the trouble off the hands of secession, except only what proceeds from the external blockade. It would do for the disunionists that which, of all things, they most desire—feed them well and give them disunion without a struggle of their own. It recognizes no fidelity to the Constitution, no obligation to maintain the Union; and while very many who have favored it are doubtless loyal citizens, it is, nevertheless, very injurious in effect.

Recurring to the action of the government, it may be stated that at first a call was made for seventy-five thousand militia; and, rapidly following this, a proclamation was issued for closing the ports of the insurrectionary districts by proceedings in the nature of blockade. So far all was believed to be strictly legal. At this point the insurrectionists announced their purpose to enter upon the practice of privateering.

Other calls were made for volunteers to serve for three years, unless sooner discharged, and also for large additions to the regular army and navy. These measures, whether strictly legal or not, were ventured upon, under what appeared to be a popular demand and a public necessity; trusting then, as now, that Congress would readily ratify them. It is believed that nothing has been done beyond the constitutional competency of Congress.

Soon after the first call for militia, it was considered a duty to authorize the commanding general in proper cases, according to his discretion, to suspend the privilege of the writ of habeas corpus, or, in other words, to arrest and detain, without resort to the ordinary processes and forms of law, such individuals as he might deem dangerous to the public safety. This authority has purposely been exercised but very sparingly. Nevertheless, the legality and propriety of what has been done under it are questioned, and the attention of the country has been called to the proposition that one who has sworn to "take care that the laws be faithfully executed" should not himself violate them. Of course some consideration was given to the questions of power and propriety before this matter was acted upon. The whole of the laws which were required to be faithfully executed were being resisted and failing of execution in nearly one third of the states. Must they be allowed to finally fail of execution, even had it been perfectly clear that by the use of the means necessary to their execution some single law, made in such extreme tenderness of the citizen's liberty that, practically, it relieves more of the guilty than of the innocent, should to a very limited extent be violated?

To state the question more directly: Are all the laws but one to go unexecuted, and the government itself go to pieces lest that one be violated? Even in such a case, would not the official oath be broken if the government should be overthrown when it was believed that disregarding the single law would tend to preserve it? But it was not believed that this question was presented. It was not believed that any law was violated. The provision of the Constitution that "the privilege of the writ of habeas corpus shall not be suspended, unless when, in cases of rebellion or invasion, the public safety may require it" is equivalent to a provision—is a provision—that such privilege may be suspended when, in case of rebellion or invasion, the public safety does require it. It was decided that we have a case of rebellion, and that the public safety does require the qualified suspension of the privilege of the writ which was authorized to be made. Now it is insisted that Congress, and not the executive, is vested with this power. But the Constitution itself is silent as to which or who is to exercise the power; and as the provision was plainly made for a dangerous emergency, it cannot be believed the framers of the instrument intended that in every case the danger should run its course until Congress could be called together, the very assembling of which might be prevented, as was intended in this case, by the rebellion.

No more extended argument is now offered, as an opinion at some length will probably be presented by the attorney general. Whether there shall be any legislation upon the subject, and if any, what, is submitted entirely to the better judgment of Congress.

The forbearance of this government had been so extraordinary and so long continued as to lead some foreign nations to shape their action as if they supposed the early destruction of our national Union was probable. While this, on discovery, gave the executive some concern, he is now happy to say that the sovereignty and rights of the United States are now everywhere practically respected by foreign powers; and a general sympathy with the country is manifested throughout the world.

The reports of the secretaries of the Treasury, War, and the Navy will give the information in detail deemed necessary and convenient for your deliberation and action; while the executive and all the departments will stand ready to supply omissions, or to communicate new facts considered important for you to know.

It is now recommended that you give the legal means for making this contest a short and decisive one: that you place at the control of the government for the work at least four hundred thousand men and $400 million. That number of men is about one tenth of those of proper ages within the regions where, apparently, all are willing to engage; and the sum is less than a twenty-third part of the money value owned by the men who seem ready to devote the whole. A debt of $600 million now is a less sum per head than was the debt of our Revolution when we came out of that struggle; and the money value in the country now bears even a greater proportion to what it was then than does the population. Surely each man has as strong a motive now to preserve our liberties as each had then to establish them.

A right result at this time will be worth more to the world than ten times the men and ten times the money. The evidence reaching us from the country leaves no doubt that the material for the work is abundant, and that it needs only the hand of legislation to give it legal sanction, and the hand of the executive to give it practical shape and efficiency. One of the greatest perplexities of the government is to avoid receiving troops faster than it can provide for them. In a word, the people will save their government if the government itself will do its part only indifferently well.

It might seem, at first thought, to be of little difference whether the present movement at the South be called "secession" or "rebellion." The movers, however, well understand the difference. At the beginning they knew they could never raise their treason to any respectable magnitude by any name which implies violation of law. They knew their people possessed as much of moral sense, as much of devotion to law and order, and as much pride in and reverence for the history and government of their common country as any other civilized and patriotic people. They knew they could make no advancement directly in the teeth of these strong and noble sentiments. Accordingly, they commenced by an insidious debauching of the public mind. They invented an ingenious sophism which, if conceded, was followed by perfectly logical steps, through all the incidents, to the complete destruction of the Union. The sophism itself is that any state of the Union may consistently with the national Constitution, and therefore lawfully and peacefully, withdraw from the Union without the consent of the Union or of any other state. The little disguise that the supposed right is to be exercised only for just cause, themselves to be the sole judges of its justice, is too thin to merit any notice.

With rebellion thus sugarcoated they have been drugging the public mind of their section for more than thirty years, and until at length they have brought many good men to a willingness to take up arms against the government the day after some assemblage of men have enacted the farcical pretense of taking their state out of the Union, who could have been brought to no such thing the day before.

This sophism derives much, perhaps the whole, of its currency from the assumption that there is some omnipotent and sacred supremacy pertaining to a state—to each state of our federal Union. Our states have neither more nor less power than that reserved to them in the Union by the Constitution—no one of them ever having been a state out of the Union. The original ones passed into the Union even before they cast off their British colonial dependence; and the new ones each came into the Union directly from a condition of dependence, excepting Texas. And even Texas in its temporary independence was never designated a state. The new ones only took the designation of states on coming into the Union, while that name was first adopted for the old ones in and by the Declaration of Independence. Therein the "United Colonies" were declared to be "free and independent states"; but even then the object plainly was not to declare their independence of one another or of the Union, but directly the contrary, as their mutual pledge and their mutual action before, at the time, and afterward, abundantly show.

The express plighting of faith by each and all of the original thirteen in the Articles of Confederation, two years later, that the Union shall be perpetual, is most conclusive. Having never been states either in substance or in name outside of the Union, whence this magical omnipotence of "state rights," asserting a claim of power to lawfully destroy the Union itself? Much is said about the "sovereignty" of the states; but the word even is not in the national Constitution, nor, as is believed, in any of the state constitutions. What is "sovereignty" in the political sense of the term? Would it be far wrong to define it as "a political community without a political superior"? Tested by this, no one of our states except Texas ever was a sovereignty. And even Texas gave up the character on coming into the Union; by which act she acknowledged the Constitution of the United States, and the laws and treaties of the United States made in pursuance of the Constitution, to be for her the supreme law of the land.

The states have their status in the Union, and they have no other legal status. If they break from this, they can only do so against law and by revolution. The Union, and not themselves separately, procured their independence and their liberty. By conquest or purchase the Union gave each of them whatever of independence or liberty it has. The Union is older than any of the states, and, in fact, it created them as states. Originally some dependent colonies made the Union, and, in turn, the Union threw off their old dependence for them, and made them states, such as they are. Not one of them ever had a state constitution independent of the Union. Of course, it is not forgotten that all the new states framed their constitutions before they entered the Union—nevertheless, dependent upon and preparatory to coming into the Union.

Unquestionably the states have the powers and rights reserved to them in and by the national Constitution; but among these surely are not included all conceivable powers, however mischievous or destructive, but, at most, such only as were known in the world at the time as governmental powers; and certainly a power to destroy the government itself had never been known as a governmental, as a merely administrative power. This relative matter of national power and state rights, as a principle, is no other than the principle of generality and locality. Whatever concerns the whole should be confided to the whole—to the general government; while whatever concerns only the state should be left exclusively to the state. This is all there is of original principle about it. Whether the national Constitution in defining boundaries between the two has applied the principle with exact accuracy, is not to be questioned. We are all bound by that defining, without question.

What is now combated is the position that secession is consistent with the Constitution—is lawful and peaceful. It is not contended that there is any express law for it; and nothing should ever be implied as law which leads to unjust or absurd consequences. The nation purchased with money the countries out of which several of these states were formed. Is it just that they shall go off without leave and without refunding? The nation paid very large sums (in the aggregate, I believe, nearly a hundred millions) to relieve Florida of the aboriginal tribes. Is it just that she shall now be off without consent or without making any return? The nation is now in debt for money applied to the benefit of these so-called seceding states in common with the rest. Is it just either that creditors shall go unpaid or the remaining states pay the whole? A part of the present national debt was contracted to pay the old debts of Texas. Is it just that she shall leave and pay no part of this herself?

Again, if one state may secede, so may another; and when all shall have seceded, none is left to pay the debts. Is this quite just for creditors? Did we notify them of this sage view of ours when we borrowed their money? If we now recognize this doctrine by allowing the seceders to go in peace, it is difficult to see what we can do if others choose to go or to extort terms upon which they will promise to remain.

The seceders insist that our Constitution admits of secession. They have assumed to make a national constitution of their own, in which of necessity they have either discarded or retained the right of secession as they insist it exists in ours. If they have discarded it, they thereby admit that on principle it ought not to be in ours. If they have retained it, by their own construction of ours, they show that to be consistent they must secede from one another whenever they shall find it the easiest way of settling their debts, or effecting any other selfish or unjust object. The principle itself is one of disintegration and upon which no government can possibly endure.

If all the states save one should assert the power to drive that one out of the Union, it is presumed the whole class of seceder politicians would at once deny the power and denounce the act as the greatest outrage upon state rights. But suppose that precisely the same act, instead of being called "driving the one out," should be called "the seceding of the others from that one," it would be exactly what the seceders claim to do, unless, indeed, they make the point that the one, because it is a minority, may rightfully do what the others, because they are a majority, may not rightfully do. These politicians are subtle and profound on the rights of minorities. They are not partial to that power which made the Constitution and speaks from the preamble, calling itself "We, the People."

It may well be questioned whether there is today a majority of the legally qualified voters of any state except perhaps South Carolina in favor of disunion. There is much reason to believe that the Union men are the majority in many, if not in every other one, of the so-called seceded states. The contrary has not been demonstrated in any one of them. It is ventured to affirm this even of Virginia and Tennessee; for the result of an election held in military camps, where the bayonets are all on one side of the question voted upon, can scarcely be considered as demonstrating popular sentiment. At such an election, all that large class who are at once for the Union and against coercion would be coerced to vote against the Union.

It may be affirmed without extravagance that the free institutions we enjoy have developed the powers and improved the condition of our whole people beyond any example in the world. Of this we now have a striking and an impressive illustration. So large an army as the government has now on foot was never before known without a soldier in it but who has taken his place there of his own free choice. But more than this, there are many single regiments whose members, one and another, possess full practical knowledge of all the arts, sciences, professions, and whatever else, whether useful or elegant, is known in the world; and there is scarcely one from which there could not be selected a president, a Cabinet, a Congress, and perhaps a court, abundantly competent to administer the government itself. Nor do I say this is not true also in the army of our late friends, now adversaries in this contest; but if it is, so much better the reason why the government which has conferred such benefits on both them and us should not be broken up.

Whoever in any section proposes to abandon such a government would do well to consider in deference to what principle it is that he does it; what better he is likely to get in its stead; whether the substitute will give, or be intended to give, so much of good to the people. There are some foreshadowings on this subject. Our adversaries have adopted some declarations of independence in which, unlike the good old one, penned by Jefferson, they omit the words "all men are created equal." Why? They have adopted a temporary national constitution, in the preamble of which, unlike our good old one, signed by Washington, they omit "We, the People," and substitute, "We, the deputies of the sovereign and independent states." Why? Why this deliberate pressing out of view the rights of men and the authority of the people?

This is essentially a people's contest. On the side of the Union it is a struggle for maintaining in the world that form and substance of government whose leading object is to elevate the condition of men—to lift artificial weights from all shoulders; to clear the paths of laudable pursuit for all; to afford all an unfettered start, and a fair chance in the race of life. Yielding to partial and temporary departures, from necessity, this is the leading object of the government for whose existence we contend.

I am most happy to believe that the plain people understand and appreciate this. It is worthy of note that, while in this the government's hour of trial large numbers of those in the army and navy who have been favored with the offices have resigned and proved false to the hand which had pampered them, not one common soldier or common sailor is known to have deserted his flag.

Great honor is due to those officers who remained true, despite the example of their treacherous associates; but the greatest honor, and most important fact of all, is the unanimous firmness of the common soldiers and common sailors. To the last man, so far as known, they have successfully resisted the traitorous efforts of those whose commands, but an hour before, they obeyed as absolute law. This is the patriotic instinct of the plain people. They understand, without an argument, that the destroying of the government which was made by Washington means no good to them.

Our popular government has often been called an experiment. Two points in it our people have already settled—the successful establishing and the successful administering of it. One still remains—its successful maintenance against a formidable internal attempt to overthrow it. It is now for them to demonstrate to the world that those who can fairly carry an election can also suppress a rebellion; that ballots are the rightful and peaceful successors of bullets; and that when ballots have fairly and constitutionally decided, there can be no successful appeal back to bullets; that there can be no successful appeal, except to ballots themselves, at succeeding elections. Such will be a great lesson of peace: teaching men that what they cannot take by an election, neither can they take it by a war; teaching all the folly of being the beginners of a war.

Lest there be some uneasiness in the minds of candid men as to what is to be the course of the government toward the Southern states after the rebellion shall have been suppressed, the executive deems it proper to say it will be his purpose then, as ever, to be guided by the Constitution and the laws; and that he probably will have no different understanding of the powers and duties of the federal government relatively to the rights of the states and the people, under the Constitution, than that expressed in the inaugural address.

He desires to preserve the government, that it may be administered for all as it was administered by the men who made it. Loyal citizens everywhere have the right to claim this of their government, and the government has no right to withhold or neglect it. It is not perceived that in giving it there is any coercion, any conquest, or any subjugation, in any just sense of those terms.

The Constitution provides, and all the states have accepted the provision, that "the United States shall guarantee to every state in this Union a republican form of government." But if a state may lawfully go out of the Union, having done so it may also discard the republican form of government, so that to prevent its going out is an indispensable means to the end of maintaining the guarantee mentioned; and when an end is lawful and obligatory, the indispensable means to it are also lawful and obligatory.

It was with the deepest regret that the executive found the duty of employing the war power in defense of the government forced upon him. He could but perform this duty or surrender the existence of the government. No compromise by public servants could, in this case, be a cure; not that compromises are not often proper, but that no popular government can long survive a marked precedent that those who carry an election can only save the government from immediate destruction by giving up the main point upon which the people gave the election. The people themselves, and not their servants, can safely reverse their own deliberate decisions.

As a private citizen the executive could not have consented that these institutions shall perish; much less could he in betrayal of so vast and so sacred a trust as these free people had confided to him. He felt that he had no moral right to shrink, nor even to count the chances of his own life, in what might follow. In full view of his great responsibility he has, so far, done what he has deemed his duty. You will now, according to your own judgment, perform yours. He sincerely hopes that your views and your action may so accord with his as to assure all faithful citizens who have been disturbed in their rights of a certain and speedy restoration to them, under the Constitution and the laws.

And having thus chosen our course, without guile and with pure purpose, let us renew our trust in God, and go forward without fear and with manly hearts.

Proclamation Authorizing a National Fast Day

August 12, 1861

Whereas, A joint committee of both houses of Congress has waited on the president of the United States and requested him to "recommend a day of public humiliation, prayer, and fasting to be observed by the people of the United States with religious solemnities and the offering of fervent supplications to Almighty God for the safety and welfare of these states, His blessings on their arms, and a speedy restoration of peace"; and,

Whereas, It is fit and becoming in all people at all times to acknowledge and revere the supreme government of God, to bow in humble submission to His chastisements, to confess and deplore their sins and transgressions in the full conviction that the fear of the Lord is the beginning of wisdom, and to pray with all fervency and contrition for the pardon of their past offenses and for a blessing upon their present and prospective action; and,

Whereas, When our own beloved country, once, by the blessing of God, united, prosperous, and happy, is now afflicted with faction and civil war, it is peculiarly fit for us to recognize the hand of God in this terrible visitation, and in sorrowful remembrance of our own faults and crimes as a nation and as individuals to humble ourselves before Him and to pray for His mercy—to pray that we may be spared further punishment, though most justly deserved, that our arms may be blessed and made effectual for the reestablishment of order, law, and peace throughout the wide extent of our country, and that the inestimable boon of civil and religious liberty, earned under His guidance and blessing by the labors and sufferings of our fathers, may be restored in all its original excellence:

Therefore I, Abraham Lincoln, President of the United States, do appoint the last Thursday in September next as a day of humiliation, prayer, and fasting for all the people of the nation. And I do earnestly recommend to all the people, and especially to all ministers and teachers of religion of all denominations and to all heads of families, to observe and keep that day according to their several creeds and modes of worship in all humility and with all religious solemnity, to the end that the united prayer of the nation may ascend to the Throne of Grace and bring down plentiful blessings upon our country.

In testimony whereof I have hereunto set my hand and caused the seal of the United States to be affixed, this twelfth day of August, A.D. 1861, and of the independence of the United States of America the eighty-sixth.

PROCLAMATION FORBIDDING RELATIONS WITH THE REBELLIOUS STATES

August 16, 1861

Whereas, On the fifteenth day of April, eighteen hundred and sixty-one, the president of the United States, in view of an insurrection against the laws, Constitution, and government of the United States which had broken out within the states of South Carolina, Georgia, Alabama, Florida, Mississippi, Louisiana, and Texas, and in pursuance of the provisions of the act entitled "An Act to Provide for Calling Forth the Militia to Execute the Laws of the Union, Suppress Insurrections, and Repel Invasions, and to Repeal the Act Now in Force for That Purpose," approved February twenty-eighth, seventeen hundred and ninety-five, did call forth the militia to suppress said insurrection, and to cause the laws of the Union to be duly executed, and the insurgents have failed to disperse by the time directed by the president; and whereas such insurrection has since broken out and yet exists within the states of Virginia, North Carolina, Tennessee, and Arkansas; and whereas the insurgents in all the said states claim to act under the authority thereof, and such claim is not disclaimed or repudiated by the persons exercising the functions of government in such states or states, or in the part or parts thereof in which such combinations exist, nor has such insurrection been suppressed by said states:

Now, therefore, I, Abraham Lincoln, President of the United States, in pursuance of an act of Congress approved July thirteen, eighteen hundred and sixty-one, do hereby declare that the inhabitants of the said states of Georgia, South Carolina, Virginia, North Carolina, Tennessee, Alabama, Louisiana, Texas, Arkansas, Mississippi, and Florida (except the inhabitants of that part of the state of Virginia lying west of the Alleghany Mountains, and of such other parts of that state, and the other states hereinbefore named, as may maintain a loyal adhesion to the Union and the Constitution, or may be from time to time occupied and controlled by forces of the United States engaged in the dispersion of said insurgents), are in a state of insurrection against the United States, and that all commercial intercourse between the same and the inhabitants thereof, with the exceptions aforesaid, and the citizens of other states and other parts of the United States, is unlawful, and will remain unlawful until such insurrection shall cease or has been suppressed; that all goods and chattels, wares and merchandise, coming from any of said states, with the exceptions aforesaid, into other parts of the United States, without the special license and permission of the president, through the secretary of the Treasury, or proceeding to any of said states, with the exceptions aforesaid, by land or water, together with the vessel or vehicle conveying the same, or conveying persons to or from said states, with said exceptions, will be forfeited to the United States; and that from and after fifteen days from the issuing of this proclamation all ships and vessels belonging in whole or in part to any citizen or inhabitant of any of said states, with said exceptions, found at sea, or in any port of the United States, will be forfeited to the United States; and I hereby enjoin upon all district attorneys, marshals, and officers of the revenue and of the military and naval forces of the United States to be vigilant in the execution of said act, and in the enforcement of the penalties and forfeitures imposed or declared by it; leaving any party who may think himself aggrieved thereby to his application to the secretary of the Treasury for the remission of any penalty or forfeiture, which the said secretary is authorized by law to grant if, in his judgment, the special circumstances of any case shall require such remission.

In witness whereof, I have hereunto set my hand, and caused the seal of the United States to be affixed.

Done at the city of Washington, this sixteenth day of August, in the year of Our Lord eighteen hundred and sixty-one, and of the independence of the United States of America the eighty-sixth.

LETTER TO
ORVILLE H. BROWNING

Executive Mansion, Washington,
September 22, 1861

My dear Sir:

Yours of the 17th is just received; and coming from you, I confess it astonishes me. That you should object to my adhering to a law which you had assisted in making and presenting to me less than a month before is odd enough. But this is a very small part. General Frémont's proclamation as to confiscation of property and the liberation of slaves is purely political and not within the range of military law or necessity. If a commanding general finds a necessity to seize the farm of a private owner for a pasture, an encampment, or a fortification, he has the right to do so, and to so hold it as long as the necessity lasts; and this is within military law, because within military necessity. But to say the farm shall no longer belong to the owner, or his heirs forever, and this as well when the farm is not needed for military purposes as when it is, is purely political, without the savor of military law about it. And the same is true of slaves. If the general needs them, he can seize them and use them; but when the need is past, it is not for him to fix their permanent future condition. That must be settled according to laws made by lawmakers, and not by military proclamations. The proclamation in the point in question is simply "dictatorship." It assumes that the general may do anything he pleases—confiscate the lands and free the slaves of loyal people, as well as of disloyal ones. And going the whole figure, I have no doubt, would be more popular with some thoughtless people than that which has been done! But I cannot assume this reckless position, nor allow others to assume it on my responsibility.

You speak of it as being the only means of saving the

government. On the contrary, it is itself the surrender of the government. Can it be pretended that it is any longer the government of the United States—any government of constitution and laws—wherein a general or a president may make permanent rules of property by proclamation? I do not say Congress might not with propriety pass a law on the point, just such as General Frémont proclaimed. I do not say I might not, as a member of Congress, vote for it. What I object to is, that I, as president, shall expressly or impliedly seize and exercise the permanent legislative functions of the government.

So much as to principle. Now as to policy. No doubt the thing was popular in some quarters, and would have been more so if it had been a general declaration of emancipation. The Kentucky legislature would not budge till that proclamation was modified; and General Anderson telegraphed me that on the news of General Frémont having actually issued deeds of manumission, a whole company of our volunteers threw down their arms and disbanded. I was so assured as to think it probable that the very arms we had furnished Kentucky would be turned against us. I think to lose Kentucky is nearly the same as to lose the whole game. Kentucky gone, we cannot hold Missouri, nor, as I think, Maryland. These all against us, and the job on our hands is too large for us. We would as well consent to separation at once, including the surrender of this capital. On the contrary, if you will give up your restlessness for new positions, and back me manfully on the grounds upon which you and other kind friends gave me the election and have approved in my public documents, we shall go through triumphantly. You must not understand I took my course on the proclamation because of Kentucky. I took the same ground in a private letter to General Frémont before I heard from Kentucky.

You think I am inconsistent because I did not also forbid General Frémont to shoot men under the proclamation. I understand that part to be within military law, but I also think, and so privately wrote General Frémont, that it is impolitic in this, that our adversaries have the power, and will certainly exercise it, to shoot as many of our men as we shoot of theirs. I did not say this in the public letter, because it is a subject I prefer not to discuss in the hearing of our enemies.

There has been no thought of removing General Frémont on any ground connected with his proclamation, and if there has been any wish for his removal on any ground, our mutual friend Sam. Glover can probably tell you what it was. I hope no real necessity for it exists on any ground.

Your friend, as ever,
A. LINCOLN

First Annual Message to Congress

December 3, 1861

Fellow Citizens of the Senate and House of Representatives: In the midst of unprecedented political troubles we have cause of great gratitude to God for unusual good health and most abundant harvests.

You will not be surprised to learn that in the peculiar exigencies of the times our intercourse with foreign nations has been attended with profound solicitude, chiefly turning upon our own domestic affairs.

A disloyal portion of the American people have during the whole year been engaged in an attempt to divide and destroy the Union. A nation which endures factious domestic division is exposed to disrespect abroad, and one party, if not both, is sure sooner or later to invoke foreign intervention.

Nations thus tempted to interfere are not always able to resist the counsels of seeming expediency and ungenerous ambition, although measures adopted under such influences seldom fail to be unfortunate and injurious to those adopting them.

The disloyal citizens of the United States who have offered the ruin of our country in return for the aid and comfort which they have invoked abroad have received less patronage and encouragement than they probably expected. If it were just to suppose, as the insurgents have seemed to assume, that foreign nations in this case, discarding all moral, social, and treaty obligations, would act solely and selfishly for the most speedy restoration of commerce, including especially the acquisition of cotton, those nations appear as yet not to have seen their way to their object more directly or clearly through the destruction than through the preservation of the Union. If we could dare to believe that foreign nations are actuated by no higher principle than this, I am quite sure a sound argument could be made to show them that they can reach their aim more readily and easily by aiding to crush this rebellion than by giving encouragement to it.

The principal lever relied on by the insurgents for exciting foreign nations to hostility against us, as already intimated, is the embarrassment of commerce. Those nations, however, not improbably saw from the first that it was the Union which made as well our foreign as our domestic commerce. They can scarcely have failed to perceive that the effort for disunion produces the existing difficulty, and that one strong nation promises more durable peace and a more extensive, valuable, and reliable commerce than can the same nation broken into hostile fragments.

It is not my purpose to review our discussions with foreign states, because, whatever might be their wishes or dispositions, the integrity of our country and the stability of our government mainly depend not upon them, but on the loyalty, virtue, patriotism, and intelligence of the American people. The correspondence itself, with the usual reservations, is herewith submitted.

I venture to hope it will appear that we have practiced prudence and liberality toward foreign powers, averting causes of irritation and with firmness maintaining our own rights and honor. Since, however, it is apparent that here, as in every other state, foreign dangers necessarily attend domestic difficulties, I recommend that adequate and ample measures be adopted for maintaining the public defenses on every side. While under this general recommendation provision for defending our seacoast line readily occurs to the mind, I also in the same connection ask the attention of Congress to our great lakes and rivers. It is believed that some fortifications and depots of arms and munitions, with harbor and navigation improvements, all at well-selected points upon these, would be of great importance to the national defense and preservation. I ask attention to the views of the secretary of war, expressed in his report, upon the same general subject.

I deem it of importance that the loyal regions of east Tennessee and western North Carolina should be connected with Kentucky and other faithful parts of the Union by railroad. I therefore recommend, as a military measure, that Congress provide for the construction of such railroad as speedily as possible. Kentucky will no doubt cooperate, and through her legislature make the most judicious selection of a line. The northern terminus must connect with some existing railroad, and whether the route shall be from Lexington or Nicholasville to the Cumberland Gap, or from Lebanon to the Tennessee line, in the direction of Knoxville, or on some still different line, can easily be determined. Kentucky and the general government cooperating, the work can be completed in a very short time, and when done it will be not only of vast present usefulness but also a valuable permanent improvement, worth its cost in all the future.

Some treaties, designed chiefly for the interests of commerce, and having no grave political importance, have been negotiated, and will be submitted to the Senate for their consideration.

Although we have failed to induce some of the commercial powers to adopt a desirable melioration of the rigor of maritime war, we have removed all obstructions from the way of this humane reform except such as are merely of temporary and accidental occurrence.

I invite your attention to the correspondence between her Britannic Majesty's minister accredited to this government and the secretary of state relative to the detention of the British ship *Perthshire* in June last by the United States steamer *Massachusetts* for a supposed breach of the blockade. As this detention was occasioned by an obvious misapprehension of the facts, and as justice requires that we should commit no belligerent act not founded in strict right as sanctioned by public law, I recommend that an appropriation be made to satisfy the reasonable demand of the owners of the vessel for her detention.

I repeat the recommendation of my predecessor in his annual message to Congress in December last in regard to the disposition of the surplus which will probably remain after satisfying the claims of American citizens against China, pursuant to the awards of the commissioners under the act of the third of March 1859. If, however, it should not be deemed advisable to carry that recommendation into effect, I would suggest that authority be given for investing the principal, over the proceeds of the surplus referred to, in good securities, with a view to the satisfaction of such other just claims of our citizens against China as are not unlikely to arise hereafter in the course of our extensive trade with that empire.

By the act of the fifth of August last Congress authorized the president to instruct the commanders of suitable vessels to defend themselves against and to capture pirates. This authority has been exercised in a single instance only. For the more effectual protection of our extensive and valuable commerce in the Eastern seas especially, it seems to me that it would also be advisable to authorize the commanders of sailing vessels to recapture any prizes which pirates may make of United States vessels and their cargoes, and the consular courts now established by law in Eastern countries to adjudicate the cases in the event that this should not be objected to by the local authorities.

If any good reason exists why we should persevere longer in withholding our recognition of the independence and sovereignty of Haiti and Liberia, I am unable to discern it. Unwilling, however, to inaugurate a novel policy in regard to them without the approbation of Congress, I submit for your consideration the expediency of an appropriation for maintaining a chargé d'affaires near each of those new states. It does not admit of doubt that important commercial advantages might be secured by favorable treaties with them.

The operations of the Treasury during the period which has elapsed since your adjournment have been conducted with signal success. The patriotism of the people has placed at the disposal of the government the large means demanded by the public exigencies. Much of the national loan has been taken by citizens of the industrial classes, whose confidence in their country's faith and zeal for their country's deliverance from present peril have induced them to contribute to the support of the government the whole of their limited acquisitions. This fact imposes peculiar obligations to economy in disbursement and energy in action.

The revenue from all sources, including loans, for the financial year ending on the thirtieth of June 1861, was $86,835,900.27, and the expenditures for the same period, including payments on account of the public debt, were $84,578,834.47, leaving a balance in the Treasury on the first of July of $2,257,065.80. For the first quarter of the financial year ending on the thirtieth of September 1861, the receipts from all sources, including the balance of the first of July, were $102,532,509.27, and the expenses $98,239,733.09, leaving a balance on the first of October 1861 of $4,292,776.18. . . .

One of the unavoidable consequences of the present insurrection is the entire suppression in many places of all the ordinary means of administering civil justice by the officers and in the forms of existing law. This is the case, in whole or in part, in all the insurgent states; and as our armies advance upon and take possession of parts of those states the practical evil becomes more apparent. There are no courts or officers to whom the citizens of other states may apply for the enforcement of their lawful claims against citizens of the insurgent states, and there is a vast amount of debt constituting such claims. Some have estimated it as high as $200 million due in large part from insurgents in open rebellion to loyal citizens who are even now making great sacrifices in the discharge of their patriotic duty to support the government.

Under these circumstances I have been urgently solicited to establish, by military power, courts to administer summary justice in such cases. I have thus far declined to do it, not because

I had any doubt that the end proposed—the collection of the debts—was just and right in itself, but because I have been unwilling to go beyond the pressure of necessity in the unusual exercise of power. But the powers of Congress, I suppose, are equal to the anomalous occasion, and therefore I refer the whole matter to Congress, with the hope that a plan may be devised for the administration of justice in all such parts of the insurgent states and territories as may be under the control of this government, whether by a voluntary return to allegiance and order or by the power of our arms; this, however, not to be a permanent institution, but a temporary substitute, and to cease as soon as the ordinary courts can be reestablished in peace.

It is important that some more convenient means should be provided, if possible, for the adjustment of claims against the government, especially in view of their increased number by reason of the war. It is as much the duty of government to render prompt justice against itself in favor of citizens as it is to administer the same between private individuals. The investigation and adjudication of claims in their nature belong to the judicial department. Besides, it is apparent that the attention of Congress will be more than usually engaged for some time to come with great national questions. It was intended by the organization of the Court of Claims mainly to remove this branch of business from the halls of Congress; but, while the court has proved to be an effective and valuable means of investigation, it in great degree fails to effect the object of its creation for want of power to make its judgments final.

Fully aware of the delicacy, not to say the danger, of the subject, I commend to your careful consideration whether this power of making judgments final may not properly be given to the court, reserving the right of appeal on questions of law to the Supreme Court, with such other provisions as experience may have shown to be necessary. . . .

The relations of the government with the Indian tribes have been greatly disturbed by the insurrection, especially in the southern superintendency and in that of New Mexico. The

Indian country south of Kansas is in the possession of insurgents from Texas and Arkansas. The agents of the United States appointed since the fourth of March for this superintendency have been unable to reach their posts, while the most of those who were in office before that time have espoused the insurrectionary cause, and assume to exercise the powers of agents by virtue of commissions from the insurrectionists.

It has been stated in the public press that a portion of those Indians have been organized as a military force and are attached to the army of the insurgents. Although the government has no official information upon this subject, letters have been written to the commissioner of Indian Affairs by several prominent chiefs giving assurance of their loyalty to the United States and expressing a wish for the presence of federal troops to protect them. It is believed that upon the repossession of the country by the federal forces the Indians will readily cease all hostile demonstrations and resume their former relations to the government. . . .

The territories of Colorado, Dakota, and Nevada, created by the last Congress, have been organized, and civil administration has been inaugurated therein under auspices especially gratifying when it is considered that the leaven of treason was found existing in some of these new countries when the federal officers arrived there.

The abundant natural resources of these territories, with the security and protection afforded by organized government, will doubtless invite to them a large immigration when peace shall restore the business of the country to its accustomed channels. I submit the resolutions of the legislature of Colorado, which evidence the patriotic spirit of the people of the territory. So far the authority of the United States has been upheld in all the territories, as it is hoped it will be in the future. I commend their interests and defense to the enlightened and generous care of Congress.

I recommend to the favorable consideration of Congress the interests of the District of Columbia. The insurrection has been the cause of much suffering and sacrifice to its inhabitants, and as they have no representative in Congress that body should not overlook their just claims upon the government. . . .

The war continues. In considering the policy to be adopted for suppressing the insurrection I have been anxious and careful that the inevitable conflict for this purpose shall not degenerate into a violent and remorseless revolutionary struggle. I have therefore in every case thought it proper to keep the integrity of the Union prominent as the primary object of the contest on our part, leaving all questions which are not of vital military importance to the more deliberate action of the legislature.

In the exercise of my best discretion I have adhered to the blockade of the ports held by the insurgents, instead of putting in force by proclamation the law of Congress enacted at the late session for closing those ports.

So also, obeying the dictates of prudence, as well as the obligations of law, instead of transcending I have adhered to the act of Congress to confiscate property used for insurrectionary purposes. If a new law upon the same subject shall be proposed, its propriety will be duly considered. The Union must be preserved, and hence all indispensable means must be employed. We should not be in haste to determine that radical and extreme measures, which may reach the loyal as well as the disloyal, are indispensable.

The inaugural address at the beginning of the administration and the message to Congress at the late special session were both mainly devoted to the domestic controversy out of which the insurrection and consequent war have sprung. Nothing now occurs to add or subtract to or from the principles or general purposes stated and expressed in those documents.

The last ray of hope for preserving the Union peaceably expired at the assault upon Fort Sumter, and a general review of what has occurred since may not be unprofitable. What was painfully uncertain then is much better defined and more distinct now, and the progress of events is plainly in the right direction. The insurgents confidently claimed a strong support from north of Mason and Dixon's line, and the friends of the Union were not free from apprehension on the point. This, however, was soon settled definitely, and on the right side. South of the line noble little Delaware led off right from the first. Maryland was made to *seem* against the Union. Our soldiers were assaulted, bridges were burned, and railroads torn up within her limits, and we were many days at one time without the ability to bring a single regiment over her soil to the capital.

Now her bridges and railroads are repaired and open to the government; she already gives seven regiments to the cause of the Union, and none to the enemy; and her people, at a regular election, have sustained the Union by a larger majority and a larger aggregate vote than they ever before gave to any candidate or any question. Kentucky, too, for some time in doubt, is now decidedly and, I think, unchangeably ranged on the side of the Union. Missouri is comparatively quiet, and, I believe, cannot again be overrun by the insurrectionists.

These three states of Maryland, Kentucky, and Missouri, neither of which would promise a single soldier at first, have now an aggregate of not less than forty thousand in the field for the Union, while of their citizens certainly not more than a third of that number, and they of doubtful whereabouts and doubtful existence, are in arms against us. After a somewhat bloody struggle of months, winter closes on the Union people of western Virginia, leaving them masters of their own country.

An insurgent force of about fifteen hundred, for months dominating the narrow peninsular region constituting the counties of Accomac and Northampton, and known as Eastern Shore of Virginia, together with some contiguous parts of Maryland, have laid down their arms, and the people there have renewed their allegiance to and accepted the protection of the old flag. This leaves no armed insurrectionist north of the Potomac or east of the Chesapeake.

Also we have obtained a footing at each of the isolated points on the southern coast of Hatteras, Port Royal, Tybee Island (near Savannah), and Ship Island; and we likewise have some general accounts of popular movements in behalf of the Union in North Carolina and Tennessee. . . .

It continues to develop that the insurrection is largely, if not exclusively, a war upon the first principle of popular government—the rights of the people. Conclusive evidence of this is found in the most grave and maturely considered public documents, as well as in the general tone of the insurgents. In those documents we find the abridgment of the existing right of suffrage and the denial to the people of all right to participate in the selection of public officers except the legislative boldly advocated, with labored arguments to prove that large control of the people in government is the source of all political evil. Monarchy itself is sometimes hinted at as a possible refuge from the power of the people.

In my present position I could scarcely be justified were I to omit raising a warning voice against this approach of returning despotism.

It is not needed nor fitting here that a general argument should be made in favor of popular institutions, but there is one point, with its connections, not so hackneyed as most others, to which I ask a brief attention. It is the effort to place *capital* on an equal footing with, if not above, *labor* in the structure of government. It is assumed that labor is available only in connection with capital; that nobody labors unless somebody else, owning capital, somehow by the use of it induces him to labor. This assumed, it is next considered whether it is best that capital shall *hire* laborers, and thus induce them to work by their own consent, or *buy* them and drive them to it without their consent. Having proceeded so far, it is naturally concluded that all laborers are either *hired* laborers or what we call slaves. And further, it is assumed that whoever is once a hired laborer is fixed in that condition for life.

Now there is no such relation between capital and labor as assumed, nor is there any such thing as a free man being fixed for life in the condition of a hired laborer. Both these assumptions are false, and all inferences from them are groundless.

Labor is prior to and independent of capital. Capital is only the fruit of labor, and could never have existed if labor had not first existed. Labor is the superior of capital, and deserves much the higher consideration. Capital has its rights, which are as worthy of protection as any other rights. Nor is it denied that there is, and probably always will be, a relation between labor and capital producing mutual benefits. The error is in assuming that the whole labor of community exists within that relation. A few men own capital, and that few avoid labor themselves, and with their capital hire or buy another few to labor for them. A large majority belong to neither class—neither working for others nor have others working for them.

In most of the Southern states a majority of the whole people of all colors are neither slaves nor masters, while in the Northern a large majority are neither hirers nor hired. Men, with their families—wives, sons, and daughters—work for themselves on their farms, in their houses, and in their shops, taking the whole product to themselves, and asking no favors of capital on the one hand nor of hired laborers or slaves on the other. It is not forgotten that a considerable number of persons mingle their own labor with capital; that is, they labor with their own hands and also buy or hire others to labor for them; but this is only a mixed and not a distinct class. No principle stated is disturbed by the existence of this mixed class.

Again, as has already been said, there is not of necessity any such thing as the free hired laborer being fixed to that condition for life. Many independent men everywhere in these states a few years back in their lives were hired laborers. The prudent, penniless beginner in the world labors for wages awhile, saves a surplus with which to buy tools or land for himself, then labors on his own account another while, and at length hires another new beginner to help him. This is the just and generous and prosperous system which opens the way to all, gives hope to all, and consequent energy and progress and improvement of condition to all. No men living are more worthy to be trusted than those who toil up from poverty; none less inclined to take or touch aught which they have not honestly earned. Let them beware of surrendering a political power which they already possess, and which if surrendered will surely be used to close the door of advancement against such as they and to fix new disabilities and burdens upon them till all of liberty shall be lost.

From the first taking of our national census to the last are seventy years, and we find our population at the end of the period eight times as great as it was at the beginning. The increase of those other things which men deem desirable has been even greater. We thus have at one view what the popular principle, applied to government through the machinery of the states and the Union, has produced in a given time, and also what if firmly maintained it promises for the future. There are already among us those who if the Union be preserved will live to see it contain 250 million. The struggle *of* today is not altogether *for* today; it is for a vast future also. With a reliance on Providence all the more firm and earnest, let us proceed in the great task which events have devolved upon us.

MESSAGE TO CONGRESS ON COMPENSATED EMANCIPATION

March 6, 1862

Fellow Citizens of the Senate and House of Representatives: I recommend the adoption of a joint resolution by your honorable bodies which shall be substantially as follows:

> *Resolved,* That the United States ought to cooperate with any state which may adopt gradual abolishment of slavery, giving to such state pecuniary aid, to be used by such state, in its discretion, to compensate for the inconveniences, public and private, produced by such change of system.

If the proposition contained in the resolution does not meet the approval of Congress and the country, there is the end; but if it does command such approval, I deem it of importance that the states and people immediately interested should be at once distinctly notified of the fact, so that they may begin to consider whether to accept or reject it. The federal government would find its highest interest in such a measure, as one of the most efficient means of self-preservation. The leaders of the existing insurrection entertain the hope that this government will ultimately be forced to acknowledge the independence of some part of the disaffected region, and that all the slave states north of such part will then say, "The Union for which we have struggled being already gone, we now choose to go with the Southern section." To deprive them of this hope substantially ends the rebellion, and the initiation of emancipation completely deprives them of it as to all the states initiating it. The point is not that *all* the states tolerating slavery would very soon, if at all, initiate emancipation; but that, while the offer is equally made to all, the more northern shall by such initiation make it certain to the more southern that in no event will the former ever join the latter in their proposed confederacy. I say "initiation" because, in my judgment, gradual and not sudden emancipation is better for all. In the mere financial or pecuniary view, any member of Congress with the census tables and treasury reports before him can readily see for himself how very soon the current expenditures of this war would purchase, at fair valuation, all the slaves in any named state. Such a proposition on the part of the general government sets up no claim of a right by federal authority to interfere with slavery within state limits, referring, as it does, the absolute control of the subject in each case to the state and its people immediately interested. It is proposed as a matter of perfectly free choice with them.

In the annual message last December, I thought fit to say, "The Union must be preserved, and hence all indispensable means must be employed." I said this not hastily, but deliberately. War has been made and continues to be an indispensable means to this end. A practical reacknowledgment of the national authority would render the war unnecessary, and it would at once cease. If, however, resistance continues, the war must also continue; and it is impossible to foresee all the incidents which may attend and all the ruin which may follow it. Such as may seem indispensable or may obviously promise great efficiency toward ending the struggle must and will come.

The proposition now made (though an offer only), I hope it may be esteemed no offense to ask whether the pecuniary consideration tendered would not be of more value to the states and private persons concerned than are the institution and property in it in the present aspect of affairs.

While it is true that the adoption of the proposed resolution would be merely initiatory, and not within itself a practical measure, it is recommended in the hope that it would soon lead to important practical results. In full view of my great responsibility to my God and to my country, I earnestly beg the attention of Congress and the people to the subject.

Telegram to General George B. McClellan

War Department, Washington City,
June 28, 1862

Major-General McClellan:

Save your army, at all events. Will send reinforcements as fast as we can. Of course they cannot reach you today, tomorrow, or next day. I have not said you were ungenerous for saying you needed reinforcements. I thought you were ungenerous in assuming that I did not send them as fast as I could. I feel any misfortune to you and your army quite as keenly as you feel it yourself. If you have had a drawn battle, or a repulse, it is the price we pay for the enemy not being in Washington. We protected Washington, and the enemy concentrated on you. Had we stripped Washington, he would have been upon us before the troops could have gotten to you. Less than a week ago you notified us that reinforcements were leaving Richmond to come in front of us. It is the nature of the case, and neither you nor the government is to blame. Please tell at once the present condition and aspect of things.

A. Lincoln

Letter to Secretary William H. Seward

Executive Mansion, June 28, 1862

My dear Sir:

My view of the present condition of the war is about as follows.

The evacuation of Corinth and our delay by the flood in the Chickahominy have enabled the enemy to concentrate too much force in Richmond for McClellan to successfully attack. In fact there soon will be no substantial rebel force anywhere else. But if we send all the force from here to McClellan, the enemy will, before we can know of it, send a force from Richmond and take Washington. Or if a large part of the western army be brought here to McClellan, they will let us have Richmond, and retake Tennessee, Kentucky, Missouri, etc. What should be done is to hold what we have in the West, open the Mississippi, and take Chattanooga and East Tennessee without more. A reasonable force should in every event be kept about Washington for its protection. Then let the country give us a hundred thousand new troops in the shortest possible time, which, added to McClellan directly or indirectly, will take Richmond without endangering any other place which we now hold, and will substantially end the war. I expect to maintain this contest until successful, or till I die, or am conquered, or my term expires, or Congress or the country forsake me; and I would publicly appeal to the country for this new force were it not that I fear a general panic and stampede would follow, so hard it is to have a thing understood as it really is. I think the new force should be all, or nearly all, infantry, principally because such can be raised most cheaply and quickly.

Yours very truly,
A. Lincoln

LETTER TO
HORACE GREELEY

Executive Mansion, Washington,
August 22, 1862

Dear Sir:

I have just read yours of the 19th, addressed to myself through the New York *Tribune*. If there be in it any statements or assumptions of fact which I may know to be erroneous, I do not now and here controvert them. If there be in it any inferences which I may believe to be falsely drawn, I do not now and here argue against them. If there be perceptible in it an impatient and dictatorial tone, I waive it in deference to an old friend, whose heart I have always supposed to be right.

As to the policy I "seem to be pursuing," as you say, I have not meant to leave anyone in doubt.

I would save the Union. I would save it the shortest way under the Constitution. The sooner the national authority can be restored, the nearer the Union will be, "the Union as it was." If there be those who would not save the Union unless they could at the same time save slavery, I do not agree with them. If there be those who would not save the Union unless they could at the same time destroy slavery, I do not agree with them.

My paramount object in this struggle is to save the Union, and is not either to save or destroy slavery. If I could save the Union without freeing any slave, I would do it; and if I could save it by freeing all the slaves, I would do it; and if I could do it by freeing some and leaving others alone, I would also do that. What I do about slavery and the colored race, I do because I believe it helps to save this Union; and what I forbear, I forbear because I do not believe it would help to save the Union. I shall do less whenever I shall believe what I am doing hurts the cause, and I shall do more whenever I shall believe doing more will help the cause. I shall try to correct errors when shown to be errors; and I shall adopt new views so fast as they shall appear to be true views. I have here stated my purpose according to my view of official duty, and I intend no modification of my oft-expressed personal wish that all men, everywhere, could be free.

Yours,

A. LINCOLN

Reply to a Committee from Chicago Religious Denominations

Asking That the President Issue a Proclamation of Emancipation

September 13, 1862

The subject presented in the memorial is one upon which I have thought much for weeks past, and I may even say for months. I am approached with the most opposite opinions and advice, and that by religious men, who are equally certain that they represent the Divine Will. I am sure that either the one or the other class is mistaken in that belief, and perhaps in some respects both. I hope it will not be irreverent for me to say that if it is probable that God would reveal his will to others, on a point so connected with my duty, it might be supposed he would reveal it directly to me; for, unless I am more deceived in myself than I often am, it is my earnest desire to know the will of Providence in this matter. And if I can learn what it is I will do it! These are not, however, the days of miracles, and I suppose it will be granted that I am not to expect a direct revelation. I must study the plain physical facts of the case, ascertain what is possible, and learn what appears to be wise and right.

The subject is difficult, and good men do not agree. For instance, the other day, four gentlemen of standing and intelligence from New York called as a delegation on business connected with the war; but before leaving two of them earnestly besought me to proclaim general emancipation, upon which the other two at once attacked them. You know also that the last session of Congress had a decided majority of antislavery men, yet they could not unite on this policy. And the same is true of the religious people. Why, the rebel soldiers are praying with a great deal more earnestness, I fear, than our own troops, and expecting God to favor their side: for one of our soldiers who had been taken prisoner told Senator Wilson a few days since that he met nothing so discouraging as the evident sincerity of those he was among in their prayers. But we will talk over the merits of the case.

What good would a proclamation of emancipation from me do, especially as we are now situated? I do not want to issue a document that the whole world will see must necessarily be inoperative, like the pope's bull against the comet! Would my word free the slaves, when I cannot even enforce the Constitution in the rebel states? Is there a single court or magistrate or individual that would be influenced by it there? And what reason is there to think it would have any greater effect upon the slaves than the late law of Congress, which I approved, and which offers protection and freedom to the slaves of rebel masters who come within our lines?

Yet I cannot learn that that law has caused a single slave to come over to us. And suppose they could be induced by a proclamation of freedom from me to throw themselves upon us, what should we do with them? How can we feed and care for such a multitude? General Butler wrote me a few days since that he was issuing more rations to the slaves who have rushed to him than to all the white troops under his command. They eat, and that is all; though it is true General Butler is feeding the whites also by the thousand; for it nearly amounts to a famine there. If, now, the pressure of the war should call off our forces from New Orleans to defend some other point, what is to prevent the masters from reducing the blacks to slavery again? For I am told that whenever the rebels take any black prisoners, free or slave, they immediately auction them off. They did so with those they took from a boat that was aground in the

Tennessee River a few days ago. And then I am very ungenerously attacked for it! For instance, when, after the late battles at and near Bull Run, an expedition went out from Washington under a flag of truce to bury the dead and bring in the wounded, and the rebels seized the blacks who went along to help, and sent them into slavery, Horace Greeley said in his paper that the government would probably do nothing about it. What could I do?

Now, then, tell me, if you please, what possible result of good would follow the issuing of such a proclamation as you desire? Understand, I raise no objections against it on legal or constitutional grounds; for, as commander in chief of the army and navy, in time of war I suppose I have a right to take any measure which may best subdue the enemy; nor do I urge objections of a moral nature, in view of possible consequences of insurrection and massacre at the South. I view this matter as a practical war measure, to be decided on according to the advantages or disadvantages it may offer to the suppression of the rebellion.

I admit that slavery is the root of the rebellion, or at least its sine qua non. The ambition of politicians may have instigated them to act, but they would have been impotent without slavery as their instrument. I will also concede that emancipation would help us in Europe, and convince them that we are incited by something more than ambition. I grant, further, that it would help somewhat at the North, though not so much, I fear, as you and those you represent imagine. Still, some additional strength would be added in that way to the war, and then, unquestionably, it would weaken the rebels by drawing off their laborers, which is of great importance; but I am not so sure we could do much with the blacks. If we were to arm them, I fear that in a few weeks the arms would be in the hands of the rebels; and, indeed, thus far we have not had arms enough to equip our white troops. I will mention another thing, though it meet only your scorn and contempt. There are fifty thousand bayonets in the Union armies from the border slave states. It would be a serious matter if, in consequence of a proclamation such as you desire, they should go over to the rebels. I do not think they all would—not so many, indeed, as a year ago, or as six months ago—not so many today as yesterday. Every day increases their Union feeling. They are also getting their pride enlisted, and want to beat the rebels. Let me say one thing more: I think you should admit that we already have an important principle to rally and unite the people, in the fact that constitutional government is at stake. This is a fundamental idea going down about as deep as anything.

Do not misunderstand me because I have mentioned these objections. They indicate the difficulties that have thus far prevented my action in some such way as you desire. I have not decided against a proclamation of liberty to the slaves, but hold the matter under advisement; and I can assure you that the subject is on my mind, by day and night, more than any other. Whatever shall appear to be God's will, I will do. I trust that in the freedom with which I have canvassed your views I have not in any respect injured your feelings.

Preliminary Emancipation Proclamation

September 22, 1862

I, Abraham Lincoln, President of the United States of America and Commander in Chief of the Army and Navy thereof, do hereby proclaim and declare that hereafter, as heretofore, the war will be prosecuted for the object of practically restoring the constitutional relation between the United States and each of the states and the people thereof in which states that relation is or may be suspended or disturbed.

That it is my purpose, upon the next meeting of Congress, to again recommend the adoption of a practical measure tendering pecuniary aid to the free acceptance or rejection of all slave states, so called, the people whereof may not then be in rebellion against the United States, and which states may then have voluntarily adopted, or thereafter may voluntarily adopt, immediate or gradual abolishment of slavery within their respective limits; and that the effort to colonize persons of African descent with their consent upon this continent or elsewhere, with the previously obtained consent of the governments existing there, will be continued.

That on the first day of January, A.D. 1863, all persons held as slaves within any state or designated part of a state the people whereof shall then be in rebellion against the United States shall be then, thenceforward, and forever free; and the executive government of the United States, including the military and naval authority thereof, will recognize and maintain the freedom of such persons and will do no act or acts to repress such persons, or any of them, in any efforts they may make for their actual freedom.

That the executive will on the first day of January aforesaid, by proclamation, designate the states and parts of states, if any, in which the people thereof, respectively, shall then be in rebellion against the United States; and the fact that any state or the people thereof shall on that day be in good faith represented in the Congress of the United States by members chosen thereto at elections wherein a majority of the qualified voters of such state shall have participated shall, in the absence of strong countervailing testimony, be deemed conclusive evidence that such state and the people thereof are not then in rebellion against the United States.

That attention is hereby called to an act of Congress entitled "An Act to Make an Additional Article of War," approved March 13, 1862, and which act is in the words and figure following:

> *Be it enacted by the Senate and House of Representatives of the United States of America in Congress assembled,* That hereafter the following shall be promulgated as an additional article of war for the government of the Army of the United States and shall be obeyed and observed as such.
>
> ARTICLE. All officers or persons in the military or naval service of the United States are prohibited from employing any of the forces under their respective commands for the purpose of returning fugitives from service or labor who may have escaped from any persons to whom such service or labor is claimed to be due, and any officer who shall be found guilty by a court-martial of violating this article shall be dismissed from the service.
>
> SECTION 2. *And be it further enacted,* That this act shall take effect from and after its passage.

Also to the ninth and tenth sections of an act entitled "An Act to Suppress Insurrection, to Punish Treason and Rebellion, to Seize and Confiscate the Property of Rebels, and for Other Purposes," approved July 17, 1862, and which sections are in the words and figures following:

SECTION 9. *And be it further enacted,* That all slaves of persons who shall hereafter be engaged in rebellion against the government of the United States, or who shall in any way give aid or comfort thereto, escaping from such persons and taking refuge within the lines of the army, and all slaves captured from such persons or deserted by them and coming under the control of the government of the United States, and all slaves of such persons found on [or] being within any place occupied by rebel forces and afterwards occupied by the forces of the United States, shall be deemed captives of war and shall be forever free of their servitude and not again held as slaves.

SECTION 10. *And be it further enacted,* That no slave escaping into any state, territory, or the District of Columbia from any other state shall be delivered up or in any way impeded or hindered of his liberty, except for crime, or some offense against the laws, unless the person claiming said fugitive shall first make oath that the person to whom the labor or service of such fugitive is alleged to be due is his lawful owner, and has not borne arms against the United States in the present rebellion, nor in any way given aid and comfort thereto; and no person engaged in the military or naval service of the United States shall, under any pretense whatever, assume to decide on the validity of the claim of any person to the service or labor of any other person, or surrender up any such person to the claimant, on pain of being dismissed from the service.

And I do hereby enjoin upon and order all persons engaged in the military and naval service of the United States to observe, obey, and enforce, within their respective spheres of service, the act and sections above recited.

And the executive will in due time recommend that all citizens of the United States who shall have remained loyal thereto throughout the rebellion shall (upon the restoration of the constitutional relation between the United States and their respective states and people, if that relation shall have been suspended or disturbed) be compensated for all losses by acts of the United States, including the loss of slaves.

In witness whereof, I have hereunto set my hand and caused the seal of the United States to be affixed.

Done at the city of Washington, this twenty-second day of September, in the year of Our Lord one thousand eight hundred and sixty-two, and of the independence of the United States the eighty-seventh.

Letter to General George B. McClellan

Executive Mansion, Washington,
October 13, 1862

My dear Sir:

You remember my speaking to you of what I called your overcautiousness. Are you not overcautious when you assume that you cannot do what the enemy is constantly doing? Should you not claim to be at least his equal in prowess, and act upon the claim?

As I understand, you telegraphed General Halleck that you cannot subsist your army at Winchester unless the railroad from Harper's Ferry to that point be put in working order. But the enemy does now subsist his army at Winchester, at a distance nearly twice as great from railroad transportation as you would have to do, without the railroad last named. He now wagons from Culpepper Courthouse, which is just about twice as far as you would have to do from Harper's Ferry. He is certainly not more than half as well provided with wagons as you are. I certainly should be pleased for you to have the advantage of the railroad from Harper's Ferry to Winchester; but it wastes all the remainder of autumn to give it to you, and, in fact, ignores the question of *time,* which cannot and must not be ignored.

Again, one of the standard maxims of war, as you know, is "to operate upon the enemy's communications as much as possible, without exposing your own." You seem to act as if this applies *against* you, but cannot apply in your *favor.* Change positions with the enemy, and think you not he would break your communication with Richmond within the next twenty-four hours? You dread his going into Pennsylvania. But if he does so in full force, he gives up his communications to you absolutely, and you have nothing to do but to follow and ruin him; if he does so with less than full force, fall upon and beat what is left behind all the easier.

Exclusive of the water line, you are now nearer to Richmond than the enemy is, by the route that you *can* and he *must* take. Why can you not reach there before him, unless you admit that he is more than your equal on a march? His route is the arc of a circle, while yours is the chord. The roads are as good on yours as on his.

You know I desired, but did not order, you to cross the Potomac below instead of above the Shenandoah and Blue Ridge. My idea was that this would at once menace the enemy's communications, which I would seize if he would permit. If he should move northward, I would follow him closely, holding his communications. If he should prevent our seizing his communications, and move toward Richmond, I would press closely to him, fight him if a favorable opportunity should present, and at least try to beat him to Richmond on the inside track. I say "try"; if we never try, we shall never succeed. If he makes a stand at Winchester, moving neither north or south, I would fight him there, on the idea that if we cannot beat him when he bears the wastage of coming to us, we never can when we bear the wastage of going to him. This proposition is a simple truth, and is too important to be lost sight of for a moment. In coming to us he tenders us an advantage which we should not waive. We should not so operate as to merely drive him away. As we must beat him somewhere or fail finally, we can do it, if at all, easier near to us than far away. If we cannot beat the enemy where he now is, we never can, he again being within the entrenchments of Richmond.

Recurring to the idea of going to Richmond on the inside track, the facility of supplying from the side away from the enemy is remarkable, as it were, by the different spokes of a wheel extending from the hub toward the rim, and this whether you move directly by the chord or on the inside arc, hugging the Blue Ridge more closely. The chordline, as you see, carries you by Aldie, Hay Market, and Fredericksburg; and you see how turnpikes, railroads, and finally the Potomac, by Aquia Creek, meet you at all points from Washington; the same, only the lines lengthened a little, if you press closer to the Blue Ridge part of the way.

The gaps through the Blue Ridge I understand to be about the following distances from Harper's Ferry, to wit: Vestal's, 5 miles; Gregory's, 13; Snicker's, 18; Ashby's, 28; Manassas, 38; Chester, 45; and Thornton's, 53. I should think it preferable to take the route nearest the enemy, disabling him to make an important move without your knowledge, and compelling him to keep his forces together for dread of you. The gaps would enable you to attack if you should wish. For a great part of the way you would be practically between the enemy and both Washington and Richmond, enabling us to spare you the greatest number of troops from here. When at length running for Richmond ahead of him enables him to move this way, if he does so, turn and attack him in rear. But I think he should be engaged long before such a point is reached. It is all easy if our troops march as well as the enemy, and it is unmanly to say they cannot do it. This letter is in no sense an order.

Yours truly,
A. LINCOLN

LETTER TO THE
ARMY OF THE POTOMAC

Executive Mansion, Washington,
December 22, 1862

To the Army of the Potomac:

I have just read your general's report of the battle of Fredericksburg. Although you were not successful, the attempt was not an error, nor the failure other than accident. The courage with which you, in an open field, maintained the contest against an entrenched foe, and the consummate skill and success with which you crossed and recrossed the river in the face of the enemy, show that you possess all the qualities of a great army, which will yet give victory to the cause of the country and of popular government.

Condoling with the mourners for the dead, and sympathizing with the severely wounded, I congratulate you that the number of both is comparatively so small.

I tender to you, officers and soldiers, the thanks of the nation.

A. LINCOLN

Letter to
Fanny McCullough

Executive Mansion, Washington,
December, 23, 1862

Dear Fanny:

It is with deep regret that I learn of the death of your kind and brave father, and especially that it is affecting your young heart beyond what is common in such cases. In this sad world of ours sorrow comes to all, and to the young it comes with bittered agony because it takes them unawares. The older have learned ever to expect it. I am anxious to afford some alleviation of your present distress. Perfect relief is not possible, except with time. You cannot now realize that you will ever feel better. Is not this so? And yet it is a mistake. You are sure to be happy again. To know this, which is certainly true, will make you some less miserable now. I have had experience enough to know what I say, and you need only to believe it to feel better at once. The memory of your dear father, instead of an agony, will yet be a sad, sweet feeling in your heart, of a purer and holier sort than you have known before.

Please present my kind regards to your afflicted mother.

Your sincere friend,
A. Lincoln

The Emancipation Proclamation

January 1, 1863

Whereas, On the twenty-second day of September, A.D. 1862, a proclamation was issued by the president of the United States, containing, among other things, the following, to wit:

> That on the first day of January, A.D. 1863, all persons held as slaves within any state or designated part of a state the people whereof shall then be in rebellion against the United States shall be then, thenceforward, and forever free; and the executive government of the United States, including the military and naval authority thereof, will recognize and maintain the freedom of such persons and will do no act or acts to repress such persons, or any of them, in any efforts they may make for their actual freedom.

> That the executive will on the first day of January aforesaid, by proclamation, designate the states and parts of states, if any, in which the people thereof, respectively, shall then be in rebellion against the United States; and the fact that any state or the people thereof shall on that day be in good faith represented in the Congress of the United States by members chosen thereto at elections wherein a majority of the qualified voters of such state shall have participated shall, in the absence of strong countervailing testimony, be deemed conclusive evidence that such state and the people thereof are not then in rebellion against the United States.

Now, therefore, I, Abraham Lincoln, President of the United States, by virtue of the power in me vested as Commander in Chief of the Army and Navy of the United States in time of actual armed rebellion against the authority and government of the United States, and as a fit and necessary war measure for suppressing said rebellion, do, on this first day of

January, A.D. 1863, and in accordance with my purpose so to do, publicly proclaimed for the full period of one hundred days from the first day above mentioned, order and designate as the states and parts of states wherein the people thereof, respectively, are this day in rebellion against the United States the following, to wit:

Arkansas, Texas, Louisiana (except the parishes of St. Bernard, Plaquemines, Jefferson, St. John, St. Charles, St. James, Ascension, Assumption, Terrebonne, Lafourche, St. Mary, St. Martin, and Orleans, including the city of New Orleans), Mississippi, Alabama, Florida, Georgia, South Carolina, North Carolina, and Virginia (except the forty-eight counties designated as West Virginia, and also the counties of Berkeley, Accomac, Northampton, Elizabeth City, York, Princess Anne, and Norfolk, including the cities of Norfolk and Portsmouth), and which excepted parts are for the present left precisely as if this proclamation were not issued.

And by virtue of the power and for the purpose aforesaid, I do order and declare that all persons held as slaves within said designated states and parts of states are, and henceforward shall be, free; and that the executive government of the United States, including the military and naval authorities thereof, will recognize and maintain the freedom of said persons.

And I hereby enjoin upon the people so declared to be free to abstain from all violence, unless in necessary self-defense; and I recommend to them that, in all cases when allowed, they labor faithfully for reasonable wages.

And I further declare and make known that such persons of suitable condition will be received into the armed service of the United States to garrison forts, positions, stations, and other places, and to man vessels of all sorts in said service.

And upon this act, sincerely believed to be an act of justice, warranted by the Constitution upon military necessity, I invoke the considerate judgment of mankind and the gracious favor of Almighty God.

In witness whereof I have hereunto set my hand and caused the seal of the United States to be affixed.

Done at the city of Washington, this first day of January, A.D. 1863, and of the independence of the United States of America the eighty-seventh.

LETTER TO GENERAL JOSEPH HOOKER

Executive Mansion, Washington, D.C.,
January 26, 1863

General:

I have placed you at the head of the Army of the Potomac. Of course I have done this upon what appear to me to be sufficient reasons, and yet I think it best for you to know that there are some things in regard to which I am not quite satisfied with you. I believe you to be a brave and skillful soldier, which of course I like. I also believe you do not mix politics with your profession, in which you are right. You have confidence in yourself, which is a valuable if not an indispensable quality. You are ambitious, which within reasonable bounds does good rather than harm; but I think that during General Burnside's command of the army you have taken counsel of your ambition and thwarted him as much as you could, in which you did a great wrong to the country and to a most meritorious and honorable brother officer.

I have heard, in such a way as to believe it, of your recently saying that both the army and the government needed a dictator. Of course it was not for this, but in spite of it, that I have given you the command. Only those generals who gain successes can set up dictators. What I now ask of you is military success, and I will risk the dictatorship. The government will support you to the utmost of its ability, which is neither more nor less than it has done and will do for all commanders. I much fear that the spirit that you have aided to infuse into the army, of criticizing their commander and withholding confidence from him, will now turn upon you. I shall assist you as far as I can to put it down. Neither you nor Napoleon, if he were alive again, could get any good out of an army while such a spirit prevails in it.

And now beware of rashness. Beware of rashness, but with energy and sleepless vigilance go forward and give us victories.

Yours very truly,
A. Lincoln

Letter to General Ulysses S. Grant

Executive Mansion, Washington,
July 13, 1863

My dear General:

I do not remember that you and I ever met personally. I write this now as a grateful acknowledgment of the almost inestimable service you have done the country. I write to say a word further. When you first reached the vicinity of Vicksburg, I thought you should do what you finally did—march the troops across the neck, run the batteries with the transports, and thus go below; and I never had any faith except a general hope that you knew better than I, that the Yazoo Pass expedition and the like could succeed. When you dropped below, and took Port Gibson, Grand Gulf, and vicinity, I thought you should go down the river and join General Banks; and when you turned northward, east of the Big Black, I feared it was a mistake. I now wish to make the personal acknowledgment that you were right and I was wrong.

Yours very truly,
A. Lincoln

LETTER TO
JAMES H. HACKETT

Executive Mansion, Washington,
August 17, 1863

My dear Sir:

Months ago I should have acknowledged the receipt of your book and accompanying kind note; and I now have to beg your pardon for not having done so.

For one of my age I have seen very little of the drama. The first presentation of Falstaff I ever saw was yours here, last winter or spring. Perhaps the best compliment I can pay is to say, as I truly can, I am very anxious to see it again. Some of Shakespeare's plays I have never read, while others I have gone over perhaps as frequently as any unprofessional reader. Among the latter are *Lear, Richard III, Henry VIII, Hamlet,* and especially *Macbeth*. I think nothing equals *Macbeth*. It is wonderful.

Unlike you gentlemen of the profession, I think the soliloquy in *Hamlet* commencing "Oh, my offense is rank" surpasses that commencing "To be or not to be." But pardon this small attempt at criticism. I should like to hear you pronounce the opening speech of *Richard III*. Will you not soon visit Washington again? If you do, please call and let me make your personal acquaintance.

Yours truly,
A. LINCOLN

LETTER TO
JAMES C. CONKLING

Executive Mansion, Washington,
August 26, 1863

My dear Sir:

Your letter inviting me to attend a mass meeting of unconditional Union men, to be held at the capital of Illinois, on the 3d day of September, has been received. It would be very agreeable for me thus to meet my old friends at my own home, but I cannot just now be absent from here so long as a visit there would require.

The meeting is to be of all those who maintain unconditional devotion to the Union, and I am sure that my old political friends will thank me for tendering, as I do, the nation's gratitude to those other noble men whom no partisan malice or partisan hope can make false to the nation's life.

There are those who are dissatisfied with me. To such I would say: You desire peace, and you blame me that we do not have it. But how can we obtain it? There are but three conceivable ways: *First*, to suppress the rebellion by force of arms. This I am trying to do. Are you for it? If you are, so far we are agreed. If you are not for it, a *second* way is to give up the Union. I am against this. Are you for it? If you are you should say so plainly. If you are not for *force* nor yet for *dissolution*, there only remains some imaginable *compromise*.

I do not believe that any compromise embracing the maintenance of the Union is now possible. All that I learn leads to a directly opposite belief. The strength of the rebellion is its military, its army. That army dominates all the country and all the people within its range. Any offer of terms made by any man or men within that range, in opposition to that army, is simply nothing for the present; because such man or men have no power whatever to enforce their side of a compromise, if one were made with them.

To illustrate: Suppose refugees from the South and peace men of the North get together in convention, and frame and proclaim a compromise embracing a restoration of the Union. In what way can that compromise be used to keep Lee's army out of Pennsylvania? Meade's army can keep Lee's army out of Pennsylvania, and, I think, can ultimately drive it out of existence. But no paper compromise to which the controllers of Lee's army are not agreed can at all affect that army. In an effort at such compromise we would waste time, which the enemy would improve to our disadvantage; and that would be all.

A compromise, to be effective, must be made either with those who control the rebel army, or with the people, first liberated from the domination of that army by the success of our own army. Now allow me to assure you that no word or intimation from that rebel army, or from any of the men controlling it, in relation to any peace compromise, has ever come to my knowledge or belief. All charges and insinuations to the contrary are deceptive and groundless. And I promise you that if any such proposition shall hereafter come, it shall not be rejected and kept a secret from you. I freely acknowledge myself to be the servant of the people, according to the bond of service, the United States Constitution, and that, as such, I am responsible to them.

But, to be plain: You are dissatisfied with me about the Negro. Quite likely there is a difference of opinion between you and myself upon that subject. I certainly wish that all men could be free, while you, I suppose, do not. Yet, I have neither adopted nor proposed any measure which is not consistent with even your view, provided you are for the Union. I suggested compensated emancipation; to which you replied you wished not to be taxed to buy Negroes. But I had not asked you to be taxed to buy Negroes, except in such way as to save you from greater taxation to save the Union exclusively by other means.

You dislike the Emancipation Proclamation, and perhaps

would have it retracted. You say it is unconstitutional. I think differently. I think the Constitution invests its commander in chief with the law of war in time of war. The most that can be said, if so much, is, that slaves are property. Is there, has there ever been, any question that by the law of war, property, both of enemies and friends, may be taken when needed? And is it not needed whenever it helps us and hurts the enemy? Armies, the world over, destroy enemies' property when they cannot use it, and even destroy their own to keep it from the enemy. Civilized belligerents do all in their power to help themselves or hurt the enemy, except a few things regarded as barbarous or cruel. Among the exceptions are the massacre of vanquished foes and noncombatants, male and female.

But the proclamation, as law, either is valid or is not valid. If it is not valid it needs no retraction. If it is valid it cannot be retracted, any more than the dead can be brought to life. Some of you profess to think its retraction would operate favorably for the Union. Why better *after* the retraction than *before* the issue? There was more than a year and a half of trial to suppress the rebellion before the proclamation was issued, the last one hundred days of which passed under an explicit notice that it was coming, unless averted by those in revolt returning to their allegiance. The war has certainly progressed as favorably for us since the issue of the proclamation as before.

I know, as fully as one can know the opinions of others, that some of the commanders of our armies in the field, who have given us our most important victories, believe the emancipation policy and the use of colored troops constitute the heaviest blows yet dealt to the rebellion, and that at least one of those important successes could not have been achieved when it was but for the aid of black soldiers.

Among the commanders who hold these views are some who have never had any affinity with what is called "abolition-ism," or with "Republican party politics," but who hold them purely as military opinions. I submit their opinions as entitled to some weight against the objections often urged that emancipation and arming the blacks are unwise as military measures, and were not adopted as such in good faith.

You say that you will not fight to free Negroes. Some of them seem willing to fight for you; but no matter. Fight you, then, exclusively, to save the Union. I issued the proclamation on purpose to aid you in saving the Union. Whenever you shall have conquered all resistance to the Union, if I shall urge you to continue fighting, it will be an apt time then for you to declare you will not fight to free Negroes. I thought that in your struggle for the Union, to whatever extent the Negroes should cease helping the enemy, to that extent it weakened the enemy in his resistance to you. Do you think differently? I thought that whatever Negroes can be got to do as soldiers, leaves just so much less for white soldiers to do in saving the Union. Does it appear otherwise to you? But Negroes, like other people, act upon motives. Why should they do anything for us if we will do nothing for them? If they stake their lives for us they must be prompted by the strongest motive, even the promise of freedom. And the promise, being made, must be kept.

The signs look better. The Father of Waters again goes unvexed to the sea. Thanks to the great Northwest for it; nor yet wholly to them. Three hundred miles up they met New England, Empire, Keystone, and Jersey, hewing their way right and left. The sunny South, too, in more colors than one, also lent a helping hand. On the spot, their part of the history was jotted down in black and white. The job was a great national one, and let none be slighted who bore an honorable part in it. And while those who have cleared the great river may well be proud, even that is not all. It is hard to say that anything has been more bravely and well done than an Antietam, Murfreesboro, Gettysburg, and on many fields of less note. Nor must Uncle Sam's web-feet be forgotten. At all the watery margins they have been present; not only on the deep sea, the broad bay, and the rapid river, but also up the narrow, muddy bayou, and wherever the ground was a little damp, they have been and made their tracks. Thanks to all. For the great Republic—for the principle it lives by and keeps alive—for man's vast future—thanks to all.

Peace does not appear so distant as it did. I hope it will come soon, and come to stay, and so come as to be worth the keeping in all future time. It will then have been proved that among free men there can be no successful appeal from the ballot to the bullet, and that they who take such appeal are sure to lose their case and pay the cost. And there will be some black men who can remember that with silent tongue, and clinched teeth, and steady eye, and well-poised bayonet, they have helped mankind on to this great consummation; while I fear there will be some white ones unable to forget that with malignant heart and deceitful speech they have striven to hinder it.

Still, let us not be oversanguine of a speedy, final triumph. Let us be quite sober. Let us diligently apply the means, never doubting that a just God, in His own good time, will give us the rightful result.

Yours very truly,
A. Lincoln

THE GETTYSBURG
ADDRESS

November 19, 1863

Fourscore and seven years ago our fathers brought forth on this continent, a new nation, conceived in liberty, and dedicated to the proposition that all men are created equal.

Now we are engaged in a great civil war, testing whether that nation or any nation so conceived and so dedicated, can long endure. We are met on a great battlefield of that war. We have come to dedicate a portion of that field, as a final resting place for those who here gave their lives that that nation might live. It is altogether fitting and proper that we should do this.

But, in a larger sense, we cannot dedicate—we cannot consecrate—we cannot hallow—this ground. The brave men, living and dead, who struggled here, have consecrated it, far above our poor power to add or detract. The world will little note, nor long remember what we say here, but it can never forget what they did here. It is for us the living, rather, to be dedicated here to the unfinished work which they who fought here have thus far so nobly advanced. It is rather for us to be here dedicated to the great task remaining before us—that from these honored dead we take increased devotion to that cause for which they gave the last full measure of devotion—that we here highly resolve that these dead shall not have died in vain—that this nation, under God, shall have a new birth of freedom—and that government of the people, by the people, for the people, shall not perish from the earth.

PROCLAMATION ON AMNESTY AND RECONSTRUCTION

December 8, 1863

Whereas, In and by the Constitution of the United States it is provided that the president "shall have power to grant reprieves and pardons for offenses against the United States, except in cases of impeachment"; and,

Whereas, A rebellion now exists whereby the loyal state governments of several states have for a long time been subverted, and many persons have committed and are now guilty of treason against the United States; and,

Whereas, With reference to said rebellion and treason, laws have been enacted by Congress declaring forfeitures and confiscation of property and liberation of slaves, all upon terms and conditions therein stated, and also declaring that the president was thereby authorized at any time thereafter, by proclamation, to extend to persons who may have participated in the existing rebellion in any state or part thereof pardon and amnesty, with such exceptions and at such times and on such conditions as he may deem expedient for the public welfare; and,

Whereas, The congressional declaration for limited and conditional pardon accords with well-established judicial exposition of the pardoning power; and,

Whereas, With reference to said rebellion, the president of the United States has issued several proclamations with provisions in regard to the liberation of slaves; and,

Whereas, It is now desired by some persons heretofore engaged in said rebellion to resume their allegiance to the United States and to reinaugurate loyal state governments within and for their respective states:

Therefore, I, Abraham Lincoln, President of the United States, do proclaim, declare, and make known to all persons who have, directly or by implication, participated in the existing rebellion, except as hereinafter excepted, that a full pardon is hereby granted to them and each of them, with restoration of all rights of property, except as to slaves and in property cases where rights of third parties shall have intervened, and upon the condition that every such person shall take and subscribe an oath and thenceforward keep and maintain said oath inviolate, and which oath shall be registered for permanent preservation and shall be of the tenor and effect following, to wit:

I, ———— ————, do solemnly swear, in presence of Almighty God, that I will henceforth faithfully support, protect, and defend the Constitution of the United States and the Union of the states thereunder; and that I will in like manner abide by and faithfully support all acts of Congress passed during the existing rebellion with reference to slaves, so long and so far as not repealed, modified, or held void by Congress or by decision of the Supreme Court; and that I will in like manner abide by and faithfully support all proclamations of the president made during the existing rebellion having reference to slaves, so long and so far as not modified or declared void by decision of the Supreme Court. So help me God.

The persons excepted from the benefits of the foregoing provisions are all who are or shall have been civil or diplomatic officers or agents of the so-called Confederate government; all who have left judicial stations under the United States to aid the rebellion; all who are or shall have been military or naval officers of said so-called Confederate government above the rank of colonel in the army or of lieutenant in the navy; all who left seats in the United States Congress to aid the rebellion; all who resigned commissions in the Army or Navy of the United States and afterwards aided the rebellion; and all who have engaged in any way in treating colored persons, or white persons in charge of such, otherwise than lawfully as prisoners of war, and which persons may have been found in the United States service as soldiers, seamen, or in any other capacity.

And I do further proclaim, declare, and make known that whenever, in any of the states of Arkansas, Texas, Louisiana, Mississippi, Tennessee, Alabama, Georgia, Florida, South Carolina, and North Carolina, a number of persons, not less than one-tenth in number of the votes cast in such state at the presidential election of the year A.D. 1860, each having taken oath aforesaid, and not having since violated it, and being a qualified voter by the election law of the state existing immediately before the so-called act of secession, and excluding all others, shall reestablish a state government which shall be republican and in nowise contravening said oath, such shall be recognized as the true government of the state, and the state shall receive thereunder the benefits of the constitutional provision which declares that "the United States shall guarantee to every state in this Union a republican form of government and shall protect each of them against invasion, and, on application of the legislature, or the executive (when the legislature can not be convened), against domestic violence."

And I do further proclaim, declare, and make known that any provision which may be adopted by such state government in relation to the freed people of such state which shall recognize and declare their permanent freedom, provide for their education, and which may yet be consistent as a temporary arrangement with their present condition as a laboring, landless, and homeless class, will not be objected to by the national executive.

And it is suggested as not improper that in constructing a loyal state government in any state the name of the state, the boundary, the subdivisions, the constitution, and the general code of laws as before the rebellion be maintained, subject only to the modifications made necessary by the conditions hereinbefore stated, and such others, if any, not contravening said conditions and which may be deemed expedient by those framing the new state government.

To avoid misunderstanding, it may be proper to say that

this proclamation, so far as it relates to state governments, has no reference to states wherein loyal state governments have all the while been maintained. And for the same reason it may be proper to further say that whether members sent to Congress from any state shall be admitted to seats constitutionally rests exclusively with the respective houses, and not to any extent with the executive. And, still further, that this proclamation is intended to present the people of the states wherein the national authority has been suspended and loyal state governments have been subverted a mode in and by which the national authority and loyal state governments may be reestablished within said states or in any of them; and while the mode presented is the best the executive can suggest, with his present impressions, it must not be understood that no other possible mode would be acceptable.

Given under my hand at the city of Washington, the eighth day of December, A.D. 1863, and of the independence of the United States of America the eighty-eighth.

Address to General Ulysses S. Grant

March 9, 1864

General Grant: The expression of the nation's approbation of what you have already done, and its reliance on you for what remains to do in the existing great struggle, is now presented with this commission constituting you Lieutenant-General of the Army of the United States.

With this high honor, devolves on you an additional responsibility. As the country herein trusts you, so, under God, it will sustain you. I scarcely need add, that with what I here speak for the country, goes my own hearty personal concurrence.

REPLY TO THE
COMMITTEE OF THE
NATIONAL UNION
[REPUBLICAN]
CONVENTION

NOTIFYING PRESIDENT LINCOLN
OF HIS RENOMINATION

June 9, 1864

Mr. Chairman and Gentlemen of the Committee: I will neither conceal my gratification nor restrain the expression of my gratitude that the Union people, through their convention, in their continued effort to save and advance the nation, have deemed me not unworthy to remain in my present position. I know no reason to doubt that I shall accept the nomination tendered; and yet perhaps I should not declare definitely before reading and considering what is called the platform. I will say now, however, I approve the declaration in favor of so amending the Constitution as to prohibit slavery throughout the nation. When the people in revolt, with a hundred days of explicit notice that they could within those days resume their allegiance without the overthrow of their institution, and that they could not so resume it afterward, elected to stand out, such amendment of the Constitution as now proposed became a fitting and necessary conclusion to the final success of the Union cause. Such alone can meet and cover all cavils. Now the unconditional Union men, North and South, perceive its importance and embrace it. In the joint names of Liberty and Union, let us labor to give it legal form and practical effect.

LETTER TO THE COMMITTEE OF THE NATIONAL UNION CONVENTION

Executive Mansion, Washington,
June 27, 1864

Gentlemen:

Your letter of the 14th instant, formally notifying me that I have been nominated by the convention you represent for the presidency of the United States for four years from the 4th of March next, has been received. The nomination is gratefully accepted, as the resolutions of the convention, called the platform, are heartily approved.

While the resolution in regard to the supplanting of republican government upon the Western Continent is fully concurred in, there might be misunderstanding were I not to say that the position of the government in relation to the action of France in Mexico, as assumed through the State Department and endorsed by the convention among the measures and acts of the executive, will be faithfully maintained so long as the state of facts shall leave that position pertinent and applicable.

I am especially gratified that the soldier and seaman were not forgotten by the convention, as they forever must and will be remembered by the grateful country for whose salvation they devote their lives.

Thanking you for the kind and complimentary terms in which you have communicated the nomination and other proceedings of the convention, I subscribe myself,

Your obedient servant,
ABRAHAM LINCOLN

Proclamation Authorizing a Day of Prayer

July 7, 1864

Whereas, The Senate and House of Representatives at their last session adopted a concurrent resolution, which was approved on the second day of July instant, and which was in the words following, namely:

That the president of the United States be requested to appoint a day of humiliation and prayer by the people of the United States, that he request his constitutional advisers at the head of the executive departments to unite with him, as chief magistrate of the nation, at the city of Washington, and the members of Congress, and all magistrates, all civil, military, and naval officers, all soldiers, sailors, and marines, with all loyal and law-abiding people, to convene at their usual places of worship, or wherever they may be, to confess and to repent of their manifold sins, to implore the compassion and forgiveness of the Almighty, that if consistent with His will, the existing rebellion may be speedily suppressed, and the supremacy of the Constitution and laws of the United States may be established throughout all the states; to implore Him, as the Supreme Ruler of the World, not to destroy us as a people, nor suffer us to be destroyed by the hostility or connivance of other nations, or by obstinate adhesion to our own counsels which may be in conflict with His eternal purposes, and to implore Him to enlighten the mind of the nation to know and do His will, humbly believing that it is in accordance with His will that our place should be maintained as a united people among the family of nations; to implore Him to grant to our armed defenders, and the masses of the people, that courage, power of resistance, and endurance necessary to secure that result; to implore Him in His infinite goodness to soften the hearts, enlighten the minds, and quicken the conscience of those in rebellion, that they may lay down their arms, and speedily return to their allegiance to the United States, that they may not be utterly destroyed, that the effusion of blood may be stayed, and that unity and fraternity may be restored, and peace established throughout all our borders.

Now, therefore, I, Abraham Lincoln, President of the United States, cordially concurring with the Congress of the United States, in the penitential and pious sentiments expressed in the aforesaid resolutions, and heartily approving of the devotional design and purpose thereof, do hereby appoint the first Thursday of August next to be observed by the people of the United States as a day of national humiliation and prayer.

I do hereby further invite and request the heads of the executive departments of this government, together with all legislators, all judges and magistrates, and all other persons exercising authority in the land, whether civil, military, or naval, and all soldiers, seamen, and marines in the national service, and all other loyal and law-abiding people of the United States, to assemble in their preferred places of public worship on that day, and there to render to the Almighty and Merciful Ruler of the Universe, such homage and such confessions, and to offer to Him such supplications as the Congress of the United States have, in their aforesaid resolution, so solemnly, so earnestly, and so reverently recommended.

In testimony whereof, I have hereunto set my hand and caused the seal of the United States to be affixed.

Done at the city of Washington this seventh day of July, in the year of Our Lord one thousand eight hundred and sixty-four, and of the independence of the United States the eighty-ninth.

PROCLAMATION ON RECONSTRUCTION

July 8, 1864

Whereas, At the late session Congress passed a bill "to guarantee to certain states whose governments have been usurped or overthrown a republican form of government," a copy of which is hereunto annexed; and,

Whereas, The said bill was presented to the president of the United States for his approval less than one hour before the *sine die* adjournment of said session, and was not signed by him; and,

Whereas, The said bill contains, among other things, a plan for restoring the states in rebellion to their proper practical relation in the Union, which plan expresses the sense of Congress upon that subject, and which plan it is now thought fit to lay before the people for their consideration:

Now, therefore, I, Abraham Lincoln, President of the United States, do proclaim, declare, and make known that while I am (as I was in December last, when, by proclamation, I propounded a plan for restoration) unprepared by a formal approval of this bill to be inflexibly committed to any single plan of restoration, and while I am also unprepared to declare that the free state constitutions and governments already adopted and installed in Arkansas and Louisiana shall be set aside and held for naught, thereby repelling and discouraging the loyal citizens who have set up the same as to further effort, or to declare a constitutional competency in Congress to abolish slavery in states, but am at the same time sincerely hoping and expecting that a constitutional amendment abolishing slavery throughout the nation may be adopted, nevertheless I am fully satisfied with the system for restoration contained in the bill as óne very proper plan for the loyal people of any state choosing to adopt it, and that I am and at all times shall be prepared to give the executive aid and assistance to any such people so soon as the military resistance to the United States shall have been suppressed in any such state and the people thereof shall have sufficiently returned to their obedience to the Constitution and the laws of the United States, in which cases military governors will be appointed with directions to proceed according to the bill.

In testimony whereof I have hereunto set my hand and caused the seal of the United States to be affixed.

Done at the city of Washington, this eighth day of July, A.D. 1864, and of the independence of the United States the eighty-ninth.

LETTER TO
HORACE GREELEY

Washington, D.C., July 9, 1864

Dear Sir:

Your letter of the 7th, with enclosures, received.

If you can find any person, anywhere, professing to have any proposition of Jefferson Davis in writing, for peace, embracing the restoration of the Union and abandonment of slavery, whatever else it embraces, say to him he may come to me with you; and that if he really brings such proposition, he shall at the least have safe conduct with the paper (and without publicity, if he chooses) to the point where you shall have to meet him. The same if there be two or more persons.

Yours truly,

A. LINCOLN

LETTER TO
ELIZA P. GURNEY

Executive Mansion, Washington,
September 4, 1864

My esteemed Friend:

I have not forgotten—probably never shall forget—the very impressive occasion when yourself and friends visited me on a Sabbath forenoon two years ago—nor has your kind letter, written nearly a year later, even been forgotten. In all, it has been your purpose to strengthen my reliance on God. I am much indebted to the good Christian people of the country for their constant prayer and consolations; and to no one of them, more than to yourself. The purposes of the Almighty are perfect, and must prevail, though we erring mortals may fail to accurately perceive them in advance. We hoped for a happy termination of this terrible war long before this; but God knows best, and has ruled otherwise. We shall yet acknowledge His wisdom, and our own error therein. Meanwhile we must work earnestly in the best light He gives us, trusting that so working still conduces to the great ends He ordains. Surely He intends some great good to follow this mighty convulsion, which no mortal could make, and no mortal could stay.

Your people—the Friends—have had, and are having, a very great trial. On principle, and faith, opposed to both war and oppression, they can only practically oppose oppression by war. For those appealing to me on conscientious grounds, I have done, and shall do, the best I could and can, in my own conscience, under my oath to the law. That you believe this I doubt not, and believing it, I shall still receive, for our country and myself your earnest prayers to our Father in heaven.

Your sincere friend,
A. LINCOLN

RESPONSE TO A SERENADE

November 10, 1864

It has long been a grave question whether any government, not too strong for the liberties of its people, can be strong enough to maintain its existence in great emergencies. On this point the present rebellion brought our government to a severe test, and a presidential election occurring in regular course during the rebellion, added not a little to the strain.

If the loyal people united were put to the utmost of their strength by the rebellion, must they not fail when divided and partially paralyzed by a political war among themselves? But the election was a necessity. We cannot have free government without elections; and if the war could force us to forego or postpone a national election, it might fairly claim to have already conquered and ruined us. The strife of the election is but human nature practically applied to the facts of the case. What has occurred in this case must ever recur in similar cases. Human nature will not change. In any future great national trial, compared with the men of this, we will have as weak and as strong, as silly and as wise, as bad and as good. Let us, therefore, study the incidents of this as philosophy to learn wisdom from, and none of them as wrongs to be revenged.

But the election, along with its incidental and undesirable strife, has done good, too. It has demonstrated that a people's government can sustain a national election in the midst of a great civil war. Until now, it has not been known to the world that this was a possibility. It shows, also, how sound and strong we still are. It shows that even among the candidates of the same party, he who is most devoted to the Union and most opposed to treason can receive most of the people's votes. It shows, also, to the extent yet known, that we have more men now than we had when the war began. Gold is good in its place; but living, brave, and patriotic men are better than gold.

But the rebellion continues, and, now that the election is over, may not all have a common interest to reunite in a common effort to save our common country? For my own part, I have striven and shall strive to avoid placing any obstacle in the way. So long as I have been here, I have not willingly planted a thorn in any man's bosom. While I am duly sensible to the high compliment of a reelection, and duly grateful, as I trust, to Almighty God, for having directed my countrymen to a right conclusion, as I think, for their good, it adds nothing to my satisfaction that any other man may be disappointed by the result.

May I ask those who have not differed with me to join with me in this same spirit towards those who have? And now, let me close by asking three hearty cheers for our brave soldiers and seamen, and their gallant and skillful commanders.

Fourth Annual Message to Congress

December 6, 1864

Fellow Citizens of the Senate and House of Representatives: Again the blessings of health and abundant harvests claim our profoundest gratitude to Almighty God.

The condition of our foreign affairs is reasonably satisfactory.

Mexico continues to be a theater of civil war. While our political relations with that country have undergone no change, we have at the same time strictly maintained neutrality between the belligerents.

At the request of the states of Costa Rica and Nicaragua, a competent engineer has been authorized to make a survey of the river San Juan and the port of San Juan. It is a source of much satisfaction that the difficulties which for a moment excited some political apprehensions and caused a closing of the interoceanic transit route have been amicably adjusted, and that there is a good prospect that the route will soon be reopened with an increase of capacity and adaptation. We could not exaggerate either the commercial or the political importance of that great improvement.

It would be doing injustice to an important South American state not to acknowledge the directness, frankness, and cordiality with which the United States of Colombia have entered into intimate relations with this government. A claims convention has been constituted to complete the unfinished work of the one which closed its session in 1861.

The new liberal constitution of Venezuela having gone into effect with the universal acquiescence of the people, the government under it has been recognized and diplomatic intercourse with it has opened in a cordial and friendly spirit. The long-deferred Aves Island claim has been satisfactorily paid and discharged.

Mutual payments have been made of the claims awarded by the late joint commission for the settlement of claims between the United States and Peru. An earnest and cordial friendship continues to exist between the two countries, and such efforts as were in my power have been used to remove misunderstanding, and avert a threatened war between Peru and Spain.

Our relations are of the most friendly nature with Chile, the Argentine Republic, Bolivia, Costa Rica, Paraguay, San Salvador, and Haiti.

During the past year no differences of any kind have arisen with any of these republics, and on the other hand, their sympathies with the United States are constantly expressed with cordiality and earnestness.

The claim arising from the seizure of the cargo of the brig *Macedonian* in 1821 has been paid in full by the government of Chile.

Civil war continues in the Spanish part of San Domingo, apparently without prospect of an early close.

Official correspondence has been freely opened with Liberia, and it gives us a pleasing view of social and political progress in that republic. It may be expected to derive new vigor from American influence improved by the rapid disappearance of slavery in the United States.

I solicit your authority to furnish to the republic a gunboat, at moderate cost, to be reimbursed to the United States by installments. Such a vessel is needed for the safety of that state against the native African races, and in Liberian hands it would be more effective in arresting the African slave trade than a squadron in our own hands. The possession of the least organized naval force would stimulate a generous ambition in the republic, and the confidence which we should manifest by furnishing it would win forbearance and favor toward the colony from all civilized nations.

The proposed overland telegraph between America and Europe, by the way of Bering Straits and Asiatic Russia, which was sanctioned by Congress at the last session, has been undertaken, under very favorable circumstances, by an association of American citizens, with the cordial goodwill and support as well of this government as of those of Great Britain and Russia. Assurances have been received from most of the South American states of their high appreciation of the enterprise and their readiness to cooperate in constructing lines tributary to that world-encircling communication. I learn with much satisfaction that the noble design of a telegraphic communication between the eastern coast of America and Great Britain has been renewed, with full expectation of its early accomplishment.

Thus it is hoped that with the return of domestic peace the country will be able to resume with energy and advantage its former high career of commerce and civilization.

Our very popular and estimable representative in Egypt died in April last. An unpleasant altercation which arose between the temporary incumbent of the office and the government of the Pasha resulted in a suspension of intercourse. The evil was promptly corrected on the arrival of the successor in the consulate, and our relations with Egypt, as well as our relations with the Barbary Powers, are entirely satisfactory.

The rebellion which has so long been flagrant in China has at last been suppressed, with the cooperating good offices of this government and of the other Western commercial states. The judicial consular establishment there has become very difficult and onerous, and it will need legislative revision to adapt it to the extension of our commerce and to the more intimate intercourse which has been instituted with the government and people of that vast empire. China seems to be accepting with hearty goodwill the conventional laws which regulate commercial and social intercourse among the Western nations.

Owing to the peculiar situation of Japan and the anomalous form of its government, the action of that empire in performing treaty stipulations is inconstant and capricious. Nevertheless, good progress has been effected by the Western powers, moving with enlightened concert. Our own pecuniary claims have been allowed or put in course of settlement, and the inland sea has been reopened to commerce. There is reason also to believe that these proceedings have increased rather than diminished the friendship of Japan toward the United States.

The ports of Norfolk, Fernandina, and Pensacola have been opened by proclamation. It is hoped that foreign merchants will now consider whether it is not safer and more profitable to themselves, as well as just to the United States, to resort to these and other open ports than it is to pursue, through many hazards and at vast cost, a contraband trade with other ports which are closed, if not by actual military occupation, at least by a lawful and effective blockade.

For myself, I have no doubt of the power and duty of the executive, under the law of nations, to exclude enemies of the human race from an asylum in the United States. If Congress should think that proceedings in such cases lack the authority of law, or ought to be further regulated by it, I recommend that provision be made for effectually preventing foreign slave traders from acquiring domicile and facilities for their criminal occupation in our country.

It is possible that if it were a new and open question the maritime powers, with the lights they now enjoy, would not concede the privileges of a naval belligerent to the insurgents of the United States, destitute, as they are, and always have been, equally of ships of war and of ports and harbors. Disloyal emissaries have been neither assiduous nor more successful during the last year than they were before that time in their efforts, under favor of that privilege, to embroil our country in foreign wars. The desire and determination of the governments of the maritime states to defeat that design are believed to be as sincere as and cannot be more earnest than our own. Nevertheless, unforeseen political difficulties have arisen, especially in Brazilian and British ports and on the northern boundary of the United States, which have required, and are likely to continue to require, the practice of constant vigilance and a just and conciliatory spirit on the part of the United States, as well as of the nations concerned and their governments.

Commissioners have been appointed under the treaty with Great Britain on the adjustment of the claims of the Hudson Bay and Puget Sound agricultural companies, in Oregon, and are now proceeding to the execution of the trust assigned to them.

In view of the insecurity of life and property in the region adjacent to the Canadian border, by reason of recent assaults and depredations committed by inimical and desperate persons who are harbored there, it has been thought proper to give notice that after the expiration of six months, the period conditionally stipulated in the existing arrangement with Great Britain, the United States must hold themselves at liberty to increase their naval armament upon the Lakes if they shall find that proceeding necessary. The condition of the border will necessarily come into consideration in connection with the question of continuing or modifying the rights of transit from Canada through the United States, as well as the regulation of imposts, which were temporarily established by the reciprocity treaty of June 5, 1854.

I desire, however, to be understood while making this statement that the colonial authorities of Canada are not deemed to be intentionally unjust or unfriendly toward the United States, but, on the contrary, there is every reason to expect that, with the approval of the imperial government, they will take the necessary measures to prevent new incursions across the border.

The act passed at the last session for the encouragement of immigration has so far as was possible been put into operation. It seems to need amendment which will enable the officers of the government to prevent the practice of frauds against the immigrants while on their way and on their arrival in the ports, so as to secure them here a free choice of avocations and places of settlement. A liberal disposition toward this great national policy is manifested by most of the European states, and ought to be reciprocated on our part by giving the immigrants effective national protection. I regard our immigrants as one of the principal replenishing streams which are appointed by Providence to repair the ravages of internal war and its wastes of national strength and health. All that is necessary is to secure the flow of that stream in its present fullness, and to that end the government must in every way make it manifest that it neither needs nor designs to impose involuntary military service upon those who come from other lands to cast their lot in our country.

The financial affairs of the government have been successfully administered during the last year. The legislation of the last session of Congress has beneficially affected the revenues, although sufficient time has not yet elapsed to experience the full effect of several of the provisions of the acts of Congress imposing increased taxation.

The receipts during the year from all sources, upon the basis of warrants signed by the secretary of the Treasury, including loans and the balance in the Treasury on the first day of July 1863, were $1,394,796,007.62, and the aggregate disbursements, upon the same basis, were $1,298,056,101.89, leaving a balance in the Treasury, as shown by warrants, of $96,739,905.73. Deduct from these amounts the amount of the principal of the public debt redeemed and the amount of issues in substitution therefor, and the actual cash operations of the Treasury were: receipts, $884,076,646.57; disbursements, $865,234,087.86; which leaves a cash balance in the Treasury of $18,842,558.71. . . .

It is of noteworthy interest that the steady expansion of population, improvement, and governmental institutions over the new and unoccupied portions of our country have scarcely been checked, much less impeded or destroyed, by our great civil war, which at first glance would seem to have absorbed almost the entire energies of the nation.

The organization and admission of the state of Nevada has been completed in conformity with law, and thus our excellent system is firmly established in the mountains, which once seemed a barren and uninhabitable waste between the Atlantic states and those which have grown up on the coast of the Pacific Ocean.

The territories of the Union are generally in a condition of prosperity and rapid growth. Idaho and Montana, by reason of their great distance and the interruption of communication with them by Indian hostilities, have been only partially organized; but it is understood that these difficulties are about to disappear, which will permit their governments, like those of the others, to go into speedy and full operation. . . .

The great enterprise of connecting the Atlantic with the Pacific states by railways and telegraph lines has been entered upon with a vigor that gives assurance of success, notwithstanding the embarrassments arising from the prevailing high prices of materials and labor. The route of the main line of the road has been definitely located for one hundred miles westward from the initial point at Omaha City, Nebraska, and a preliminary location of the Pacific Railroad of California has been made from Sacramento eastward to the great bend of the Truckee River in Nevada.

Numerous discoveries of gold, silver, and cinnabar mines have been added to the many heretofore known, and the country occupied by the Sierra Nevada and Rocky mountains and the subordinate ranges now teems with enterprising labor, which is richly remunerative. It is believed that the produce of the mines of precious metals in that region has during the year reached, if not exceeded, $100 million in value.

It was recommended in my last annual message that our Indian system be remodeled. Congress at its last session, acting upon the recommendation, did provide for reorganizing the system in California, and it is believed that under the present organization the management of the Indians there will be attended with reasonable success. Much yet remains to be done to provide for the proper government of the Indians in other parts of the country, to render it secure for the advancing settler, and to provide for the welfare of the Indian. The secretary reiterates his recommendations, and to them the attention of Congress is invited. . . .

The war continues. Since the last annual message all the important lines and positions then occupied by our forces have been maintained and our arms have steadily advanced, thus liberating the regions left in rear, so that Missouri, Kentucky, Tennessee, and parts of other states have again produced reasonably fair crops.

The most remarkable feature in the military operations of the year is General Sherman's attempted march of three hundred miles directly through the insurgent region. It tends to show a great increase of our relative strength that our general in chief should feel able to confront and hold in check every active force of the enemy, and yet to detach a well-appointed large army to move on such an expedition. The result not yet being known, conjecture in regard to it is not here indulged.

Important movements have also occurred during the year to the effect of molding society for durability in the Union. Although short of complete success, it is much in the right direction that twelve thousand citizens in each of the states of Arkansas and Louisiana have organized loyal state governments, with free constitutions, and are earnestly struggling to maintain and administer them. The movements in the same direction more extensive though less definite in Missouri, Kentucky, and Tennessee, should not be overlooked. But Maryland presents the example of complete success. Maryland is secure to liberty and union for all the future. The genius of rebellion will no more claim Maryland. Like another foul spirit being driven out, it may seek to tear her, but it will woo her no more.

At the last session of Congress a proposed amendment of the Constitution abolishing slavery throughout the United States passed the Senate, but failed for lack of the requisite two-thirds vote in the House of Representatives. Although the present is the same Congress and nearly the same members, and without questioning the wisdom or patriotism of those who stood in opposition, I venture to recommend the reconsideration and passage of the measure at the present session. Of course the abstract question is not changed; but an intervening election shows almost certainly that the next Congress will pass the measure if this does not. Hence there is only a question of *time* as to when the proposed amendment will go to the states for their action. And as it is to so go at all events, may we not agree that the sooner the better? It is not claimed that the election has imposed a duty on members to change their views or their votes any further than, as an additional element to be considered, their judgment may be affected by it. It is the voice of the people now for the first time heard upon the question. In a great national crisis like ours, unanimity of action among those seeking a common end is very desirable—almost indispensable. And yet no approach to such unanimity is attainable unless some deference shall be paid to the will of the majority simply because it is the will of the majority. In this case the common end is the maintenance of the Union, and among the means to secure that end such will, through the election, is most clearly declared in favor of such constitutional amendment.

The most reliable indication of public purpose in this country is derived through our popular elections. Judging by the recent canvass and its result, the purpose of the people within the loyal states to maintain the integrity of the Union was never more firm nor more nearly unanimous than now. The extraordinary calmness and good order with which the millions of voters met and mingled at the polls give strong assurance of this. Not only all those who supported the Union ticket, so called, but a great majority of the opposing party also may be fairly claimed to entertain and to be actuated by the same purpose. It is an unanswerable argument to this effect that no candidate for any office whatever, high or low, has ventured to seek votes on the avowal that he was for giving up the Union. There have been much impugning of motives and much heated controversy as to the proper means and best mode of advancing the Union cause, but on the distinct issue of Union or no Union the politicians have shown their instinctive knowledge that there is no diversity among the people. In affording the people the fair opportunity of showing one to another and to the world this firmness and unanimity of purpose, the election has been of vast value to the national cause.

The election has exhibited another fact not less valuable to be known—the fact that we do not approach exhaustion in the most important branch of national resources, that of living men. While it is melancholy to reflect that the war has filled so many graves and carried mourning to so many hearts, it is some relief to know that, compared with the surviving, the fallen have been so few. While corps and divisions and brigades and regiments have formed and fought and dwindled and gone out of existence, a great majority of the men who composed them are still living. The same is true of the naval service. The election returns prove this. So many voters could not else be found. The states regularly holding elections, both now and four years ago, to wit, California, Connecticut, Delaware, Illinois, Indiana, Iowa, Kentucky, Maine, Maryland, Massachusetts, Michigan, Minnesota, Missouri, New Hampshire, New Jersey, New York, Ohio, Oregon, Pennsylvania, Rhode Island, Vermont, West Virginia, and Wisconsin, cast 3,982,011 votes now, against 3,870,222 cast then, showing an aggregate now of 3,982,011. To this is to be added 33,762 cast now in the new states of Kansas and Nevada, which states did not vote in 1860, thus swelling the aggregate to 4,015,773 and the net increase during the three years and a half of war to 145,551. . . . To this again should be added the number of all soldiers in the field from Massachusetts, Rhode Island, New Jersey, Delaware, Indiana, Illinois, and California, who by the laws of those states could not vote away from their homes, and which number cannot be less than ninety thousand. Nor yet is this all. The number in organized territories is triple now what it was four years ago, while thousands, white and black, join us as the national arms press back the insurgent lines. So much is shown, affirmatively and negatively, by the election. It is not material to inquire how the increase has been produced or to show that it would have been greater but for the war, which is probably true. The important fact remains demonstrated that we have *more* men *now* than we had when the war *began;* that we are not exhausted nor in process of exhaustion; that we are *gaining* strength and may if need be maintain the contest indefinitely. This as to men. Material resources are now more complete and abundant than ever.

The national resources, then, are unexhausted, and, as we believe, inexhaustible. The public purpose to reestablish and maintain the national authority is unchanged, and, as we believe, unchangeable. The manner of continuing the effort remains to choose. On careful consideration of all the evidence accessible it seems to me that no attempt at negotiation with the insurgent leader could result in any good. He would accept nothing short of severance of the Union, precisely what we will not and cannot give. His declarations to this effect are explicit and oft repeated. He does not attempt to deceive us. He affords us no excuse to deceive ourselves. He cannot voluntarily reaccept the Union; we cannot voluntarily yield it. Between him and us the issue is distinct, simple, and inflexible. It is an issue which can only be tried by war and decided by victory. If we yield, we are beaten; if the Southern people fail him, he is beaten. Either way it would be the victory and defeat following war. What is true, however, of him who heads the insurgent cause is not necessarily true of those who follow. Although he cannot reaccept the Union, they can. Some of them, we know, already desire peace and reunion. The number of such may increase. They can at any moment have peace simply by laying down their arms and submitting to the national authority under the Constitution. After so much the government could not, if it would, maintain war against them. The loyal people would not sustain or allow it. If questions should remain, we would adjust them by the peaceful means of legislation, conference, courts, and votes, operating only in constitutional and lawful channels. Some certain, and other possible, questions are and would be beyond the executive power to adjust; as, for instance, the admission of members into Congress and whatever might require the appropriation of money. The executive power itself would be greatly diminished by the cessation of actual war. Pardons and remissions of forfeitures, however, would still be within executive control. In what spirit and temper this control would be exercised can be fairly judged of by the past.

A year ago general pardon and amnesty, upon specified terms, were offered to all except certain designated classes, and it was at the same time made known that the excepted classes were still within contemplation of special clemency. During the year many availed themselves of the general provision, and many more would, only that the signs of bad faith in some led to such precautionary measures as rendered the practical process less easy and certain. During the same time also special pardons have been granted to individuals of the excepted classes, and no voluntary application has been denied. Thus practically the door has been for a full year open to all except such as were not in condition to make free choice; that is, such as were in custody or under constraint. It is still so open to all. But the time may come, probably will come, when public duty shall demand that it be closed and that in lieu more rigorous measures than heretofore shall be adopted.

In presenting the abandonment of armed resistance to the national authority on the part of the insurgents as the only indispensable condition to ending the war on the part of the government, I retract nothing heretofore said as to slavery. I repeat the declaration made a year ago, that "while I remain in my present position I shall not attempt to retract or modify the Emancipation Proclamation, nor shall I return to slavery any person who is free by the terms of that proclamation or by any of the acts of Congress." If the people should, by whatever mode or means, make it an executive duty to reenslave such persons, another, and not I, must be their instrument to perform it.

In stating a single condition of peace I mean simply to say that the war will cease on the part of the government whenever it shall have ceased on the part of those who began it.

LETTER TO GENERAL WILLIAM T. SHERMAN

Executive Mansion, Washington,
December 26, 1864

My dear General Sherman:

Many, many thanks for your Christmas gift, the capture of Savannah.

When you were about leaving Atlanta for the Atlantic coast, I was anxious, if not fearful; but feeling that you were the better judge, and remembering that "nothing risked, nothing gained," I did not interfere. Now, the undertaking being a success, the honor is all yours; for I believe none of us went further than to acquiesce.

And taking the work of General Thomas into the count, as it should be taken, it is indeed a great success. Not only does it afford the obvious and immediate military advantages; but in showing to the world that your army could be divided, putting the stronger part to an important new service, and yet leaving enough to vanquish the old opposing force of the whole— Hood's army—it brings those who sat in darkness to see a great light. But what next?

I suppose it will be safe if I leave General Grant and yourself to decide.

Please make my grateful acknowledgments to your whole army—officers and men.

Yours very truly,
A. LINCOLN

Letter to General Ulysses S. Grant

Executive Mansion, Washington,
January 19, 1865

Lieutenant-General Grant:

Please read and answer this letter as though I was not president, but only a friend. My son, now in his twenty-second year, having graduated at Harvard, wishes to see something of the war before it ends. I do not wish to put him in the ranks, nor yet to give him a commission, to which those who have already served long are better entitled and better qualified to hold. Could he, without embarrassment to you, or detriment to the service, go into your military family with some nominal rank, I, and not the public, furnishing his necessary means? If no, say so without the least hesitation, because I am as anxious and as deeply interested that you shall not be encumbered as you can be yourself.

Yours truly,
A. Lincoln

Second Inaugural Address

March 4, 1865

Fellow Countrymen: At this second appearing to take the oath of the presidential office there is less occasion for an extended address than there was at the first. Then a statement somewhat in detail of a course to be pursued seemed fitting and proper. Now, at the expiration of four years, during which public declarations have been constantly called forth on every point and phase of the great contest which still absorbs the attention and engrosses the energies of the nation, little that is new could be presented. The progress of our arms, upon which all else chiefly depends, is as well known to the public as to myself, and it is, I trust, reasonably satisfactory and encouraging to all. With high hope for the future, no prediction in regard to it is ventured.

On the occasion corresponding to this four years ago all thoughts were anxiously directed to an impending civil war. All dreaded it, all sought to avert it. While the inaugural address was being delivered from this place, devoted altogether to *saving* the Union without war, insurgent agents were in the city seeking to *destroy* it without war—seeking to dissolve the Union and divide effects by negotiation. Both parties deprecated war, but one of them would *make* war rather than let the nation survive, and the other would *accept* war rather than let it perish, and the war came.

One-eighth of the whole population was colored slaves, not distributed generally over the Union, but localized in the southern part of it. These slaves constituted a peculiar and powerful interest. All knew that this interest was somehow the cause of the war. To strengthen, perpetuate, and extend this interest was the object for which the insurgents would rend the Union even by war, while the government claimed no right to do more than to restrict the territorial enlargement of it. Neither party expected for the war the magnitude or the duration which it has already attained. Neither anticipated that the *cause* of the conflict might cease with or even before the conflict itself should cease. Each looked for an easier triumph, and a result less fundamental and astounding. Both read the same Bible and pray to the same God, and each invokes His aid against the other. It may seem strange that any men should dare to ask a just God's assistance in wringing their bread from the sweat of other men's faces, but let us judge not, that we be not judged. The prayers of both could not be answered. That of neither has been answered fully. The Almighty has His own purposes. "Woe unto the world because of offenses; for it must needs be that offenses come, but woe to that man by whom the offense cometh."

If we shall suppose that American slavery is one of those offenses which, in the providence of God, must needs come, but which, having continued through His appointed time, He now wills to remove, and that He gives to both North and South this terrible war as the woe due to those by whom the offense came, shall we discern therein any departure from those divine attributes which the believers in a living God always ascribe to Him? Fondly do we hope, fervently do we pray, that this mighty scourge of war may speedily pass away. Yet, if God wills that it continue until all the wealth piled by the bondsman's two hundred and fifty years of unrequited toil shall be sunk, and until every drop of blood drawn with the lash shall be paid by another drawn with the sword, as was said three thousand years ago, so still it must be said, "The judgments of the Lord are true and righteous altogether."

With malice toward none, with charity for all, with firmness in the right as God gives us to see the right, let us strive on to finish the work we are in, to bind up the nation's wounds, to care for him who shall have borne the battle and for his widow and his orphan, to do all which may achieve and cherish a just and lasting peace among ourselves and with all nations.

TELEGRAMS TO
SECRETARY
EDWIN M. STANTON

City Point, Virginia,
April 2, 1865, 8:30 A.M.

Hon. E. M. Stanton, Secretary of War:

Last night General Grant telegraphed that General Sheridan, with his cavalry and the Fifth Corps, had captured three brigades of infantry, a train of wagons, and several batteries; the prisoners amounting to several thousand.

This morning General Grant, having ordered an attack along the whole line, telegraphs as follows:

Both Wright and Parke got through the enemy's lines. The battle now rages furiously. General Sheridan, with his cavalry, the Fifth Corps, and Miles's Division of the Second Corps, which was sent to him this morning, is now sweeping down from the west.

All now looks highly favorable. General Ord is engaged, but I have not yet heard the result in his front.

A. LINCOLN

City Point, April 2, 11:00 A.M.

Dispatches are frequently coming in. All is going on finely. Generals Parke, Wright, and Ord's lines are extending from the Appomattox to Hatcher's Run. They have all broken through the enemy's entrenched lines, taking some forts, guns, and prisoners.

Sheridan, with his own cavalry, the Fifth Corps, and part of the Second, is coming in from the west on the enemy's flank. Wright is already tearing up the Southside Railroad.

A. LINCOLN

City Point, Virginia,
April 2, 2:00 P.M.

At 10:45 A.M. General Grant telegraphs as follows:

Everything has been carried from the left of the Ninth Corps. The Sixth Corps alone captured more than three thousand prisoners. The Second and Twenty-fourth Corps captured forts, guns, and prisoners from the enemy, but I cannot tell the numbers. We are now closing around the works of the line immediately enveloping Petersburg. All looks remarkably well. I have not yet heard from Sheridan. His headquarters have been moved up to Banks's house, near the Boydton road, about three miles southwest of Petersburg.

A. LINCOLN

City Point, Virginia,
April 2, 8:30 P.M.

At 4:30 P.M. today General Grant telegraphs as follows:

We are now up and have a continuous line of troops, and in a few hours will be entrenched from the Appomattox below Petersburg to the river above. The whole captures since the army started out will not amount to less than twelve thousand men, and probably fifty pieces of artillery. I do not know the number of men and guns accurately, however. A portion of Foster's Division, Twenty-fourth Corps, made a most gallant charge this afternoon, and captured a very important fort from the enemy, with its entire garrison. All seems well with us, and everything is quiet just now.

A. LINCOLN

TELEGRAM TO
MARY TODD LINCOLN

City Point, Virginia, April 2, 1865

Mrs. Lincoln:

At 4:30 P.M. today General Grant telegraphs that he has Petersburg completely enveloped from river below to river above, and has captured, since he started last Wednesday, about twelve thousand prisoners and fifty guns. He suggests that I shall go out and see him in the morning, which I think I will do. Tad and I are both well, and will be glad to see you and your party here at the time you name.

A. LINCOLN

TELEGRAMS TO
SECRETARY
EDWIN M. STANTON

City Point, Virginia,
April 3, 1865, 8:30 A.M.

Hon. E. M. Stanton, Secretary of War:

This morning Lieutenant-General Grant reports Petersburg evacuated, and he is confident that Richmond also is.

He is pushing forward to cut off, if possible, the retreating rebel army.

A. LINCOLN

City Point, Virginia,
April 3, 1865, 5:00 P.M.

Hon. Edwin M. Stanton, Secretary of War:

Yours received. Thanks for your caution, but I have already been to Petersburg. Stayed with General Grant an hour and a half and returned here. It is certain now that Richmond is in our hands, and I think I will go there tomorrow. I will take care of myself.

A. LINCOLN

LAST PUBLIC ADDRESS

ON RECONSTRUCTION

Washington, D.C., April 11, 1865

Fellow Citizens: We meet this evening not in sorrow, but in gladness of heart. The evacuation of Petersburg and Richmond, and the surrender of the principal insurgent army, give hope of a righteous and speedy peace, whose joyous expression cannot be restrained. In the midst of this, however, He from whom all blessings flow must not be forgotten.

A call for a national thanksgiving is being prepared, and will be duly promulgated. Nor must those whose harder part gives us the cause of rejoicing be overlooked. Their honors must not be parcelled out with others. I myself was near the front, and had the pleasure of transmitting much of the good news to you. But no part of the honor for plan or execution is mine. To General Grant, his skillful officers, and brave men, all belongs. The gallant navy stood ready, but was not in reach to take active part. By these recent successes, the reinauguration of the national authority—reconstruction—which has had a large share of thought from the first, is pressed much more closely upon our attention. It is fraught with great difficulty. Unlike a case of war between independent nations, *there is no authorized organ for us to treat with*—no one man has authority to give up the rebellion for any other man. We simply must begin with and mould from disorganized and discordant elements. Nor is it a small additional embarrassment that we, the loyal people, differ among ourselves as to the mode, manner, and measure of reconstruction. As a general rule, I abstain from reading the reports of attacks upon myself, wishing not to be provoked by that to which I cannot properly offer an answer. In spite of this precaution, however, it comes to my knowledge that I am much censured for some supposed agency in setting up and seeking to sustain the new state government of Louisiana. In this I have done just so much and no more than the public knows. In the annual message of December 1863, and the accompanying proclamation, I presented a plan of reconstruction, as the phrase goes, which I promised, if adopted by any state, would be acceptable to and sustained by the executive government of the nation. I distinctly stated that this was not the only plan which might possibly be acceptable, and I also distinctly protested that the executive claimed no right to say when or whether members should be admitted to seats in Congress from such states. This plan was in advance submitted to the then Cabinet, and approved by every member of it. One of them suggested that I should then and in that connection apply the Emancipation Proclamation to the theretofore excepted parts of Virginia and Louisiana; that I should drop the suggestion about apprenticeship for freed people, and that I should omit the protest against my own power in regard to the admission of members of Congress. But even he approved every part and parcel of the plan which has since been employed or touched by the action of Louisiana. The new constitution of Louisiana, declaring emancipation for the whole state, practically applies the proclamation to the part previously excepted. It does not adopt apprenticeship for freed people, and is silent, as it could not well be otherwise, about the admission of members to Congress. So that, as it applied to Louisiana, every member of the Cabinet fully approved the plan. The message went to Congress, and I received many commendations of the plan, written and verbal, and not a single objection to it from any professed emancipationist came to my knowledge until after the news reached Washington that the people of Louisiana had begun to move in accordance with it. From about July 1862, I had corresponded with different persons supposed to be interested in seeking a reconstruction of a state government for Louisiana. When the message of 1863, with the plan before mentioned, reached New Orleans, General Banks wrote me that he was confident that the people, with his military cooperation, would reconstruct substantially on that plan. I wrote to him and some of them to try it. They tried it, and the result is known. Such has been my only agency in getting up the Louisiana government. As to sustaining it my promise is out, as before stated. But, as bad promises are better broken than kept, I shall treat this as a bad promise and break it, whenever I shall be convinced that keeping it is adverse to the public interest; but I have not yet been so convinced. I have been shown a letter on this subject, supposed to be an able one, in which the writer expresses regret that my mind has not seemed to be definitely fixed upon the question whether the seceded states, so called, are in the Union or out of it. It would perhaps add astonishment to his regret were he to learn that since I have found professed Union men endeavoring to answer that question, I have purposely forborne any public expression upon it. As appears to me, that question has not been nor yet is a practically material one, and that any discussion of it, while it thus remains practically immaterial, could have no effect other than the mischievous one of dividing our friends. As yet, whatever it may become, that question is bad as the basis of a controversy, and good for nothing at all—a merely pernicious abstraction.

We all agree that the seceded states, so called, are out of their proper practical relation with the Union, and that the sole object of the government, civil and military, in regard to those states, is to again get them into their proper practical relation. I believe that it is not only possible, but in fact easier, to do this without deciding or even considering whether those states have ever been out of the Union, than with it. Finding themselves safely at home, it would be utterly immaterial whether they had been abroad. Let us all join in doing the acts necessary to restore the proper practical relations between these states and the Union, and each forever after innocently indulge his own opinion whether, in doing the acts he brought the states from without into the Union, or only gave them proper assistance, they never having been out of it. The amount of constituency, so to speak, on which the Louisiana government rests, would be more satisfactory to all if it contained fifty thousand, or thirty thousand, or even twenty thousand, instead of twelve thousand, as it does. It is also unsatisfactory to some that the elective franchise is not given to the colored man. I would myself prefer that it were now conferred on the very intelligent, and on those who serve our cause as soldiers. Still, the question is not whether the Louisiana government, as it stands, is quite all that is desirable. The question is, Will it be wiser to take it as it is and help to improve it, or to reject and disperse? Can Louisiana be brought into proper practical relation with the Union sooner by sustaining or by discarding her new state government? Some twelve thousand voters in the heretofore slave state of Louisiana have sworn allegiance to the Union, assumed to be the rightful political power of the state, held elections, organized a state government, adopted a free-state constitution, giving the benefit of public schools equally to black and white, and empowering the legislature to confer the elective franchise upon the colored man. This legislature has already voted to ratify the constitutional amendment recently passed by Congress, abolishing slavery throughout the nation. These twelve thousand persons are thus fully committed to the Union and to perpetuate freedom in the state—committed to the very things, and nearly all things, the nation wants—and they ask the nation's recognition and its assistance to make good this committal. Now, if we reject and spurn them, we do our utmost to disorganize and disperse them. We, in fact, say to the white man: You are worthless or worse; we will neither help you nor be helped by you. To the blacks we say: This cup of liberty which these, your old masters, held to your lips, we will dash from you, and leave you to the chances of gathering the spilled and scattered contents in some vague and undefined when, where, and how. If this course, discouraging and paralyzing both white and black, has any tendency to bring Louisiana into proper practical relations with the Union, I have so far been unable to perceive it. If, on the contrary, we recognize and sustain the new government of Louisiana, the converse of all this is made true. We encourage the hearts and nerve the arms of twelve thousand to adhere to their work, and argue for it, and proselyte for it, and fight for it, and feed it, and grow it, and ripen it to a complete success. The colored man, too, in seeing all united for him, is inspired with vigilance, and energy, and daring to the same end. Grant that he desires the elective franchise, will he not attain it sooner by saving the already advanced steps towards it, than by running backward over them? Concede that the new government of Louisiana is only to what it should be as the egg is to the fowl, we shall sooner have the fowl by hatching the egg than by smashing it.

Again, if we reject Louisiana, we also reject one vote in favor of the proposed amendment to the national Constitution. To meet this proposition, it has been argued that no more than three fourths of those states which have not attempted secession are necessary to validly ratify the amendment. I do not commit myself against this, further than to say that such a ratification would be questionable, and sure to be persistently questioned, while a ratification by three fourths of all the states would be unquestioned and unquestionable. I repeat the question, Can Louisiana be brought into proper practical relation with the Union sooner by sustaining or by discarding her new state government? What has been said of Louisiana will apply to other states. And yet so great peculiarities pertain to each state, and such important and sudden changes occur in the same state, and withal so new and unprecedented is the whole case, that no exclusive and inflexible plan can safely be prescribed as to details and collaterals. Such exclusive and inflexible plan would surely become a new entanglement. Important principles may and must be inflexible. In the present situation as the phrase goes, it may be my duty to make some new announcement to the people of the South. I am considering, and shall not fail to act, when satisfied that action will be proper.